RELATIONSHIP

Jesus' **Blueprint** for New Converts… & **All** His Church!

THE Lamb's BOOK

Jonathan & Jeanette Gainsbrugh

JOSHUA PUBLISHING

DEDICATION:

Lord Jesus Christ, I first of all must thank You, for You alone are our supreme Shepherd-King; You are my own personal Lord and Savior. You have supremely cared not only for us all...but You have supremely loved, cared for, protected & blessed me! THANK YOU!

As a freshly saved, newborn lamb in God's flock and Eternal Kingdom (at the long overdue age of 23, Lord Jesus, Your commitment to RELATIONSHIP with me, (and Your 'agape love') has carried me thru the fire & flood. I THANK YOU, LORD JESUS!

My darling wife Jeanette, my co-author, and faithful, loving, life-mate of 33 years, to you I owe an un-payable debt of gratitude. You've "stayed the course" & hung in through thick & thin. I love you! To our four lambs: Heaven, Christmas, Christian & Grace: thanks for loving me & and for being the four most precious lambs in my world! I LOVE AND THANK YOU!

Blessings beyond any words are each precious, God-sent partner-pastor & monthly missions-pledging church. Pastor: you who have joined our National Lamb-Care Network (and to your board, leaders & whole church) are due an eternal debt of gratitude. Thank y-o-u for each Sunday service, every missions love-offering, each one-time (& ongoing gift) and monthly pledge. To our current... and future... partner pastors: as any missionary, I couldn't go unless you faithfully send! Your Great Co-Mission heart, life & help are so vital! THANK YOU!

Saints one-and-all: sacrificially-giving friends & family, loving & committed blood-brothers & sisters across this country, spread over the 10,000's of miles I've traveled teaching the "Feed My Lambs" seminar to 1, 000's of pastors and God's people. In every place, God touches individual hearts to become an ongoing part of our national Lamb-Care prayer & monthly missions-support team. Grandmas & Grandpas, widows & widowers, young & old, singles, long-married's & newlyweds, church planters & veteran pastors...

You know who you are and Jesus knows who you are as well.

Jesus promised in Mark 9:41... "Anyone who gives you a cup of cold water in My Name because you belong to Christ, certainly will not lose his reward."

All you who gave both great and small, one-time and on-going, you who sacrificed and made a one-year pledge (all who fulfilled their pledge & many who went far beyond), to you I say: you indeed are my co-authors; Y-o-u are the ones who truly have written this book!

This is my inadequate thanks. To ALL those who helped me write this book as my co-authors, I would like to extend my extreme, and never-ending gratitude!

IT WILL BE WORTH IT ALL... WHEN WE SEE JESUS!

"As is his part that goes down to the battle, so shall be his part that stayeth by the stuff... They shall part and part alike." I Samuel 30:24

CONTENTS

I. NEW FOUNDATIONS FOR A "WORLD-CLASS "LAMBERY":

II. JESUS' PERSONAL STYLE OF CONVERT - CARE:

III. NEW- BORN ANALOGIES:

IV: IMPLEMENTATION & TRACKING:
CHANGING YOUR CHURCH'S CONVERT-CARE

FOREWORD:

YOUR CHURCH...
A WORLD CLASS "LAMBERY"

This book is written and sent forth to be a "catalyst." The dictionary defines catalyst as: "An active ingredient, that when placed into a combination with another item (or several in a mixture) causes that beginning entity to behave in a different, desired way." 'Synergist' is the best synonym I could find!

The spiritual "catalytic-converter" effect this author desires (and prays for), is that the nurture and care of New Believers in Jesus Christ, (His very own blood-bought precious lambs), would be improved not only at **YOUR** church, but at churches across your city and state, across our nation... and around the world!

I pray this book becomes a great, inspiration, and "Holy-provocation": a tool that you bring back to your church to increase its excellence. My heartbeat is to equip Pastors and God's people everywhere, to better fulfill Jesus' words in John 21:15... "If you love Me... feed My lambs! 1st!"

Ephesians 4:11-14 says: "God gave the five-fold ministry to equip the saints... for their work of ministry!" Our job as ministers and pastors is, to not just "do" ministry, but to equip **ALL** of God's people: "the saints". The five-fold ministry is called of God to train and develop **ALL** of God's people into an ever more effective, growing ministry team!

This book has 4 main sections, based on the 4 sessions of the "Feed My Lambs" seminar, which I hope will be brought into your church & citywide area, either live or on video.

In 1914, the Assembly of God's 341 founders signed their names to this statement: "We dedicate ourselves to the greatest evangelism this world has ever seen". I am grateful, honored and sincerely glad to be a part of that same, ongoing commitment nearly 100 years later! I was led to Christ (and into salvation) through Assembly of God people, who knew and believed in the power of the saving blood of Jesus Christ!

They believed that God's Son didn't just come to merely model a perfect, moral, righteous life, nor that we should just believe in the Sermon on the Mount's inspiring beatitudes, to assure oneself of Heaven.

These blood-washed, born-again people knew instead, that the Bible says: "if righteousness comes by (our) works, Christ died in vain." They knew God's Amazing Grace personally in a life-changing **RELATIONAL** way: not as a mere popular folk song, but as a life-changing, soul-saving reality and eternal Relationship!

John Wesley and The "Moravian Effect"!

John Wesley, was aboard ship in mid-ocean, headed toward America, to preach and convert the "heathen" in the colonies. Wesley wrote in his Journal (Fri.Jan.23, 1736): (Pg. 14 & 15, Journal of John Wesley, Oxford Univ.)

"In the morning the 3rd storm increased. As I stepped out of the cabin door, the sea came over the side of the ship. I was vaulted over with water in a moment and so stunned, I scarce expected to lift my head up again, til the sea should give up her dead! But thanks to God, I received no hurt at all.

Every 10 minutes came a shock against the side of the ship, which one would think should dash the planks in pieces. Later, I went to the German Moravians aboard. Here was an opportunity to see whether they were delivered from the spirit of fear. Amid a psalm starting their service on deck, the sea broke over, split the main-sail in pieces, covered the ship & poured in between the decks as if the great deep had already swallowed us up!

A terrible screaming began among the English on board. The Germans calmly sung on. I asked one of them afterward: "were you not afraid?" He answered: "I thank God, no." I asked "But were not your women & children afraid?" He replied mildly, "No; our women and children are not afraid to die."

Wesley later wrote: **"I came, Oh Lord, to convert the heathen, but who, Oh Lord, shall convert me?" In days following, Wesley repeatedly asked himself: did he have THEIR kind of faith and THEIR kind of assurance? When he found the answer to be "No", he committed himself deeper and deeper to prayer (and to God) for the answer. Returning to England, he searched the scriptures, eventually attending an Aldersgate meeting where his heart was "wonderfully and strangely warmed". He prayed there and recieved his sure and eternal salvation by faith.**

Author's Prayer for this Book

My prayer is that this book has a life-changing effect on you... and your church! Through additional copies, I pray a revolution of ever-improving "lamb-care " will sweep this nation, and around the globe, producing, not just much fruit but as Jesus said in John 15:8 &16: "much fruit that remains."

Jesus was to John, (as Jesus Himself must be to us also), much more than an impersonal concept of truth. Rather, Truth is a Unique and Eternal Person, and a glowing, growing, personal relationship... with our Lord Jesus Christ!

Section I: Chapter 1
"I AM A LAMB"

I am a lamb! I'm just now only 8 days old! They say I weigh just 4 1/2 pounds, just a bit more than a housecat. I don't even think I look like a sheep! Tiny, frail, wobbly, furry & fuzzy long, l-o-n-g legs! Baby lambkin... yup, that's me! Though I am so tiny, I'm growing, though I can't tell it from day-to-day! The older sheep tower over me. I'll probably never be big like my older brothers & sisters, certainly never as big as mom & pop!

I was born early morning, just one week ago yesterday. It's sure great to be alive, to finally be here "on the outside!" While I was inside my momma sheep (My mom's name is Ewe-nice), I wondered what it would be like out here! I am so excited to be here! It's wonderful to be with all the flock, though I'm the runt and the tiniest of them all!

While being here is great, it sure is scary! So much I don't know! So much to learn! Everyone seems to know so much, and me, I know just about nothing... so far! I wonder if they ever were lambs themselves? I wonder if they ever felt this helpless & tiny... as I feel most of the time!

Scary Night Sounds:

At night, after dark, I hear the strangest, most frightening howling sounds. It scares the jeewilligers out of me! The grown-up sheep in the flock tell me these sounds are killer animals. "Predators"... I think they call'em. I'm told these "predators" love to prey especially on the unsuspecting, youngest lambs of the flock, especially on lambs 8 days old or less! Veeerrrrrrrrrrrry scccccaaaaaaaarrrrrry!

They also tell me o-u-r Shepherd is the Greatest. I'm sure He is! He carries me around so gently, in His strong, secure arms. I actually hate for Him to ever put me down, except that now & then I do get to "eat".

Well, actually I can't eat yet, I o-n-l-y drink! It's only Mom's milk for now! I can't even chew the tenderest, green grass yet! You see, I don't have any teeth! Not even baby teeth! But someday, in a few months, I hope I will!

Our Shepherd has the kindest, gentlest voice. He tells me to not be afraid of the killer-wolves & howling coyotes. I'm confident I can always race back to the Shepherd in time, if need be. Sometimes I just get "curious". It just comes over me, at the oddest times! I start to wander off... first in my mind... then with my feet! I wander from the Shepherd, from Mom & Pop...

and from the rest of the flock. Yesterday I "suddenly" found myself looking over the edge of a steep cliff. Promise you won't tell anyone, but I almost slipped! I felt a sort of rush and thrill, even though I know I could have fallen and been hurt, or worse: died!

I hope I never forget what it was like... to be a wee, little, newborn baby lamb... like I am right now!

They tell me just this year alone, five other newborn lambs were destroyed! Two by "cliff-diving", and three other newborn lambs were carried off as 'dinner' by wolves and mountain lions. A-L-L 5 died from this "curiosity" thing, bit-by-bit straying past the edges of the flock. Of all horrible things, three were actually eaten by those hellish "predator" creatures. I can't imagine wolves really being this mean: can they be?

Still somehow, I just keep wandering off.

I envy the older sheep! They all seem so strong, so wise & secure, so confidently content to stay close to the Shepherd. He must really be as good as they say He is. I hope someday I'll learn to be content staying close to Him, and trust Him as much as they do!

For now, it's one day at a time for me. I guess I'll learn and survive, if they (Mom, Pop, the flock & our Shepherd) all keep on faithfully loving and caring for me! Life ahead sometimes excites me, but sometimes it scares me so much, I shiver and shake, especially at night... in the dark.

I'm just so glad I have a family to "family" me, and a loving, watchful Shepherd (and His faithful sheepdogs) to "Shepherd" me and protect me. Other lambs have made it, despite the five lamb-kin this year who didn't.

I hope and pray I can survive & grow up too!

I hope I live long enough to become a big sheep someday too... just like the others in my flock!

PS. If (and when) I ever become a full-grown sheep, someday maybe I'll even have a little lamb of my own. Lord, I promise I'll take such good, diligent, watchful care of it, so it will live to grow up tall and strong like it's dad and be able then to raise a healthy, family of his own.

I hope I never forget what it was like... to be a wee, little, newborn baby lamb... like I am right now!

"Lord, please help me never to forget!"

Chapter 2
A TALE OF TWO LAMBS...
& ONE WORLD-CLASS LAMBERY

Billy was broke and broken. Billy Smithston had tried all the world had to offer: drugs, sex, rock-n-roll, life in the "fast lane", "pedal-to-the-metal": You name it, he'd done it! Way past sick and tired of being "sick & tired, "Billy was tired of living. He was looking for an answer: any answer... to his broken, hopeless messed-up "excuse-of-a-life"!

He had just turned 29. His money was gone...and so were his wife, kids, house, job & dreams! He had no future and hated his present and past! Suicide loomed in his thinking. He was constantly depressed, even in his "better" times. He had fallen through society, like the Flying Wallendas, and was now living in a crash pad with his fast-lane "friends". They "helped" him deliver drugs "to pay his 'fair' share" of the rent and food! He didn't mind risking his life in these sometimes lethal drug deals. What the 'H!'": for Billy to live was "hell" enough; why care about any "hell" beyond! He could "care less" about life after death. His real question was: Would there ever again be l-i-f-e (for him) ...real, satisfying l-i-f-e.... before death?

He'd heard of secular rehab houses and their low success rate. He'd also heard of a Christian rehab "Teen Challenge" (or whatever). He might give them a try... but how? Any Christian friends? Billy knew a few Bible thumpers! But a r-e-a-l Christian friend? Someone truly interested in him? No way! All they wanted was a quick prayer & then? "Poof!" Nothing! That's what! Nothing... after the prayer!"

Billy had already done the "pray the prayer" number four times the last two years! "Here today, gone tomorrow!" Sort of like a religious "one-night stand"... he thought to himself! Maybe it was just praying the prayer with somebody that they got off on!

Now compare "Billy's story" above with Jim's new-birth story at church #2: a world-class "lambery"!

Jim was also broke & broken (just like Billy), but not a-f-t-e-r getting saved at his church! Jim's life was also shattered in 1,000 pieces, like a beer bottle thrown in a rage against a brick wall. Jim's new-birth story is different, because of Steve, his good friend, who worked on the assembly line with Jim at the Chevy plant. Steve wasn't perfect, just a genuine Christian. He faithfully attended a caring, growing local church with his family. When

3

Jim's car broke down, Steve picked him up 10 consecutive workdays, until payday when Jim could get his car fixed.

Jim's story is also different... because he got saved at Steve's church: a world-class 'lamb-ery'!

Way, way back, (long before coming to Christ... or ever dreaming of church), Jim had been deathly sick and couldn't go to work. Missing Jim at work, Steve had 1st phoned, then stopped by after work with food & help. He prayed with Jim, helped Jim write out & mail some overdue bills, made an ATM deposit for Jim and had even taken the trash out in sub-zero weather! Unbelievable, Steve even did a load of laundry for his unsaved buddy Jim, while Jim was burning up with a fever for three days.

This new life in Christ that Steve said so wonderfully changed his life ten years back, sounded like it had really filled the empty place in Steve's life. Jim increasingly wanted that same empty place filled in his own life as well. Jim hungered, not for a religious belief, but for the same joy-giving relationship Steve had obviously found: a real, loving "personal connection" with this amazing, always-there, life-changing Jesus! Steve shared with Jim, Jesus' promise, that He would come into Jim's heart & life, and that He'd never, ever leave or abandon him! Steve patiently listened to (& answered) all of Jim's questions (even the "dumb" ones!) One night, Jim asked Steve to pray a salvation-prayer with him to meet this Jesus!

What did Jim's church do for him after praying the salvation prayer? I'll let Jim tell you in his own words:

"FAMILY! ...In one word, these church people were 'instant family' to me! They 'family-ed' me! This church connected with me & carried me as a new believer. I knew nothing of the Bible, Nada! Zip! Zero! But, "overnight", I had dozens of friends & family... that I had never met before! They convinced me that "God's will" was (& would always be) the ultimate, very b-e-s-t plan for my life!

They regularly and lovingly checked up on me and cared for me from "Day One"! I sensed they weren't snooping, but just showing they really cared. Right off, they were committed to my success & to my "making it" as a new "lamb" in their Lord's precious flock! Thank God, they somehow knew their caring relationship with me, was even more important than Bible knowledge. They knew that relationship was God's "umbilical cord" for the new Life-Force to flow into my life. I didn't care how much they knew, (Bible or otherwise), until they showed me how much they cared. And care for me they did! In a very impressive way!.

Day One:

Coming forward at that Sunday morning service's altar call, I prayed the salvation prayer. I couldn't believe it! When I peeked through my closed eyes, two altar workers had joined me. They wept tears of joy along with my tears of sorrow. They hugged me and sincerely shared my new-birth joy! They invited me out with them for a meal immediately following, which I of course took them up on! I had nowhere to go, and was glad to see they weren't in a hurry to dump me and be with their older, Christian "church-crowd" friends.

Before I even left the altar, they gave me a new Bible signed by the Pastor & also a pocket-size New Testament to keep with me. They also gave me a copy of the "Jesus Video" to take home, and a framed 8x11 "New Birth certificate", signed by Pastor & staff! They also gave me one other very special gift: an audio-tape cassette of that very same Sunday AM service's sermon & altar call; the one where God touched & changed my heart & life forever! It was like the entire church "took me under their wing". They also gave me a full size (and also a laminated wallet-size) list of all local Christian radio & Christian TV station call-letters, channel #'s and times. It also had Christian web-sites, 24-hour toll-free 800 prayer-counseling lines, a weekly church schedule & other city-wide Christian activities. I tuned in the local Christian K-LUV radio station that same afternoon on the way home in my car. Due to that local Christian resource sheet, I've been listening to Christian radio ever since!

They linked me up, right at the altar with a "big-brother" friend, Wally, to meet weekly with me. They asked me if I'd like an easy, 3-week, 30-minute start-up Bible study. I said yes and In the weeks and months following, Wally and I became great friends in the Lord. We still are, Praise God!

They gave me a "Welcome to the Family" audio-tape message from Pastor (with a few congregation changed-life testimonies thrown in) on side 1. It also had great, upbeat worship & praise music on side 2. They said praise music (in my early mornings) would help wake me up better than coffee. They were right! They told me their "Welcome to the Family" meal-team had me lined up for a meal at someone's home the next 4 Sundays after AM service! This sounded warm, inviting & welcoming to me. To them, I wasn't a one-time "bag-em & tag-em" number to write down on a salvation "score card" or tally sheet!

That very same Sunday night, they picked me up & took me to one of their "TLC" small home-group meetings. I loved it! More "instant family!" In less than two hours, I met a dozen new, accepting & encouraging friends. Several lived right near me. Four separate brothers gave me their phone # (& also a wallet-sized group members' name & phone list) & told me: "call anytime." One guy took me to play golf with him that following week. We had food at the home group meeting's start, sang, shared, prayed, then later they took me out for pizza.

The very first week: They told me that God would never, NEVER leave me, but also that satan would lie to me big-time & try to discourage me, especially during my 1st week in Christ! They told me satan's #1 "anti new-birth lie" was to tell me the very next morning: "it was all emotion... you've been manipulated... don't give up your old counter-culture friends... etc.! That's why they called me that 1st Monday morning for a 30 second prayer... to let me know they'd be praying for me all during that day!

Later that same first week, Steve took me to a local Christian bookstore. He said: "Go ahead & buy a CD! Your choice! We're buying!" He put on a few upbeat, Christian groups he liked: I found one I liked! Steve said: "The church family is covering it as a 1st week re-birthday gift to you from them all!" Our church also had a contemporary Christian music CD & video Lending Library that all new believers can borrow from. Boy, did I ever use & love that Lending Library! It cost me zip! What a great loving, lamb-care church the Lord birthed me into! Yeah God!

> **Steve took me to a local Christian bookstore and said, "Go ahead pick a CD! We're buying!**

The 1st Month: Unbelievable as it sounds, they actually did have a "New Believer Welcome-to-the-Family" meal team! For the next four Sundays in a row (after church), I met four really great, loving families. I shared meals at their homes on those 1st 4 Sundays after getting saved! These folks are now some of my closest Christian friends. We always hug when we see each other on Sundays. Hugs really do beat drugs!

The 1st Quarter: Our Sr. Pastor also holds a quarterly, special get-together & meal at his home (can you believe it), for all their recent new believers. It was great getting to know "Pastor B" & his wife a bit. He shared some personal, funny stories of his own early days as a believer. Additionally, the church held a semi-annual one-night weekend retreat for their new believers with key staff, Board & "Convert-Care Team" members there. All this helped me develop relationships. It really made me feel like I was a valuable and wanted part of their family!

1st Year: Last week I just celebrated my 1st re-Birthday, being 1 year old now that I have been "born again" in the Lord Jesus! I didn't think the church would remember my salvation date from a year ago, but they did! They helped me give a brief two minute testimony on Sunday AM. Steve's Sunday School class sang "Happy Re-birthday" to me! They even had a few gift-wrapped Christian books & presents for me... and a cake! I broke into tears in the pulpit, though I tried not to. I thanked them all, each and every one, for being such a caring church & connecting me in so many wonderful ways. I thanked them for praying for me, (as I found out they had done & still do) at every monthly church-board meeting. You see, they pray over a list of the most recent "salvations", going back one full year! I thanked them all for caring for me, and for teaching me that Salvation is a Relationship: a growing, exciting relationship with Jesus. Thank God its a Lifestyle... not a religion!

I thanked them all for not leaving me to flounder as a "baby Christian."

I thanked them for all they had done for me from "Day One": the meals together (both meals "out" & also meals "in" at the meal-team's homes), for the Jesus Video gift & the New Birth certificate, for the local-area Christian radio (& TV) info sheet, the pastor's "Welcome to the Family" gift tape, the start-up 3-week Bible Study, the TLC small group connection, all the friendships, and rides to the small group, the free music CD tape at the Christian Bookstore, and the weekly snack-packs they'd faithfully sent me every single week (starting that 1st Monday) for my 1st six consecutive weeks! This was so thoughtful, with handwritten notes & small encouraging daily "New Life" items & devotionals, mini-booklets, etc. for me to read, spiritually "nibble on" and pray over. I started keeping these little Gospel items in my locker at work, in my car, bathroom, living room, etc., as I, day-by-day and step-by-step, got used to living for (and walking with) my Lord Jesus!

Now someday I want to pass on this great Lamb-care blessing! Someday I want to be part of my church's Convert-Care Team! It has meant everything to me. Without it, I'd probably have fallen away and been just another missing "convert statistic", who prayed the prayer... but then what? For now, they tell me to not worry about it, to just keep on feasting on God's Word, praying, being faithful in church attendance, and growing in the Lord!"

This is n-o-t really the story of two churches! You see, church #1 is the "same" church as church #2!

The very same pastor... at the very same church... changed his priority and heart. He became interested in feeding Jesus' lambs first, as our Lord Himself so clearly said we should, prioritized their care in John 21:15!

Once the pastor decided to place caring for the lambs 1st... much of the rest of their improved care is merely an implementation of a few of the many ideas and strategies in "The Lambs' Book". "The Lamb's Book" was written to have this very same effect in churches just like his... and yours... across our nation and our world!

Chapter 3
"THE SILENCE OF THE LAMBS"

Across the USA, for decades, millions of conversions have been reported annually. Millions of converts are reported by scores of denominations, by 100's of evangelists and Evangelistic Associations, and by 10,000's of additional non-tallied, local-church outreach events.

Cummulatize all the crusades, 1,000's of individual evangelists (& para-church) ministries nation-wide, along with hundreds of 24-hour Christian radio and television stations, and other mass media. Still atop all this, are unreported results of the personal soul-winning efforts of 50 million American evangelical Christians attending one-third million American evangelical churches!

All these "millions" of annual converts not-withstanding, internationally respected Christian author and demographer George Barna (www.barna.org) reports that U.S.A. Christianity has not grown in the last twenty years: either numerically... nor in influence!

You can't fill a sieve with water... unless...

The Bible, God's unchanging Holy Word, says: "It is required of a man that a steward be found faithful." (I Corinthians 4:2.) Do we, as God's faithful stewards, dare to ask the ever-challenging question: w-h-y no growth?

How can millions of converts result in zero growth in American churches, year after year?

More importantly, if we dare ask "why," are we willing to listen (and implement) God's strategic answer to correct this sub-Biblical plateau?

Why has all this massive, sincere, dedicated evangelistic effort (& billions of dollars in church expenditure) left zero growth in America? How can millions of converts result in "zero sum" growth in American Christianity and in 300,000 Christ-preaching churches?" While the USA population increased 50 million... why didn't the churches grow as well?

You can't correct what you don't detect

What has happened... is a "paralysis of non-analysis"! There is little (or no), accurate comparing between the reported annual Convert totals, with the truer indicator of a church's (or denomination's) health: namely its cumulative, Sunday AM gain, loss, or non-growth.

This lack of retention and tracking often occurs during rapid growth or revival periods. However, a church (movement or organization) will always eventually rise or fall... to its level of care! Eventually the lack of tracking (previously overshadowed by a period of tremendous growth), will begin... by its absence... to play a larger and larger role.

An increasing awareness grows of the huge discrepancy between the massive harvest totals reported in the field and abysmally low number (and volume) of sheaves actually making it back into the barn! Jamie Buckingham wrote: "The truth will set you free... but first it may make you miserable!"

What will it take to change... and why change at all?

The common thought in the "Laodicean" America church is: "Well, isn't the American church (& Christianity in general), doing alright? Why talk about need for change at all? Churches are putting up larger, more elegant buildings. The president is a born-again Christian. Surely things are on the upswing, aren't they?

Assimilation: one indispensable, missing ingredient!

Assimilation in a church, in one sentence, is: "Making insiders out of outsiders", making friends out of strangers and making family out of friends! Assimilation is helping people to connect: intentionally assisting people to belong. For "if people don't belong... before too long... they're gonna say... so long!"

How do brown cows... produce white milk...
which becomes yellow butter?

Assimilation is a p-r-o-c-e-s-s that is wonderfully parallel to the following analogy! Assimilation enables a brown and white cow to eat green grass, then turn that into white milk, which then becomes yellow butter, which then is transformed into orange cheddar cheese. This may then process into a T-bone steak with black char-broiled grill marks across it.

This transformation process parallels the process of the assimilation of visitors and converts at a church, which is vastly under-taught. It is the crucial dynamic that ultimately determines whether a-n-y church (or denomination) will grow, plateau, or decline!

Assimilation is the cognitive, scientific study (and a-r-t) of understanding (and improving) the dynamics of how Visitors, New Converts, as well as New and Regular Members, become an ongoing, connected, healthy, growing part of a church family or whether they leave: out "the Back Door!"

Every church and believer must become more skilled in understanding the "how and why" of these costly people-losses, and how to reverse or better yet, prevent, those loss-factor dynamics as well!

Jesus said: "I will b-u-i-l-d My Church"... not plateau it!

Church decline must be seen as totally unacceptable! Jesus said He would build His church and the gates of hell would N-0-T prevail against it. When we see entire Districts (representing hundreds of churches each) reporting thousands, even ten thousands of converts, but zero Sunday morning growth, something is drastically wrong! The cross is not a minus. Rather, the cross is the greatest "plus sign" in history! What will turn this minus (horizontal) sign into a plus....will be prayer, and a willingness to re-think and re-calibrate our care of Jesus' precious lambs... the growth edge of the flock!

One leading denomination exemplifies the many... in today's contemporary, flat-lined American religious landscape!

The Assemblies of God USA is frequently referred to by many national Church Growth experts, (along with many news articles & media) as currently the "fastest growing, American evangelical denomination." This statement is true referring to AG overseas missions and stats, but sadly not in the USA!

Overseas: The Assemblies Of God has Been Modeling constant, u-p-w-a-r-d Growth!

Assembly of God Division of Foreign Missions reports that AG churches (outside America) grew by 3.5 million overseas in one year... a rate of almost 10,000 per day! The statistics show a different picture here at home!

At home... "The Trunk has Shrunk!"

While the branches (overseas missions) have grown phenomenally, at home here in the USA, the international "sending base" has had a different result.

How could 4 million converts in 12,000 churches in 10 years create a Sunday AM gain of only 240,000?

During the decade of the 1990's, (named by the USA Assemblies as their "Decade of Harvest"), 12,000 American AG churches reported an annual average of over 300,000 converts (1/3 of a million) yearly conversions. A total of 4.2 million USA converts were reported for the decade of the 1990's in 12,000 American Assembly of God churches!

95% of the harvest is missing!

An even greater un-addressed problem is that these staggering ongoing losses are not seen as a cause for grave concern. These losses should trigger immediate, ongoing, result-producing corrective action from all levels of leadership: national, district (or state), sectional and e-v-e-r-y local church level!

Has a new millennium brought improvement to these Convert losses?

Year 2000... U.S.A. National #'s: Any sign of Improvement?

Statistics for year 2000 are cause for even more alarm than the preceding 1990's decade!

In the year 2000, 486,339 reported converts in American AG churches resulted in a national Sunday AM decrease of - 9,683 (almost a minus-10,000!)

This was the first Sunday AM decline in the last three decades (without a major national reason) to account for it!

In the year 2000, twenty-six of 58 American AG districts, (representing 1,000's of AG churches & 100,000's of believers), reported a minus (or Sunday AM decline). This meant 46% (almost h-a-l-f) of all USA AG districts decreased.

One larger district reported the highest year 2000 total number of converts: ...52,798... while simultaneously reporting a Sunday AM decrease in their 261 churches! Another US district reported a minus - 4,535 Sunday AM, while at the same time reporting 22,576 converts!

*In AG polity, one state is usually a district. Larger states sub-divide into 2 or 3 districts.

If God is not into #'s...
why did our Lord Jesus Christ use specific #s
in His parables, His ministry & bless them
in the Book of Acts?

One pastor of a church running several thousand on Sunday AM, heard me use the above #s and said to me: "I've heard your #'s!... So what!"

Some say that "God is N-O-T into numbers." Wait a minute! Isn't Numbers the 4th book in the Bible?

Jesus Himself used specific #'s for a specific reason. Specific numbers help to eliminate "fog". In the natural, heavy fog prevents one from either driving very fast or making much progress. Where there is heavy fog, one can not accurately see or assess where one is going. Sometimes airports are totally shut down because of extreme fog, and then no planes are even allowed to take off!

> **How can you add 26,000 converts to 430 churches... and come up with a minus anything?**

Another district with 430 churches (year 2000 alone), reported 26,390 converts... yet this "produced"... a district-wide Sunday AM decrease of a minus - 755!

11

> **"I've pastored this church 4 years and we've recorded 7,894 converts, but somehow we've not grown."**

One particular pastor came to me for help and consultation. During our time together, at lunch, this frustrated pastor picked up a paper napkin and slowly, deliberately wrote on it the following equation: 7, 8 9 4 = O. This pastor told me the meaning, as he explained: "I've been pastor at our church just over 4 years. In all that time, we have recorded 7,894 converts, but somehow the church has not grown any larger from when I came 4 years ago!"

"What About Other Denominations?"

The Navigators Christian Ministries, (a globally-respected discipleship ministry founded by Dawson Trotman) states that in a national research survey they conducted that "not one county in the USA gained in church attendance... in the entire last decade."

Parallel with other Historical Holocausts

This "Silence of the Lambs" (Jesus' millions of missing lambs) issue... has historic parallels in the horrific U.S. Slavery/Abolition struggle, as well as Nazi Germany's attempted genocide of the Jews... a-n-d the current ongoing U.S. Holocaust of 40 million + deliberate abortion-deaths of precious, pre-born American children!

As the following paragraphs illustrate, every genocidal holocaust included the rationalization, excuse, and deception that: "the victims are 'non-persons' ...they are n-o-t to be pitied or defended, for they don't deserve protection... because of their apparent "non-person-hood!"

HOLOCAUST #1:
Slavery and the British Empire

Slavery in the "Christian" British empire was: a "silent holocaust" that eventually was "wiped out! British statesman, William Wilberforce, spoke fearlessly and continually for eighteen long years against slavery, from 1788... until it was finally abolished on March 25, 1806.

Wilberforce introduced his first anti-slavery motion in the British House of Commons in 1788, and brought it back every year. For eighteen long years, Wilberforce confronted his colleagues in the British Parliament, ever increasingly bringing the issue to public (and to legislative) awareness.

He eventually spearheaded a committee to gather information on (and bring to light) the inhumane mistreatment and actual murders of slaves that commonly occurred in the global, British slaving "enterprise."

John Wesley (Wilberforce's contemporary and ally), wrote him the following letter... Feb 24, 1791: (a full 15 years before British slavery was finally toppled and outlawed!)

"*Dear Sir:* **Unless the divine power has raised you up to be as "Athanasius against the world", I see not how you can go through your glorious enterprise in opposing that execrable villainy, which is the scandal of religion, of England, and of human nature. Unless God has raised you up for this very thing, you will be worn out by the opposition of men and devils. But if God be for you, who can be against you? Are all of them stronger than God? Oh be not weary of well doing! Go on, in the Name of God, in the power of His might, until even American slavery (the vilest that ever saw the sun) shall vanish away before it. Reading this morning a tract written by a poor African, I was particularly struck by the circumstance, that a man who has black skin, being wronged or outraged by a white man, can have no redress; it being a LAW in our colonies that the OATH of a black man against a white goes for nothing. What villainy is this! That He Who has guided you from youth, may continue to strengthen you in this and all things is the prayer of, dear sir, Your affectionate servant",** - John Wesley

> "**I've pastored this church 4 years and we've recorded 7,894 converts, but somehow we've not grown.**"

John Newton (former slave-trader... eventual composer of "Amazing Grace") himself... later in his own life... became William Wilberforce's revered Pastor!

Little known, is the fact that John Newton, 'converted from a life of evil as a British slave-trader from Africa to the British West Indies', would eventually became world-renowned as the composer of the best known hymn of all time: "Amazing Grace."

In his later years, this same John Newton grew into full time ministry and actually became William Wilberforce's pastor. Newton was so aware of the indescribable horrors & inhumanity of the slave trade, that he continually breathed new inspiration & hope into Wilberforce, urging him to stay in Parliament and fight slavery legislatively. Newton's prayers and insistence that Wilberforce would eventually win... and that the evil slave trade would finally be abolished forever in Britain (& her colonies) ...finally prevailed!

In 1806, after 18 long years of Wilberforce's continual efforts, the British empire's corrupt slave trade was finally ended. Due to an ever-increasing public outcry, Parliament was finally persuaded to abolish the profit-driven trade of human lives, an evil no Christian nation ever should have tolerated!

Continual outcry, attention and constant gaining of momentum, resources, power and allies... finally toppled the powerful British slave trade!

HOLOCAUST #2:
Slavery in the United States

AMERICA'S SLAVERY "HOLOCAUST" WAS ALSO ABOLISHED
O-N-L-Y THROUGH CONTINUAL OUTCRY & PUBLIC ATTENTION!

It was sixty long years a-f-t-e-r the British Parliament abolished slavery... before slavery was outlawed on the Western side of the North Atlantic, resolving it once and for all through the American Civil War (1860-1864.)

"Non-Personhood"

Slaves were considered "things" and thus, as non-persons had no "rights". The infamous, historic "Dredd Scott" U.S. Supreme Court decision (in 1857) stated: "Slaves in the United States were legally 'not-persons:' Therefore, slaves were N -O -T legally protected by our constitutional and moral laws." This holocaust-justifying "Dredd Scott" decision furthermore stated: "slaves were "things", "mere property", to do with as their owners willed. These slaves could be bought, sold, traded, mistreated, beaten, (even killed) at will...by those that "legally owned" them!

What brought America's "slavery holocaust" to its demise?

Once again, it was only the courageous, sacrificial efforts of out-spoken, anti-slavery abolitionists in the North, notably among them John Brown, Steven Douglas, and President Abraham Lincoln, who ended this Holocaust. The fiery, abolitionist writing of others, publicizing the sub-human mis-treatment of slaves, brought slavery to the boiling point and national crisis, splitting the country in the Civil War.

"UNCLE TOM'S CABIN":
The Awesome Power of One Courageous Book!

The courageous writing of Mrs. Harriet Beecher Stowe paved the way with her anti-slavery masterpiece: "Uncle Tom's Cabin". It was an instant national best-seller, and sold 300,000 copies in 1850 (its first year in print) in the USA alone! This one volume, more than any other, informed, inflamed & mobilized millions into action to see that slavery in the USA was A-B-O-L-I-S-H-E-D!

Lincoln, when he 1st met Mrs. Stowe at Gettysburg said, "So you're the little lady who started all this!"

When Abraham Lincoln first met this fiery authoress at Gettysburg after the Civil War's ending, he was quoted as having said to her: "So you're the little lady that started all of this!"

IT WILL TAKE A SIMILAR OUTCRY TO STOP THE
HOLOCAUST OF MILLIONS OF NEW CONVERT "LAMBS"!

14

HOLOCAUST #3:
The Genocidal Jewish Holocaust in Nazi Germany

In 1936, the Supreme Tribunal of Nazi Germany declared that Jews were "n-o-t persons", therefore n-o-t protected by the "laws" of Nazi Germany!

Once again the de-personalization and "un-person-hood"-ing of victims is seen as a common tactic, in BOTH previous and subsequent holocausts! Germany's Third Reich only achieved their barbaric extermination of six-million Jewish people, by committing mass murders under cover of "darkness!" Hitler's initial, genocidal years & atrocities were hidden from international awareness, behind electrified barbed wire and the concrete walls of Nazi concentration camps. Myriad atrocities and unimaginable horrors were perpetrated: the torture, abuse & murder of literally millions of precious fellow human beings went on... undetected... and unchecked!

Only after the word got out internationally, as the news media documented Hitler's inhumane butchery and gas-chamber slaughters, was the international community aroused sufficiently to bring the Nazi reign of terror... to a long-overdue end.

HOLOCAUST #4:
the American Abortion Holocaust
40 Million Victims... One Every 20 Seconds!

"Deliver those who are drawn toward death, and hold back those stumbling to the slaughter".

January 23, 1973 was the initial date of the US Supreme Court's infamous - anti-Christian "Roe v. Wade Decision", which first "legalized" abortion by the highest court in our land. The highest court in our land supposedly "legalized" the taking of a life... (spelled m-u-r-d-e-r) ...of millions of pre-born children 'in utero' across the United States: another "legalized holocaust"!

Since that fateful date in 1973, the American abortion Holocaust has seen doctors (and abortion mills) across our land profit billions of dollars while taking the lives of 40 million....never-to-be born precious children at the rate of 1.5 million deaths per year. God's Word speaks to this indefensible slaughter.

"Deliver those who are drawn toward death, and hold back those stumbling to the slaughter". If you say, "Surely we did not know this," ...does not He Who weighs the hearts consider it? He Who keeps your soul, does He not now know it? And will He not render to each man according to his deeds." Proverbs 24: 11, & 12

Once again, the Holocaust victims are robbed of their personhood and legitimacy. As in prior holocausts, ...the helpless (in this case, precious unborn children) are crudely... cruelly... and conveniently... classified as

15

"non - persons". They are subsequently seen as "legally" n-o-t deserving of the protection of our constitution and laws.

In the case of Roe V. Wade, Norma McCorvey (known by the pseudonym Jane Roe) was the plaintiff versus Henry Wade, the Dallas District Attorney. Norma McCorvey) was the "then" pregnant mother-to-be, who fought for the right to legally "abort" her child.

As the trial dragged on and on, the baby was actually born. Norma McCorvey was unable to take her child's life through "legal" abortion. Instead, she gave her up for adoption. Today, 30 years later, Miss Norma McCorvey is a nationally known Christian pro-life spokesperson. Her life-story and autobiographical book, titled: "Won By Love" is available through Christian Bookstores. She (& her ministry) can be reached at (214) 343-1069, Box 550626 Dallas, TX 75355, or her ministry web site: www.roenomore.org. Her current emphasis is to overturn Roe V. Wade, to force the courts to de-legalize abortion (www.operationoutcry.org). She asks Christians every-where to pray (Isaiah 28:14-22), that this 'death covenant' will be annulled

The national news media, have lent their full complicity to this U.S. abortion holocaust. Pro-life agencies & ministries repeatedly assert it is impossible to get the liberal-biased media to show a picture of an aborted child both "in- utero", and after its life is been so tragically, violently... taken!

" If wombs had windows... abortion would end tomorrow."

The most frequently asked question by young ladies moving toward an abortion is: "IS THIS REALLY A BABY?" The standard pro-choice (pro-death) response is: "No, it's just a glob of tissue, just a "fish" or a mere, pre-human, unconscious, and unfeeling "appendage".

However, the Bible refers to an unborn child as a "brephos" (Greek word for a young child: for both the pre-born & newly born). God's Holy Word uses the personal pronouns of "my", "he" and "me", (not "thing") in referring to the pre-born.

Both Jeremiah, the "weeping prophet" and John the Baptist were sanctified "from their mother's womb." Scripture says: "The babe leaped for joy", referring to pre-born, "in-utero" John the Baptist, in Mary's cousin Elizabeth's womb. (Luke 1:44).

He (not "it")... as a person... (while still an embryo and a growing, living, h-u-m-a-n fetus), the 'person' (John the Baptist, pre-born)..."leaped for joy"...when Mary (pregnant with the Lord Jesus Christ) entered into the same room.

"And it happened, when Elizabeth heard the greeting of Mary, that the babe leaped in her womb; and Elizabeth was filled with the Holy Spirit. Then she spoke out with a loud voice and said, " Blessed are you among women, and blessed is the fruit of your womb!"

"But why is this granted to me, that the mother of my Lord should come to me? For indeed, as soon as the voice of your greeting sounded in my ears, the babe leaped in my womb for joy." – Luke 1: 41-44)

"Things" do not have joy! Globs of tissue or inanimate objects do not have joy...nor other human emotions! To the contrary, human persons, and personalities, yes, even pre-born human beings (gestating "in–utero") according to God's Eternal Word, ... did...and still do ...experience joy! That is, until their precious & precarious life is "snuffed out".

A third of all USA High School graduating classes are "not there". This is the chilling & staggering proportion of children "legally" aborted across America in the last three decades since the "Roe v. Wade Decision"!

HOLOCAUST #5:
The New Convert Loss Epidemic

THE NEW CONVERT- LOSS HOLOCAUST MUST BE STOPPED!

The Silence of the lambs... devouring millions of Jesus' missing lambs... is just as serious a Holocaust... with, even more chilling and devastating... eternal consequences!

We live in an increasingly, un-shockable, de-sensitized culture. In the popular 1990's movie "The Silence of the Lambs" (& now completed gruesome trilogy), the main character is one Hannibal Lector (portrayed by Anthony Hopkins). This diabolical, menace unveils to us the sick mind of a cannibalistic, perverse criminal psychiatrist & psychopath.

The degenerate mind of a human cannibal is presented as "palatable", illustrating the escalating social desensitization prevalent in media. The mainstream acceptance of previous "outrage", sub-human topics such as human cannibalism (in our nation's theaters) reveals our culture's advanced state of decay!

Media critics estimate that children watch and see 60,000 cumulative TV murders in their 1,000's of hours of TV viewing throughout their impressionable K-12 years.

IT WILL TAKE A CONTINUED, LOUD OUTCRY TO BRING THE HOLOCAUST OF NEW CONVERT 'LAMBS' TO THE LIGHT & TO AN END!

What Part Will You Personally Play in Ending This National Convert Holocaust?

Will you be part of the solution to turn around this "Holocaust" and loss of millions of Jesus' blood-bought, new-born "lambs?" Will y-o-u add your voice, your prayers, your effort, your finances and connections? How large a portion of this solution will you allow your life, talents and resources to be (and become) in our Lord's hands?

Will you join the growing ranks and raise an outcry on behalf of the millions of missing lambs, bringing lamb-care to the forefront of concern and action... in America's 1/3 million evangelical churches?

Our Lord Jesus Himself said:

"*If You Love Me... Feed my Lambs*" (John 21:15)
If not you... then who?
If not now... then when?
And if not at your church ....then where?

**"Lift your voice for those that perish.
Do not say, I knew it not...**

for He that knows the heart..... knows yours,
...and He knows that you knew"
Proverbs 24:11 & 12

Chapter 4
"IF YOU LOVE ME FEED MY ___"
Jesus under-emphasized John 21:15 Priority

O ne Bible passage familiar to most believers occurs shortly after Jesus' resurrection, at the end of John's Gospel. Here we see Jesus again meeting His disciples at the shores of the Sea of Galilee. It was an intentional repeat of the same life-changing spot Jesus HAD first met them. They had been out all night long fishing for fish... when Jesus had come along "fishing" for "filet-of-*soul*" (& catching) them!

> **They had been fishing for fish... when Jesus had come along "fishing" for (& catching) them!**

In John 21, we find Peter and six other of Jesus' disciples out on the lake of Galilee in their boat (100 yards... or a 'football field length' off-shore). Jesus is on the shore unrecognized by them. He calls out to them: "Have you caught any fish?" The disciples out on the lake answer "No...", exactly as they had done when Jesus met them 3 years earlier. (John 21:4 & Luke 5:5)

Once again, just as before, when Jesus first called them, He instructs them to cast their nets on the "r-i-g-h-t" side of their ship (21:6). Obeying Jesus' instructions, they unexpectedly once again catch a miraculous haul of 153 large fish (John 21:10).

At the moment of this miracle, John says to "Rocky" (Simon Peter): "Heh, you guys, it's the Lord!" Impulsive as always, "Mr. Impetuosity" (Peter) jumps overboard & swims the 100 yards to shore, leaving the other disciples on board to haul in the net & row the heavy boat (& heavy load of fish) ashore.

When they arrive on shore, Peter & Jesus await them, Jesus (as always) is ready to greet and to feed them!

God's Living Word, JESUS, (the ever-fresh spiritual Bread of Life) not only once again feeds His "lambs" hungry stomachs... but again combines this with His true aim: nourishing their immortal souls & spiritual Life! Simultaneously, Jesus graciously meets their temporal needs with these 153 sellable, large fish, to help them pay their power bill, mortgage payments, etc.

"Come and have breakfast!", the Master calls!

Scripture tells us that Jesus has a fire blazing with both fish & bread broiling on a blazing fire, ready to feed His hungry disciples. Jesus warmly invites them to also bring some of the fish they have just caught (John 21:10) ...as well as to: "Come and have breakfast!" (King James: "Come and dine!")

19

Jesus switches the subject on them!

Jesus suddenly switches the topic of the conversation from "fish" to "lambs and sheep".

While enjoying their Divine Chef's (the Lord of Hosts) cooking and cuisine, the disciples also might have been day-dreaming... fast-forwarding to the testimonial use of "the miracle catch of fish," and centerfold photo-essay their miracle-catch would soon become!

Seemingly, out of the blue, Jesus pulls them back to reality. He switches the subject suddenly from their breakfast "miracle fish catch" to something else! Swifter & deeper than the most skillful surgeon, with one soul-piercing question to Peter, Jesus changes the conversation to the topic closest to His own heart: not fish, bur rather care & nurture of His lambs!

One catches " fish"...but one must continually, day by day... Care for lambs!

Fish have water to protect them, but lambs have nothing to protect them except a shepherd, sheepdogs & (if they're fortunate), the rest of the flock.

As Jesus opens this lamb-care subject, He intentionally f-i-r-s-t brings the subject immediately to the feeding of the smallest, youngest & newest members of the flock: His lambs! O-n-l-y a-f-t-e-r the perishable baby lambs are cared for... does Jesus continue on to feeding His sheep!

The question Jesus asked 3 Times... "The rest of the story!"

Most believers know well that Jesus asked Peter three times: "Peter, do you love Me?" But most have never really heard the rest... and best... of this story! When asked to complete Jesus' words to Peter: "Peter, if you love Me more than these... f e e d M y... (blank:_____)", 90 % of all believers & pastors (even 40-year life-time pastors) commonly reply that Jesus said: "Feed My S-H-E-E-P!"

"Feed My sheep..." is W-R-O-N-G!

This "sheep" answer is wrong! At best, it is only partially right! We shrug off the difference as if there were none! In sequence, it is n-o-t the r-i-g-h-t answer... NOT at all! It is true Jesus asked Peter three times (John 21:15,16&17) the same question: "Do you love ME?" It's also true as Jesus asks "Do you love Me" (the 2nd & 3rd time) (v.16&17), Jesus does reply: "Feed My SHEEP!"

What is totally untaught here... is:

What is totally untaught is the clear, inarguable fact that B-E-F-O-R-E Jesus told Peter : "Feed My sheep" even one time.(Jn.21:16)... and before Jesus said: "Feed My Sheep the 2nd time (21:17)

Jesus first (intentionally & clearly) told Peter:
"If you really love Me, Peter...: Feed My L–A–M–B–S! "
Clearly, in John 21:15, we see...
...that JESUS PUT THE LAMBS... F–I–R–S–T!

How common is this wrong answer:

Most Biblically literate people on a church staff will wrongly answer "Sheep!" Most church boards, deacons, and committed leadership will also answer: "Sheep." Shockingly, most pastors will also wrongly answer "Sheep" as well! Jesus did N-O-T say: "Feed MY sheep" first!

Making a mountain out of a mole hill... or
...a molehill... out of a Mountain!

At first, one might say: this is making a mountain out of an inconsequential mole-hill. But when understood properly, we see:

...making a mole-hill... out of a mountain!

Just exactly how 'Under-emphasized' is Jesus "lamb – first" priority?

I contacted 26 Superintendents whose districts had declined! I asked them: "Have you ever heard of a seminar on caring for new converts, that lasted four hours... or longer." One by one, each told me they'd never heard of a convert-care seminar that long or comprehensive.

There couldn't be that much to learn, could there?

Not making a mountain out of a mole hill... but... making a molehill... out of a Mountain!

Is there a Bible College or Seminary in the nation that devotes an entire semester course to the nurture of New Converts? I've heard of only one, North Central Bible College in Minneapolis. I'd love to hear of 1,000's more! Could there be that much to learn? Perhaps we should end the book here, call it a 21 page booklet, and "let class out early." How difficult can lamb-care be?

However, if we have never even heard that Jesus put the lambs 1st, what else haven't we heard : such as "what does that mean, how did Jesus model that Himself with His disciples, what are we to do, how should we change, what, where, who, when, etc.?

Contrary to our popular American-church "McChristian" drive-through, church-culture, there are numerous life-&-death things to learn about better nurturing of Jesus' newborn lambs.

How exactly did Jesus put the Lambs F-i-r-s-t?

In John 21:15, Jesus First... very clearly... said:
"Feed My L–a–m–b–s ".

In John 21:15,
The exact Greek words for "Feed My Lambs" are:
*"**Boske** (Feed), **Ta** (My)... and*
***Arnia** (lambs), **Mou** (of Me)*

"B O S K E "

> The Greek words for "Feed My Lambs" are: "Boske (Feed), Ta (My)... and Arnia (lambs), Mou (of Me).

"Boske", in the New Testament Koinei Greek, means to "feed".

However, it doesn't merely mean to bring the animal to the food. Rather, it means to nurture and to bring the food to the animal. There's a vast, life-and-death difference: particularly in context of Jesus' instructions and the immediacy of newborn nurture!

It is the difference between needing to nurture a baby, contrasted with assuming that a baby (just like an adult) will come to the food, and (as any developed adult), responsibly feed itself!

All lambs are sheep... but not all sheep are lambs!

To treat a lamb as a sheep, would be as criminally negligent as treating a baby as an adult! "Boske" (as far as feeding Jesus' precious lambs) means to bring the food to the baby, not throwing a flake of alfalfa into the corral & expecting the horse (or live-stock) to come to it.

There is an understood nurturing pro-activity, even in Jesus' first words. "If you "agape" Me, Peter...bring the food & nourishment to... deliberately take extra-special care... to feed MY lambs... f-i-r-s-t!

God is Love... But... "Love is n-o-t God!"

All syllogisms don't work as well backwards as forwards. One clear and easy example is I John 4: 8, that tells us : "God is love." While this is Holy Scripture and certainly, forever true, the reverse of the "verse" is n-o-t true! "God is love... but "Love is n-o-t God"! (God is Light... but Light is not God!)

"A R N I A "

The explicit, distinct Greek word here "ARNIA" is the unique word for "lamb". It's only found here in John 21:15, in the 1st of these three consecutive:

"Feed MY ___ " passages (John 21:15, 16 & 17)

Jesus uses the specific word: "Arnia". This word "Arnia", (lamb in the Greek), is an entirely separate, different word for "lamb", distinctly separate from the Greek word "probata" for "sheep."

"Arnia" (used here for lamb) is the very-same word found in Revelation chapters 5,6,7,14, 21 & 22... referring to the "Lamb of God... found worthy to open the seals... the Lamb of God... slain b-e-f-o-r-e the foundation of the world."

This is distinctly a Lamb... a sacrificial, harmless, helpless, vulnerable l-a-m-b, not merely an adult s-h-e-e-p. Jesus' cousin, John the Baptist, sees Jesus coming to be baptized by him in the River Jordan, and exclaims: "Behold the L A M B... of God... " (not the "S-h-e-e-p" of God)... W h o takes away the sin of the world." (John 1:29 & John 1:36)

All lambs are sheep... but not A-L-L sheep are lambs!

The distinctly different word for "sheep" (used by Jesus in both of the next two verses (John 21:16 &17) is the Greek word "PROBATIA", the specific Greek word for "sheep". "Probatia" is used 14 times in John 10, which we know as the "Good Shepherd" chapter!

All lambs are sheep... but not A-L-L sheep are lambs!

Look again, even more closely still, at our three targeted verses: John 21:15-17. Interestingly, in John 10, the Greek word for lamb ("arnia") isn't found: not even once in the 42-verse Good Shepherd chapter!

" M o u "

"Mou" then is the fourth and final word in Jesus' phrase "Feed MY lambs": ("Boske Ta Arnia Mou") in John 21:15! As Jesus uses the word "Mou" in His instructions to Peter, this is the Greek 1st person possessive pronoun for: "My." Jesus is telling us they are not our lambs, nor our church's lambs!

We forget so easily and so quickly exactly Whose lambs they are!

We call them o-u-r lambs, o-u-r church's, or our denomination's converts. Whose lambs are they?

They are not o-u-r lambs.

They are His!

These are His lambs...not ours!

These are Jesus' personal, blood-washed lambs, and His alone!

They are His: ...only being entrusted to us to be treasured, protected, and loved. They are His... for us to be held accountable for.

Jesus precisely and preciously calls them H-I-S lambs. Indeed, that is exactly what...and exactly Whose... they really are! They are lambs born

23

> **They are lambs born "out of Jesus' heart", out of His Spirit, out of His very own spiritual womb and passion**

"out of Jesus' heart", out of His Spirit, out of Jesus Christ's very own spiritual womb and passion:... born out of His passion, death, resurrection and Grace!

They are lambs born out of Jesus' actual suffering, His flogging, His death and His precious Life-blood, given so freely to birth them... and you and me... on Calvary's cruel cross.

God puts His wisdom on the "simple-side of complex":

Our Father-God must regularly bring His genius, wisdom, and planning way, way down... to our level of comprehension. We believe Colossians 2:3, that "all the treasures of wisdom and knowledge are hidden in Christ in God." God must often bring things down to our level. In Isaiah 55:5 & 6 God states plainly:

"My ways are not your ways and My thoughts are not your thoughts.
But as the Heavens are higher than the earth, so are My ways higher than
your ways and My thoughts higher than your thoughts."

Sometimes, God even has to say something to us more than once. ("Heads are closed and eyes are bowed!") Paul writes in Ephesians 1:17-18:

(1:17) **"I keep asking that the God of our Lord Jesus Christ, the glorious Father, may give you the Spirit of wisdom & revelation, so that you may know Him better."**

(1:18) **"I pray also that the eyes of your understanding may be enlightened (illuminated & flooded with Light), so you may know the hope into which He has called you, the riches of His glorious inheritance in the saints, and His incomparably great power toward us who believe."**

Now that we've established that Jesus put the lambs f-i-r-s-t, ...we next need to determine... exactly w-h-y Jesus did that... and h-o-w we must follow His perfect example!

Chapter 5
WHY JESUS PUT THE LAMBS... F-I-R-S-T!

As we begin exploring more deeply the reason(s) "WHY?" Jesus put the lambs f-i-r-s-t (in John 21:15), let's refresh our memory as to exactly who is the enemy of our souls, the enemy of God and His Kingdom. All that God loves, the enemy, satan hates. Thus, we also know that all satan hates, God loves!

If the lambs are so extremely precious to our Lord Jesus, is it any wonder that they become a number one target for the enemy of God's Kingdom.

One pastor said to me, in a semi-mocking way in a public meeting: "What's the big deal? What's the difference between a sheep and a lamb, anyway?" The difference is obvious: ...A lamb is nothing... if not a b-a-b-y sheep!

Jesus knew what He was talking about when He said "F-I-R-S-T!"

God's redeemed people consistently respond incorrectly with the word "sheep," when asked to complete Jesus' statement to Peter: "If you love Me, feed MY _____ ."

What we are hearing voiced in this response is "the majority voice."

Indeed, the grown-up sheep are numerically... the "majority" of the flock! The adult sheep are the "majority voice" of the flock!

However... Jesus did N-O-T say: "Feed My sheep! "
FIRST HE SAID: "FEED MY LAMBS!"

Jesus put the lambs F-I-R-S-T!

30 Years of ministry and I never heard those 5 words! Throughout my 30 + years of traveling ministry, I've preached in over 500 churches, training 1,000's of ministers in the US (and abroad). I've also listened to 1,000's of sermon hours of Christian radio and television. I spent 10 years researching the Body of Christ's resources producing a 750 page Christian Resource Directory, listing 20,000 ministry resources under 400+ ministry areas. Yet, I never once heard those f-i-v-e k-e-y w-o-r-d-s pinpointing what so drastically ails America's 300,000 "plateaue"-ed, evangelical churches. I never heard anyone say these 5 words representing Jesus' heart.

Jesus put the lambs F-I-R-S-T!

"JESUS PUT THE LAMBS... FIRST!"
What do these five key words
"Jesus put the lambs f-i-r-s-t" ...mean?

Just meditating on these five words helps us see Jesus quite intentionally, d-i-d put the care of His lambs first. Once we recognize this intentional priority of Jesus, it then raises a galaxy of other parallel, connected, secondary questions.

Most readers have also never heard these 5 words either! Sad but true, most pastors, preachers, church boards, deacons, and leadership teams have also never heard those five words. I ask each reader to stop a moment & repeat these five one-syllable words aloud to himself (or herself) for emphasis: the five words of Jesus' heartbeat in John 21:15: Jesus put the lambs f-i-r-s-t!

Jesus didn't put the lambs second! Jesus didn't put the lambs third! Quite, intentionally, He put the lambs f-i-r-s-t! Now since Jesus put the lambs first, we must ask ourselves:

Q: Why did Jesus put the lambs first?

Q: How did He put the lambs f-i-r-s-t?

Q: Where and when did Jesus put the lambs f-i-r-s-t ?

Q: What does it mean: "to put the lambs first?"

How are we to follow Jesus' command and example, in our own churches & convert-care methods, putting our own lambs (really HIS lambs) F I R S T?

"How to destroy a flock...:

Wiser than any earthly shepherd, Jesus knew that to protect & grow a flock, A-L-L of the sheep are indeed very important. A-L-L the Good Shepherd's sheep are deeply loved, cherished, protected, and fed by their Good Shepherd!

However TV cartoon-land's "Wiley Coyote" ...or the dumbest...and hungriest... of predators... certainly knows the easiest way to destroy a flock is not to directly attack the shepherd. Nor is the easiest "attack–path" to out-fight a pack of sharp-toothed, loud-barking sheep-dogs. To attack and out-wrestle the big daddy ram with his 24-inch long "killer" horns is also not the wisest strategy to take.

The "thinking" predator knows all he needs do, to destroy a flock... is, by stealth, to attack & pick off the newborn, defenseless baby lambs!

All a predator needs do... to wipe out a flock...
...is target & kill the vulnerable, naïve & helpless
baby lambs.

26

Satan Loves "Lamb-Chops"

The easiest prey, and the most tender, effortless meal in the entire flock for a famished predator (be it mountain lion, wolf, coyote or bear) is a tender, naïve, defenseless, newborn lamb! The lambs are the easiest, tastiest, and most naturally "tenderized" meal. Simultaneously, these new-born lambs are also the one single "meal" (& loss) that is absolutely the most damaging loss to a flock... and its future!

The lambs are the easiest "fast food"

Lambs are unquestionably the easiest "fast food". Baby lambs are a predator's "dream come true" during each Spring's "lamb-ing" season! Tender lambs are the effortless meal: the perfect "snack-food!" Lambs are the food of "least resistance!" "More taste... with... less killing!" Lambs are the most trouble-free, risk-free "drive-by: a perennial source of quick, instant "drive-thru" meals "to go"!

The "lamb's- face" is the "feeding place" for a predator, especially if the lambs' only defense: (the shepherd, the sheepdogs & other full-grown sheep) are busy elsewhere feeding themselves, or not vigilantly guarding the youngest, tastiest new members of the flock: the l-a-m-b-s!

King David the "shepherd boy"... protected his father's lambs

> **"I was keeping my father's flock, when a bear and a lion came & grabbed a lamb out of the flock."**

We see young David, the sweet psalmist of Israel, as a faithful teenage shepherd boy in 1 Samuel 17:34-36. Here David writes of this undeniable "lamb–preference" of predators. Notice, the predators' (both the lion & the bear's) preference in "meal choice". In e-a-c-h instance, the predator took... a lamb!

David continues: "Each time, when the lion & bear rose up against me, I rescued the lamb from out of the predator's mouth, and killed these predators (slaying both the bear and the lion)."

David... a God-Pleasing... "lamb-saver!"

David repeatedly (and faithfully) rescued his father's l-a-m-b-s out of the mouth of certain death.We know this faithful, young shepherd boy, David, was divinely and eternally rewarded for his diligence by God Himself (His Heavenly Father). David's future reward was to eventually be put in charge of an infinitely greater responsibility. God made David King over Israel, God's very own personal flock!

All lambs are sheep...
but not all sheep are lambs:

All lambs are sheep!... but not A-l-l sheep are lambs! Lets look at this closer!

The Sheep are the "n-o-w" of the flock"

Yes, indeed, the grown sheep are the "now" ... and the strength of the flock. The grown-up mature sheep are the fleece and milk producers, and the sheep are the reproducers. The sheep are even the lamb and mutton producers! The grown up sheep are the current value of the flock.

Alvin Toffler, a leading, best-selling futurist, wrote a book titled: "Future Shock." Many churches, movements & denominations are overdue for a drastic, irreversible Future s-h-o-c-k...if they don't realize the precious, perishable lambs...are the future of their flock!

The majority of the flock are
grown sheep... not baby lambs.
The lambs are the minority of the flock!

The majority of the flock are grown sheep....not baby lambs.

The lambs are the minority of the flock. The mature, wiser sheep know better than to stray. They eat more, and know & trust the shepherd's presence, guidance, protection and provision.

Full-grown sheep are also larger, louder and more visible. They generally live longer**, specifically because they've learned to stay close to the their Shepherd. **That is...I F they manage to survive this most vulnerable growth stage: their 1st week, 1st month, 1st quarter & 1st year as perishable baby lambs!

Shepherds don't produce sheep: sheep do!
Actually... sheep don't produce sheep...
sheep produce lambs!

The lambs... are the future of the flock!! ...and a flock... without lambs... is a Flock ...without a Future!

Shepherds protect, feed, nurture... and lovingly lead their sheep and flocks. However, it is n-o-t the shepherds who produce sheep for their flock. All wise shepherds know that...Shepherds don't produce sheep: Sheep produce sheep.

Actually... sheep don't produce sheep: Sheep produce l-a-m-b-s! If the lambs are protected, they will grow up to become sheep that will produce more lambs. In turn, if they (the new lambs), are nurtured & protected, they too will grow up to become sheep...to produce more lambs for their Shepherd. These, (in time), as nurtured baby lambs, will also grow up... etc.!

As the lambs are methodically, unnoticeably.. and mercilessly "picked off" one by one, the flock will, at first, gradually stop growing, then plateau. Slowly but steadily, the flock will decrease in number, plateau & transition from non-growth into a slow, steady, decline and fade into non-existence.

The sheep are the strength and "the N–O–W"
of the flock!! ...but the lambs...
are the future of the flock!!
...and a flock... without lambs...
is a FLOCK... WITHOUT A FUTURE!

This then is exactly W-H-Y Jesus put the lambs f—i—r—s—t!

This is why Jesus told us (as His followers)...to also put HIS lambs... first! This is just one of many, other vital reasons w-h-y the lambs need our top attention, protection & care:

Jesus said to Peter (& says to each of us today as His disciples") " IF you love Me..... F e e d M y l a m b s....first!."

Reflection & challenge questions
to improve lamb-care at your church

Q1) What part of "feeding His lambs" is Jesus calling you to in days ahead?

Q2) What is your church's annual, quarterly & monthly "lambs-loss" factor?

Q3) Do you lose more lambs at your church from "active attack" by wolves:..
...or by passive neglect and a lack of intentional, systematic relationship, nurturing, connective, care-giving?

It is way past time to do something pro-active, in an ongoing, intentional and corrective way.

Isn't it past time to change this Great Co-Mission "O-m-m-i-s-s-i-o-n"... into a progressively improved intention and fulfillment of our Lord's loving command & priority...

TO F-I-R-S-T FEED HIS LAMBS!

Chapter 6
THE BIBLE SAYS "BE DILIGENT TO K-N-O-W"

Too many churches suffer from... 'terminal fog'! Many pastors are so busy "putting out (legitimate) fires", that they sometimes can't see the forest for the trees. Many pastors are 'driving' in a "fog" of imprecise information. This ministry "fog" prevents the very growth and church health that they are working so hard to achieve.

" A Paralysis of Non-Analysis "

The majority of pastors are not in a paralysis of analysis... but rather the very opposite: a "paralysis of non-analysis!"

Pastors know they have visitors, but aren't sure how many.

They know they have new members, but aren't sure how many they keep... or lose... within what time-frame, ...much less the reasons why... or why not.

Pastors, by and large, know they have converts praying to receive Christ at their altars...but they don't know how many, nor who they are, how they're doing, and who's doing what for them.

> *" Be diligent to know the state of your flocks... and look well to your herds."*
> *Proverbs 27:23*

To fulfill Jesus command and priority to "put the lambs (H-i-s lambs) f-i-r-s-t," in (caring for new converts)... we must know who they are... where they are... how they're doing... and who is or isn't connecting w-i-t-h them. It is a pure matter of life... and death!

Below, let's review a few Biblical verses that deal with the Diligence and proper "care-giving" that excellent shepherding... and lamb-care... require.

Proverbs 27:23 originally related to a flock of four-legged sheep and goats. It also applies to a flock of two-footed sheep... most specifically, two-footed "lambs": new believers that Jesus wants supremely cared for and nurtured.

The word "Be", (starting this scripture) is an imperative! God's Word tells us: "You must be diligent to "k-n-o-w:" not guess, assume, hope so... think so...or maybe so! We are to "k-n-o-w so."

I rejoice that in First John chapter 5 verse 13, John wrote:
"these things are written to you who believe on (into) the Name of Jesus Christ, that you may k-n-o-w that you have Eternal Life."

30

"Knowing" is so different from guessing!...
God wants us to k-n-o-w that we are saved,
both now... and forever!

The command is to "BE" diligent. It is n-o-t an option or a multiple choice, to chose to be diligent or to not be diligent.

Diligence is defined in the dictionary as: "the proper amount of care, effort or concern required by a given situation."

Luke 15:4-7 The Diligent Shepherd...
...and the 100 sheep!

"What man of you having a hundred sheep, if he loses one, does not leave the 99 and go after the one until he finds it. And when he finds it, he joyfully puts it on his shoulders ...and goes home. Then he calls his friends and neighbors together and says, rejoice with me; I have found my lost sheep. I tell you, that in the same way, there will be more rejoicing in heaven over one sinner who repents, than over ninety-nine righteous persons who do not need to repent."

Here in Luke 15:4-7 Jesus tells a simple story that most long-time believers have heard often! We may think there's nothing new to learn here. That's the problem.

This diligent shepherd that Jesus describes, discovers that he is missing ONE lamb from his flock. This shepherd has an obvious 1% loss factor!

Let's look again at the 1st part of Luke 15:4
Jesus says this Shepherd H-A-S 100 sheep... not 99!

This is n-o-t the story of the 99! This i-s the story of the 1-0-0! Contrary to the name of the song in the hymnbooks titled "The Ninety and Nine", this is n-o-t the story of the ninety and nine. Rather... this i-s the story of the diligent shepherd who "h-a-d" 100 sheep.

We've been mis-programmed once again. Most Christian's call this story "the shepherd and the 99", ...or "the shepherd with the one missing sheep." But how does Jesus refer to it.

God "counts" (& sees) differently than we do!

Jesus starts out the entire story, saying: "What man of you, h -a-v-i-n-g..."

Notice! Jesus doesn't say the shepherd past tense..."used to have", the visible "truth" of the matter here. No! Jesus starts the whole story saying: "What man of you "h-a-v-i-n-g"!

"Having" is present tense, it is "now", current and ongoing. The word "h-a-d" would be past tense, and at first glance, more accurate.

We could say: "Jesus, You've got it wrong. The shepherd (past tense) "had" 100 sheep, but now he's lost one. He now only h-a-s present (visible, here & now in the fold).. he now h-a-s o-n-l-y 99! He h-a-s only 99! Lord, You're mis-counting. The shepherd already counted, and he only h-a-s ninety and nine!"

When God is "wrong"...

Of course, God is always "right", even when He's "wrong", for God is never wrong & always right! Right? Even when we think God is wrong, He's right & we're wrong. Sometimes we're so "right" when we're wrong. We must let God show us where we're wrong to make us right. Am I wrong or right?

Look closer! Jesus is teaching us here a vital principal... of Shepherding! Look closer and you'll see Jesus is teaching here a vital principal of flock-care! He is saying the shepherd "h-a-s"... not only those i-n the fold, but also those o-u-t-s-i-d-e the fold. Jesus is saying the shepherd h-a-s those w-i-t-h him by his side.

> **This principle means the pastor "h-a-s" those there on Sunday and those "not t-h-e-r-e"!**

However, he also "h-a-s" those n-o-t with him, those n-o-t by his side. This is a "do-or-die" principle of caring for Jesus' lambs, as well as the rest of His (and our) flock.

This principle means the pastor "h-a-s" those that are there on Sunday AM in the sanctuary, and those that are "not t-h-e-r-e"!

The Sunday School teacher "has" those present in class Sunday AM, and also "has" those absent!

Same with the Men's ministry, Women's Ministry, missionettes, youth and children's pastors and most particularly, the Convert-Care pastor or Lamb-care overseer at every church.

He detects... and corrects... a 1% Loss – Factor!

The Luke 15 shepherd had only a 1% loss factor! How many pastors dream they'd have only a 1% loss factor? That's where we want to bring your church's lamb-care. We can learn from this Luke 15 shepherd!

We cannot correct what we first don't d-e-t-e-c-t

When we look at this shepherd's diligence, we see immediately that we can not correct... what we first don't detect. The only way this shepherd knew he was missing any sheep at all, was that he first had to be spiritual...(and diligent enough)... to count!

Spiritual enough... to Count!

"Spiritual enough to count"! A 4-word phrase too many Christians have never heard of. Tragically, millions have incorrectly been taught the exact opposite of these vital truths!

Country Living in the
California Sierra foothills

We currently live in lovely country outside Sacramento, in the Sierra foothills. We have 7 sheep & goats that my wife principally takes diligent care of. I love to say we're "hillbilly's", because Jesus was! He was also from the hill-country, up Nazareth way in Northern Israel. For us, even with less than a dozen animals in our "flock", it is impossible to tell if there are 6 or 7 there... if one is missing... stuck in field fence or barbed wire or worse... unless you conscientiously stop and C-O-U-N-T them!

Now, if it's that hard to track less than a dozen, how did the diligent Luke 15 shepherd know that just o-n-e... was missing out of his flock...a flock more fourteen times our flock's size! Quite simply... he had to count!!

A national lamb-care revolution c-o-u-l-d come out of your town! Your church could model world-class lamb-care! It could begin in y-o-u-r church! "Can any good thing come out of Nazareth?" (John 1:46) A infinitely good thing did come out of Nazareth! A tremendous "good thing" can come out of your town. Are you willing to change and believe God for improvement?

From 85% of Retention of Lambs to 100 %

I've often shown a video clip of an AG pastor friend in North Carolina, who did a lamb-care project with us. He had been retaining 85%

> **"Jonathan, we were keeping 85% of our converts... but now we're keeping 100% of our converts."**

of his converts! He started implementing the principles the Lord's given me to share and called after a year to say: "Jonathan, we were keeping 85% of our converts... but now we're keeping 100% of our converts."

We, as pastors, have never heard that! Praise God. They say, "If it ain't broke, don't fix it!" But if its broke, we need to... fix it!! And so we shall!

The "Retention Dimension"

The "retention dimension" requires our full attention! If we increase the attention, we will increase our retention! I'm gonna ask you to go back to your church and try to track your converts from the last year. I've talked with "leading", cutting-edge pastors all across this country. They repeatedly have no answer when I ask them who their 50 or 100 converts were from last year, ...much less any idea of how they're doing... where they are... who's feeding them, etc.

I spoke with one leading pastor recently who is a brilliant, creative and dedicated. His church is growing, and they're in a new million-dollar plus facility, with lots of room to grow! I asked him: "How many converts did you have last year?" He said about a hundred." I said: "Who are they? Do you have a list? How are they doing? Where are they?"

He sheepishly replied: "I really don't know, but I know now that I need to know! We need a better system & ministry for our new believer 'lambs'."

Ezekiel 34: The "N-e-g-l-i-g-e-n-t" Shepherds

Next let's look at Ezekiel chapter 34 (Jeremiah 23 is almost identical). We see the opposite of diligent, the "N-e-g-l-i-g-e-n-t" shepherds! Both chapters read: "Woe be to the shepherds of the house of Israel." (Zeke 34:4). This is not commendation, but blistering condemnation! God says:

"Woe be to the shepherds": who are negligen... n-o-t diligent! Woe be to the shepherds of the house of Israel, who have not strengthened the weak, nor bound up the broken, nor have you healed the sick... nor brought back the wandering strays...nor searched for the lost. So they were scattered because there was no shepherd, and when they were scattered, they became food for all the wild animals. My sheep wandered over all the mountains and on every high hill. They were scattered over the whole earth, and no one searched or looked for them." (Ezekiel 34:4-6)

"Un-Shepherds"

God Himself , the "Ultimate Shepherd of a-l-l Shepherds: ...calls these extremely negligent shepherds: "Un-Shepherds". "These are shepherds who are... n-o-t shepherds", in the same way that "7 Up" calls itself the "un-cola"! However (unlike the cola), this comes with a blistering, excoriating condemnation from God Almighty, regarding the lack of care for His special people: His flock! This is not the "Well done, Good and faithful servant"! This is the "un-done"....the not even "medium rare!"

> **We too often forget, that Satan is the ultimate predator. He is out to destroy each of Jesus' lambs!**

In a recent San Diego tragedy, a next-door neighbor man, was out in the bars with the mother of a 10 year old girl. At 2 AM, as the girl's mother (God-appointed guardian & care-giver) was still getting high, drinking in the bar, this "predator neighbor" slid back into her house (next door to his). While the husband slept "like a rock", this child-pornographer predator kidnapped & killed that innocent child. These parents, not worthy of the title, were: really "UN-parents", or "NO-parents" at all!

Our hearts shudder hearing such tragedies. However, we too often forget, that Satan is the ultimate predator. He, Abaddon (the Destroyer), is out to destroy every one of Jesus' lambs left unattended and vulnerable to his slaughtering desires and designs.

Faithfulness... n-o-t fruitfulness ?
Matthew 25: Faithfulness & Fruitfulness are
n-o-t un-connected Dynamics!

One popular, un-scriptural heresy in today's non-growing American evangelical Church is that: "God is into faithfulness, N-O-T fruitfulness".

Too often, on Christian radio, I have heard nationally acclaimed media preachers boldly, and i-n-c-o-r-r-e-c-t-l-y proclaim that faithfulness and fruitfulness are mutually exclusive, unconnected terms. They simplistically preach that God is only into faithfulness... regardless of fruitfulness!

All Bible students know Jesus' parable of the Good Master in Matthew chapter 25. He entrusts 5, 2 & 1 "talents" (large sums of his money) to three of his servants before leaving on a lengthy business trip. He tells them one thing: "Occupy" till I come.

Part of the confusion here is ignorance of the King James term "Occupy" which clearly meant to "trade, invest or do business" (to make a profit)" with these large, valuable amounts... until the Master returned!

We also know that on the Master's return (Matthew 25:19-27), the servant given the 5 "talents" did invest and he i-n-c-r-e-a-s-e-d his five to ten. The returning Master sees his fruitfulness, and says: "Well done, good and FAITHFUL " and rewards him bountifully!

Similarly (in Matthew 25:23), the servant receiving the 2 talents doubles his two to four! The returning Master seeing the fruitfulness says: "Well done, good and FAITHFUL servant"...enter into the joy of your Lord."

But the servant given the 1 talent, being afraid... suspicious and accusatory of His Master, went and buried his talent. Upon the Master's return, he gives back the one "talent" he originally had been given. He had taken his one, and "grew" it to... one. No growth! There was no "fruitfulness"... and the Master was not pleased! Not exactly!

The Master does n-o-t say: "Well done...
Good and faithful!"

The Master does n-o-t- say "Well done...good and faithful...", as he did the two previous times! Rather than a commendation for faithfulness a-p-a-r-t from fruitfulness, he gives a blistering condemnation!

Seeing not an iota or shred of fruitfulness (or even an attempt), the Master says: "You wicked, no good, lazy, e-v-i-l servant." (Matthew 25:26) The master doles out an unending time of penalty and punishment for the servant who believed faithfulness ... was totally independent of fruitfulness.

God is extremely "into"
Faithfulness and Fruitfulness as Well!

God is extremely "i-n-t-o", (expectant of and blessed by) both faithfulness and fruitfulness! Our Lord is "into" one as much as the other. He is also "i-n-t-o" both the circulatory system a-n-d respiratory system He designed and placed in every human being.

Which is more important? They both are!
Is God desiring, requiring & expecting... faithfulness or fruitfulness?
The correct answer is YES!

Chapter 7
"A GREAT COMMISSION AUDIT"

Isaiah 40:11 truly shows the heart of Jesus our Great Shepherd and the Bishop of our souls.

> "*He shall tend His flock like a Shepherd,*
> *...He shall carry the lambs in His arms*
> *...He shall carry them in His bosom... (close to His heart)*
> *...and He shall gently lead those that are with young"* Isaiah 40:11

This is a great verse to memorize and to have our church boards memorize (as well) in the context of lamb-care. This verse is the heartbeat of our great Shepherd and Lord. Let's look closely at the four parts of this verse here, that describes Jesus' tender heart! Are the lambs included... and if so, in exactly how many of these four parts?

Part 1: "He shall tend His flock like a Shepherd."
(Yes, the lambs are there!)
Part 2: "He shall carry the lambs in His arms.."
(lambs" are there also!)
Part 3: "He will carry them close to His heart"
(Carrying lambs, not rams, Amen!")
Part 4: "He will gently lead those that are with their young"
(lambs once again!)

Four parts out of four! This makes a comprehensive statement for those with ears to hear God's great Fatherly heartbeat. The all-time Pattern Shepherd's heart beats loudly in this verse for His tender lambs.

Jesus truly reflected our Heavenly Father's heartbeat, to "put the lambs first."...when He prioritized the care of His frail, perishable, blood-bought lambs!

Jeremiah 13:20

A wonderfully, haunting & convicting verse in Jeremiah 13:20 reads: "Where now is thy flock? Thy beautiful flock that was given thee?"

Brothers and Sisters. The lambs are so very precious to our dear Lord Jesus. How can we learn to better care for each of them and see that not one of them is lost?

"Honey... 4 out of 5's not bad!"

A humorous, instructive story tells of a father who decided to give his wife a weekend Saturday afternoon "sanity break." He takes their five kids

"Honey... 4 out of 5's not bad!"

with him for the afternoon, to the movies & the park, and finally for ice cream.

On returning, his wife asks him, "Did you all have fun?" He replies: "Yes, we had a blast!" His wife says: "Honey, that's great, but darling, we have five children...I only see four?" To this the husband replies: "Yes sweetheart, I know we have 5 kids, ...but four out of five's not bad!"

"Four-out-of-five" is b-a-d!

Again, we realize that we can NOT correct... what we first don't detect!

If we will...increase our intention... to increase our attention... we will of course, increase our retention! Increasing our intention & attention ...will cut the fog that blinds thousands of churches as to who their converts are, how they're doing, and who's doing what for (and with) them.

Parable of the Church Treasurer:

What would we say of a church treasurer who delivered the following report at their church's annual Business Meeting! He stands up & says:
"I have good news and bad news. The Good News, first off, is that the general tithes and offerings of the church tripled this past year!" Everyone attending breaks into applause, praising God. He continues: "The bad news, folks, is that I (& we as a church board) can't seem to account as to where 96% of our increased income went (or even is)."

"...and the wheat... He will gather in His barn..."

John the Baptist said that when the greater One, Jesus, came, He (Jesus) would baptize with the Holy Spirit and with fire, and that the fire would burn up the chaff. "His winnowing fork is in His hand, to clear His threshing floor and to gather the wheat into His barn." (Luke 3:17)

The Greek word: 'apotheke' here in Luke 3:17 denotes a granary or repository, a place of separation & preservation for putting away & laying aside! What then is "the wheat" that Luke 3 refers to here?

The wheat is none other than each new soul eternally born-again into God's blood-washed family! What is the "barn"? Jesus inferred that the harvest would not only be reaped out in the fields, but would responsibly & properly, be brought into the barn: into the Church.

Not just the Church Universal... but into the local church family, to the people of God: for nurture, feeding, protection & God-honoring care!

Pastors who can't say "Who or where" ...last year's harvest is!

As we look back at the diligent shepherd so highly commended in Luke 15, we can see Jesus teaching diligence as a prototype of the ultimate, vigilant care of our Heavenly Father for e-a-c-h of His sheep... and lambs. Jesus hero-izes that shepherd's diligence. He was both spiritual enough... to count... and then cared enough to CORRECT his mere 1% loss factor. He seeks and finds his one, precious lost l-a-m-b!

I worked a year with another leading pastor. His church grew his first six years, plateau-ed the next two, then began declining his next two years. This pastor said to himself: *"I am not going to tolerate this decline,"* and called me in to work with him.

This pastor was open to improving the care and tracking systems at his church. He openly admitted that of 50 converts reported the previous year, there was no list, nor conscientious care-giving system of who or where these lambs were, how they were doing, nor who was nurturing them.

If people (and lambs) are not missed at a church... its not t-h-e-i-r fault!

Increase the "Attention" ...and the "Retention" m-u-s-t improve!

Because "we can't correct... what we first don't detect, "we implemented tracking both converts and regular attendees and absentees. As we increased the "attention" at this church, their retention not only skyrocketed, but Sunday AM decline stopped. New growth began!

If it is the shepherd's principal job to protect, provide for and prosper his flock, then tracking & care are paramount! "The less we track, the more will fall through the crack", especially the babies!

Jesus put the lambs first: dare we do otherwise?

Greenspan and M.R.G.

My father spent years on the Presidential Council of Economic Advisors for U.S. Presidents Kennedy, Eisenhower, and Truman. My Dad commuted regularly to Washington, DC in this regard, while he also worked at the National Industrial Conference Board in NYC. He also taught economics at New York University (NYU). I often show a picture of him in the White House's Oval Office with "JFK", John F. Kennedy, our 35th US President.

The mark of a teacher, in Jesus' words, is not just the teacher himself, but also the student! My father's graduate-assistant at NYU was Allan Greenspan, now the world's most famous economist & chairman of the Federal Reserve Board. An internet search of Gainsbrugh & Greenspan pulls up an interesting article. Allan speaks of my father being "his old professor", then working for my Dad. If you asked him who taught him economics, he would say: Martin Gainsbrugh!

A "Kingdom Economist"

God has called me, not to be an economist working with our Gross National Product, or the New York Stock Exchange, but something eternally even more valuable: God's Kingdom and the eternal "Flock Exchange!"

"One Soul is worth more than?"

We too lightly say one soul is worth more than all the diamonds in the entire world. But what does our church budget say... about Jesus' top priority of putting His lambs f-i-r-s-t??

Later in this book we will cover "lamb-care and church budgets." Which one receives more attention at monthly Church Board meetings: the outlay of corruptible dollars or the priceless treasure of each new convert born into any local church's congregation?

A Great Commission Audit:

God will hold us accountable for His flock....not only for His sheep...but most especially His lambs...which He has clearly instructed us in John 21:15 ...to feed first!

Any church can and will become a "world-class lambery"...as it increases its i-n-t-e-n-t-i-o-n... to increase its a-t-t-e-n-t-i-o-n... onto the r-e-t-e-n-t-i-o-n, of His lambs!

Our Lord is more than ready, willing, and able, to teach us better, practical, more effective ways... to care for and feed each lamb He sends us.

Chapter 8
"BABY" JOHN: THE LAMB'S BELOVED LAMB

Did Jesus Himself personally put His twelve lambs first?

A-f-t-e-r His triumphal resurrection, Jesus very clearly, specifically prioritized the future-care of His lambs as His top priority.

Jesus put the lambs F-I-R-S-T!

Jesus placed nurturing & feeding His lambs B-E-F-O-R-E the feeding of His sheep! (John 21:5-17).

Jesus put the lambs f-i-r-s-t! We see this unmistakably in John 21:15, although most of us have n-e-v-e-r heard those five words before!

Putting the lambs... F-I-R-S-T... was n-o-t a "new teaching" from Jesus:

Jesus was not dispensing a new doctrine or as sudden "off-the-cuff", discipleship method, when He told them this at the Sea of Galilee after His resurrection!

Jesus had A-L-W-A-Y-S put H-i-s 12 lambs f-i-r-st!

Since Jesus "put His lambs first", ...it logically follows that He also expects us to obediently follow His example... and do the same! As our faultless Shepherd, Model Disciple-Maker, Great Comission-er and Teacher, Jesus a-l-w-a-y-s modeled f-i-r-s-t what He wanted His followers to do, to say... and to be!

How did Jesus "put His lambs f-i-r-s-t" ...with His 12?

Question: "How many of the 12 disciples were newborn "lambs" when Jesus 1st called them?"

Answer: Of course: A-L-L twelve of t-h-e-m were new believers & "lambs" when Jesus first called them!

Jesus clearly had an individualized, special relationship with e-a-c-h of His chosen "twelve". Jesus loved each one of His original twelve in a unique & special way, just as He lovingly deals with each of us, in a very intimate, personalized manner.

A closer look at Jesus' relationship with "Baby John" The many "names" of John!

John the disciple is best known as author of the 4th Gospel, the Gospel of John: (Matthew, Mark, Luke & John). He is also known as John, the brother of James (Matthew 4:21) and as John, the son of Zebedee (Lk.5:8/Mk 1:19), as well as John, the author of his 3 epistles: 1st, 2nd & 3rd John. John also authored the book of Revelation and is called by some: *"John the Revelator,"* and *"St. John the Divine,"*

Best known of all, he's called: *"John the Beloved"*. Even more than these names, John is known as *"The Apostle of Love."*

With 21 chapters in the Gospel of John, 22 chapters in Revelation & seven more chapters in his three epistles (1st, 2nd & 3rd John), John's combined writings make him the 2nd most voluminous New Testament author, writing a total of 50 chapters, out of 260 in all the New Testament!

John was "The baby" and y-o-u-n-g-e-s-t of Jesus' 12 disciples.

John wrote almost one-fifth (20%) of the New Testament. Only the Apostle Paul wrote more chapters, with Paul penning nearly 1/3 of the New Testament scriptures! Together, the two of them: ...Paul & John... wrote over 50%... more than 50% of the entire New Testament!

It's easy to see how and why the great Apostle Paul produced such a prodigious, writing output. After all, Paul was one of the superior intellects and "great minds" of his day. Paul held the equivalent of a world-class rabbinical "Ph.D.", and was trained at the feet of Gamaliel, (Acts 22:3, 5:34). Rabbi Gamaliel was the most internationally-known, renowned Jewish scholar and intellectual/theologian of his time!

But John ? A scholar? A "deep thinker?" The "baby" of the twelve, ...as a trained or prodigious author? Where did "this" come from?

What was it that developed, grew and discipled John into a world-class, deep-hearted, spiritual leader?

Let's take a much closer look at the life of this disciple John, the "baby" of them all!

John: "The baby" and y-o-u-n-g-e-s-t of the 12

Church historians agree that John not only lived to an older age than any of Jesus' other original 12, but also that John was the y-o-u-n-g-e-s-t, the "baby" of the twelve. "Baby John was the "teenager" of the bunch.

"Thunderbolts: ...the Thunder-Brothers!"

John and his brother James were the ones Jesus nicknamed (Boanerges: *"thunderbolts"*- the sons of thunder). Jesus nicknamed them this early on! The nickname sounds like its straight out of the WWF: the World Wrestling Federation!

This same "baby John" (and his brother James) wanted to call down lightning (as Elijah did in I Kings 18: 23-38). In the Luke's ninth chapter, John is quoted saying: *"Lord, shall we call down fire & burn up the Samaritans"*.

This stemmed from John (& his brother Jimmy's (Jame's) shared anger over the half-breed, despised Samaritans refusing to give Jesus (& His advance team) "the keys to their city" and a proper Messianic welcome. (Lk.9:51-55/Mark 3:17).

Who can forget Jesus' quick rebuke to His two rash, young, fireball "followers", James and John. Hear again Jesus' extremely stern rebuke: "You know not what manner of Spirit you are of. The Son of Man is come to save men's lives, not to destroy them." (Luke 9:55 & 56)

How did this young *"fire-ball"* zealot, *"Baby-John"*, the same one Jesus told: "You don't know what manner of spirit you are of" (Lk.9:55),...metamorphose and become known universally in his later years as John: "the Apostle of Love"!

From "Thunder-Bolt" to "The Apostle of Love"

Church history tells us this same youngest disciple, John, in his elderly years, was noted, for repeating one phrase over & over. Wherever the Elderly Apostle John went and ministered, he preached the same Scriptural theme. He became known for saying one thing over and over to those around him: *"Little children...love one another!"*

John's "Life-Change" was
A Relationally–Powered "Heart-Change":

It was this frequently repeated phrase of saying: "Little children, love one another", ...and John's deep Spirit of God's Divine, Agape love, that displayed the deep life-change in John's heart. This alone earned him the nickname most believers know him by today: ...John "THE APOSTLE OF LOVE."

How did Jesus' discipling practices affect John so deeply? ... so permanently? ...so divinely? In the next few pages, we will look more intensively at Jesus' Convert-Care and discipleship technique, specifically with: "Baby John".

"Baby John" was the 'b-a-b-y': the " lamb" of the 12!

Because John was the youngest... he was also the most vulnerable... the "lamb" among the "Lamb's" other twelve disciples (& lambs).

(Mark.3:14-8). John was perhaps 15-17 years old when our Lord Jesus first called John at the Galilee seashore, to follow Him and become a "Kingdom-Fisher" for the souls of mankind. (Matthew 4:19-21)

Apparently... Jesus gave "baby John" some "special" ...relational treatment!

Jesus already had an undeniable, wide-open, magnetic-love for the beauty and tenderness of children, especially the youngest. Jesus'

> **Jesus' words warn not only child abusers... but convert neglectors" as well!**

twelve disciples quickly learned to n-e-v-e-r again attempt to exclude children, or treat little ones as unimportant!

Jesus Himself said: "Do N–O-T forbid (or prevent) the little children from coming to Me, for of such is the Kingdom of Heaven." (Matthew 19:14, Mark 10:13-16). When asked: "who was greatest in His Kingdom", Jesus set a little child in their midst, and then went on to say: "Unless you become like one of these little ones, you will never e-v-e-n enter into the Kingdom of Heaven."(Matthew 18:1-3)

Jesus' words echo through the centuries, to warn not only child abusers, but child excluders... and "convert neglectors" as well. Jesus said: "Whoever stumbles or offends one of these little ones that believe in Me, better for them to have a millstone tied round their necks and cast into the depths of the sea." (Matthew 18:5)

Why was John the only one specifically referred to (5 times) as "the disciple whom Jesus loved?" (John 13:23, 19:26, 20:2, 21:7 & 21:20)

We know Jesus deeply and perfectly loved A-L-L His disciples, especially His chosen, initial twelve. Jesus recognized they were the most vulnerable, the most easily hurt, quickly discouraged, misunderstood and taken advantage of. We see this in Jesus' constant, delicate and loving interaction whenever He was with the children. We also see it in Jesus' personal concern & care for "baby John"

Jesus put John, "the lamb of all His twelve lambs"... F-i-r-s-t!

Jesus put John, "the l-a-m-b of all His twelve lambs" ...f-i-r-s-t! Jesus intentionally showed this prioritizing of the youngest & weakest, in His own obvious, intimate, deliberate and intentional care for "baby John!"

"Baby John:
One of Jesus' inner circle of "The Three" but... "Why?"

Why was "baby John " one of Jesus' inner circle of 3?

John was undeniably in Jesus' "inner circle of the 3". Like millions of other believers, I've repeatedly read over & over that John was one of Jesus' "inner three." I never stopped to ask why.

Peter, James and John:
Jesus' "inner circle of three"

Jesus kept these "inner 3" (Peter, James & John) with Him several times, when He put all the others out...or kept them at a distance.

Jesus modeled this before (& while) resurrecting Jairus' daughter (Mark 5:37). Again, only the "Three" went up on the Mount of Transfiguration with Jesus, to behold Moses & Elijah and Jesus' face morphing, showing His inner, Eternal Reality & God-Head. Jesus' face became bright as lightning! Only Jesus' inner 3 got to hear these greater "three-some" talk of Jesus' upcoming pre-planned "departure" (and Exodus) out of this world, and approaching return to the Father in glory! (Matthew 17:1-3 & Mk. 9:2).

The 3rd time "the inner triad" are seen with Jesus, they are brought alongside our Lord (by Jesus Himself), to pray with Him in the Garden of Gethsemane (Mark 14:33). Jesus takes "the 3" a 'stone's throw' apart with Him, to pray with Him in His hour of maximum trial and stress.. We know, of course, all three "fell asleep", not once, but three times!

Perhaps you, (just as I) have for years, thought Peter, James & John were "the inner three" because they were the most spiritual! (Well, maybe not Peter!) Could it not also be true, that Jesus had a special bond & feeling for John, the lamb (the "baby" of the group?) ...because "baby John" was indeed the very youngest of the 12?

In a healthy family system, the oldest and strongest looks out for, protects... and nurtures... the very youngest and weakest among the siblings!

A healthy family always looks out for and protects its youngest and most vulnerable members.

In a healthy family, a loving, o-l-d-e-r brother always looks out for & protects the younger children, most especially... the very y-o-u-n-g-e-s-t! ...the most intentionally!

God the Father is the original Creator and designer of the Family, as well as the originator of, maximal, healthy loving relationships. Since Jesus obviously modeled perfect relationships His entire life-time here on earth, He clearly loved all 12 of His lambs with His perfect, Divine, 'agape' l-o-v-e.

"Baby" John's Gospel:
85% Different from the other three!

Taking a closer Biblical look at Jesus' special relationship with "Baby John", we see John's Gospel is disproportionately ... almost totally unique ... from the other three Gospels. Only in John's Gospel do we see over 85% more unique vignettes that are "non-synoptic" (not mentioned in the other 3 "synoptic" (largely similar) Gospels: Matthew, Mark & Luke).

It seems as if John had his own special relationship with Jesus! Indeed, he obviously did! One massive example of these differences: John's coverage & treatment of the Last Supper: John's Gospel gives it 5 entire chapters... the three other Gospels give it one chapter each!

John gives the Last Supper five entire chapters... the three other gospels give it only 1 chapter each.

John's Gospel alone spends more time on the Last Supper with His Lord, (five entire chapters: John 13-17,) than the entire other three Gospels do combined!

John was in a "zone" with His Lord. John's quite obvious intimate relationship with His Lord just would not allow him to leave out or leave unrecorded so many absolute scores of key verses revealing the depths and dimensions of our Lord's loving heart there at this last Passover on earth they shared, before He was to go to the cross!

Jesus "washed their feet" ...and so much more:

We can see the Gospel of John's uniqueness everywhere. Let's start with St. John chapter 13. One might begin in a-n-y one of Gospel of John's 21 chapters, and immediately see the unique differences, passages and the events only recorded by John and preserved for us... for all eternity!

As John 13 begins, we see an intimate insider's view of Jesus and His 12 disciples at their final meal together, before Jesus' betrayal, trials, suffering and crucifixion.

All of the following is unique to John's Gospel, and found nowhere else in any of the other three Gospels of Matthew, Mark and Luke: ...only to be found in the Gospel of "Baby John:" ...and "Baby John" alone!

Chapter 9
ONLY IN "BABY" JOHN'S GOSPEL DO WE FIND...

As John 13 begins, we view a unique "insiders" Last Supper snapshot album of Jesus and His 12. John treats us to an incredible, lavishly written, series of intimate "Kodak moments" and "Memorex" 'live' Word-recordings at this special Last Supper... with his precious... Heaven-sent Lord.

Here in John's Gospel alone, we see Jesus take off His outer garment, girding a towel, taking up a Servant's bowl and beginning to wash each of His disciples' feet. (John 13:1-12)

Only "Baby John" ...had his head on Jesus' breast.

Only John records Peter saying: "Lord, You'll never wash my feet," as well as Peter's following response when Jesus says: "If I don't wash you, you have no part in Me". Only John records for us "Rocky's" foot-in-mouth words here (Peter in Greek is Petros, "little rock", or "Rocky"), followed by the drastic, "in-character" change in Peter's response. Peter's humbled reply is: "In that case, Lord, wash my hands & my feet also" ("douse me" -colloquially, as one paraphrase reads: "give me the full works").

Only "Baby John" ...had his head on Jesus' breast" (John 13:23)

Jesus Celebrates The Last Supper as He Himself becomes the Passover Lamb". Breaking the Passover loaf and passing the Passover cup to His twelve, Jesus celebrates the N-E-W Covenant & ultimate eternal meaning of the Passover, Jesus reveals Himself as God's Eternal, only-begotten Sacrificial Passover Lamb... to be slain for the Sin of the e-n-t-i-r-e world! Jesus remarks that one of those present will soon betray Him.

In John 13:23 we read: "Peter beckoned to the disciple whom Jesus loved" (meaning "baby John"). Peter asks John, to ask exactly whom Jesus was referring to. None of the others apparently felt close enough to ask Jesus directly. The k-n-e-w the "Betrayer" (whoever he was) certainly was n-o-t John.

Here in John 13 we also uniquely read:
"The one who had his head on Jesus' breast"...
and... the "one whom Jesus loved".

Again, who was this? Why... it was John! More precisely: "baby" John!

John is the only one in all 89 chapters of the 4 Gospels ever mentioned as "having his head on Jesus' breast."(John 13:23) The King James version puts it even more intimately: "Now there was leaning on Jesus' bosom one of Jesus' disciples, whom Jesus loved."

Was this a singular occurrence, or had it happened before? Scripture doesn't tell us specifically yes or no. Perhaps the other eleven had elsewhere, also put their head on Jesus' chest. Regardless, whether it was commonplace, occurred elsewhere (unlikely), or if this was a unique occurrence, no other mention is made of it.

O-n-l-y the Gospel of "baby John" mentions this intimate passage and revealing detail of the heart-warming, "touch-ability and wide-open "relationality" of Jesus with His f-i-r-s-t disciples.

Listening to a human heartbeat!!

Perhaps Jesus especially wanted this youngest discile to become His very closest!

Have you ever heard the sound of a human heartbeat? Most of us have, either on video or media, either through a physician's stethoscope, or "the real thing." ...l-i-v-e! Is it coincidence that John "the baby" (the youngest), was the one held closest to Jesus' chest? lub... dub... lub-dub... lub-dub!!

What effect did listening to Jesus' actual heartbeat ...have on "Baby John"?

Here John is the only one of the disciples ever referred in Scripture as: "the disciple whom Jesus loved (the Greek word: "agape") once again clearly referring to "Baby John." We see this phrase used here (in John 13:23) for the first time, in this heart-beat listening passage!

"Import" this listening to a human heartbeat... into y-o-u-r own personal experience. How many actual human heartbeats have you listened to in your entire life-time? One or two... perhaps five... probably no more than a dozen, unless you're in the medical profession.

What impact did each heartbeat you've listened to... have on you? "Heart-beat listening" usually only occurs between people with whom one has an extremely close relationship: a mother, father, husband & wife, sister or brother, parent or child. Few others!

What effect did listening to Jesus' heartbeat actually have on "baby John." We may never know exactly, but perhaps the rest of this chapter highlighting some of the countless specific, unique differences of John's Gospel (& life) ...may give us a slight idea as to the "closer" relationship "Baby John" enjoyed!

48

"Listening to the Heart-Beat of God...!"

"Baby John" heard the 'heart-drums' of God's perfect, pure, Agape-love in his Master's heart! Wouldn't your own eardrums and spirit have also leapt for joy, as John the Baptist did in Elizabeth's womb! God's perfect, pure eternal love... resounding in each of Jesus' heartbeats was a unique privilege for "baby John", perhaps like none the other disciples ever had!

What effect did listening to Jesus' heartbeat actually have on "Baby John"?

Think of the effects of this! Divine intimacy, relationship enrichment & immeasureably deep, fellowship. Since "life-change" takes place in relationship... not in isolation... this "heartbeat listening" must have been unlimited, rich soil for "Baby John's" spirit, faith & Christian "life-walk" to grow up in!

Just exactly how different & unique is "baby John's" Gospel ...anyway?

Just a " few" unique things from "baby John's" Gospel :

John's Gospel is so extremely unique & different. Over 85% of it is "non-synoptic", (totally unique) to John's writing, not found elsewhere in either Matthew, Mark or Luke.

O-n-l-y John 1: records Jesus' eternally majestic words: "In the beginning was the Word (Logos) and the Word was with God & the Word was God."(John 1:1) The Greek here actually reads: "and the Word was with God...and **God was the Word!**" Again, o-n-l-y John's glorious first chapter reads: "And the Word was made flesh & dwelt among us... and we beheld His glory (majesty, splendor), as of the only Begotten (Unique Son) of the Father, full of Grace and truth." (John 1:14) Only John 1 also records John the Baptist's eternally significant words: "Behold the Lamb of God, Who takes away the Sin of the world." (John 1:29 & 1:36)

O-n-l-y John 2: records Jesus' 1st miracle, turning the "wedding water" into wine, at the wedding feast in Cana of Galilee. (John 2:1-11)

O-n-l-y John 3: records Jesus' life-changing encounter with Nicodemus and Jesus' unique, inviting and wonderful words: "Unless a man is born again (Greek word: 'anothen'... 'again' .or 'from above' or "from the top"), he will never see or enter the Kingdom of Heaven." (Jn. 3:3,5,7)

O-n-l-y "baby John's" chapter 3 also contains the world's most well-known Bible verse... John 3:16: "For God so loved (agape...& prized) the world, that He gave His only Begotten Son... that whosoever believes in (into) Him, shall not perish, but have Everlasting Life."

O-n-l-y John 4: records Jesus at Jacob's well, wooing & winning the outcast, 5-time divorcee Samaritan woman's heart & life with His words: "God is a Spirit, and those who worship Him must worship Him in Spirit and in Truth" (John 4:24) .

O-n-l-y "baby John" as well (in chapter 4) records Jesus' words and wide-open promise of providing the Living Water: "He that drinks of this water shall thirst again. But He that drinks of the water I give him, shall never thirst, but the water that I give him shall become a fountain (& well), springing up within him, watering him with the water of Eternal Life." (John 4:13 & 14)

O-n-l-y John 5: records Jesus' healing this particular man who was crippled 38 years, lying helpless beside the Bethesda pool. (John 5:1-8)

O-n-l-y "Baby John's" Gospel chapter 5: also records Jesus' amazing promise of Eternal Life n-o-w: "He that hears My words, and believes on Him that sent Me, shall not come into condemnation, but is already passed from (out of) Death... into L-i-f-e!" (John 5:24)

O-n- l-y John 6 records Jesus' eternal promise: "I AM the Bread of Life. He that comes to Me shall never hunger, and He that believes on Me shall never thirst." (John 6:35)

O-n-l-y "baby John" chapter 6 also records Jesus' welcoming promise: "He that comes to Me, I will in no way cast out" (John 6:37)

O-n-l-y John 7 records Jesus' invitation: "If any man thirst, let him come to Me & drink. As the scripture promises: ...out of his heart shall flow rivers of Living Water" (John 7:37 & 38)

O-n-l-y John chapter 8 records Jesus' encounter with the Pharisees and the woman caught in adultery, & Jesus' words: "Let him who is without sin cast the first stone." (John 8:7), as well as Jesus' wide-open, declaration of His Deity: "Before Abraham was born, I AM." (John 8:58) (Greek 'ego eimi')

O-n-l-y John 9: reports Jesus & the man born-blind, being healed and his age-enduring testimonial words: "I once was blind, but now I see." (John 9:25)

O-n-l-y John 10: records Jesus' words: "I am the Good Shepherd"... and all the rest of the beautiful "Good Shepherd & His sheep" passage's forty-two verses as well.

O-n-l-y "baby John" in chapter 10: also records Jesus' age-abiding words: "The thief comes only to kill, steal, and destroy. I am come that you may have Life, and that you may have Life more abundantly (in all its Divine, overflowing, fullness)" (John 10:10)

O-n-l-y John 10 as well quotes Jesus' words: "No man takes My life. I lay it down freely... I give My sheep Eternal Life. No man can snatch them out of My hand. They shall never perish. My Father, Who has given them to

Me, is greater than all. No one is able to snatch them out of My Father's hand. I and My Father are one." (John 10:28-30)

O-n-l-y John 11: tells us of Lazarus' death & resurrection, and Jesus' Death-conquering words: "I AM The Resurrection and The Life. He that believes in Me, though he were dead shall live, and he that lives and believes in Me shall never die."(John 11:25,26)

O-n-l-y "baby John" in John 11:35: also records the great words that show us Jesus' tender, heart of compassion, telling us that ... "Jesus wept!"

O-n-l-y John 12: records Jesus' words: "Unless a grain of wheat fall into the ground and die, it abides alone. But if it die, it shall bear much fruit." (John 12:24,25)

Only "baby John's" twelfth chapter also records for us Jesus' memorial words: "And I... if I be lifted up from (Greek `ek": out of) the earth, I will draw all men unto Me." (John 12:32)

Let's take a c-l-o-s-e-r look...
at "baby John's" 5 chapters on the Last Supper.
(Matthew, Mark & Luke A-L-L cover the Last Supper with one chapter each).

Why did John write more about the Last Supper... than all 3 other Gospel authors combined?

Following are just a few, unique "Last Supper words" ...that o-n-l-y `Baby John' recorded!

O-n-l-y John 13: records our great Lord Jesus (Servant of all servants) washing the disciple's feet. John starts his 5 chapters on the Last Supper, and this footwashing event, with revealing words of incredible intimate, spiritual detail & depth.

O-n-l-y "baby John" 13: also records for us Jesus' one New Commandment: "this one new commandment I give you, that you love (agape) one another, even as I have loved you!" (John13:34).

O-n-l-y John 13:35 records: "By this shall all men know that you are My disciples, by the (Agape) love you have... one to another." Unbelievably, not one of the other Gospels even mentions these two verses & also miss so many of "baby John's" quotes of Jesus' matchless words.

O-n-l-y John 13:23 records: "Baby John's" head (at the Last Supper) being laid down on Jesus' breast.

O-n-l-y John 14:6 records: "In My Father's house are many mansions. I go now to prepare a place for you." (John 14:3)

O-n-l-y "baby John" in John 14 also records: "I am the Way, the Truth & the Life. No man comes to the Father, except through Me." (John 14:6)

Hello! The "lights were on... but was anybody else at h-o-m-e?"

Were the other disciples not even aware of the majesty & beauty of these eternally precious, beautiful Words of Life Jesus was speaking to them?

Did n-o-t the others hear these words also?

O-n-l-y John 14: records Jesus' mentioning the promise of sending the Comforter, the Holy Spirit (in John 14:16), not even mentioned at all by Matthew, Mark & Luke's Gospels.

O-n-l-y John 15: records Jesus' saying: "I AM the True Vine, you are the branches" (John 15:1-16) as well as Jesus' entire True Vine, Vineyard & branches discourse (only found in John).

Only John 15 also records (then repeats) Jesus' new command: in John 15:12... "This is My commandment, that you love (agape) one another, as I have loved you."

O-n-l-y "baby John" chapter 15 also records Jesus' words: "Greater love has no man than this, that a man lay down his life for his friends." (John 15:13)

O-n-l-y John 16 records: "If I go, I will send you the Comforter, the Holy Spirit, to help you." (John 16:7-11) No other Gospel even mentions the Holy Spirit as the Comforter!

O-n-l-y 'Baby John' in 16:33 gives Jesus' world-conquering victory promise: "In the world you shall have tribulation, but be of good cheer, for I have overcome the world (kosmos). (*He that created the 'Kosmos' could certainly over-come it! (that is: the kosmos (world) that He created.)

O-n-l-y "baby John" in chapter 17 records: Jesus' High Priestly intercessory prayer for us all in John 17:1-26. "Father, I pray that they may be one, even as We are One, that the world may believe that You have sent Me" ...and so much more!

Also, only John records in John 17:23: "Father that You would show them, that You have loved them, even as You have loved Me."

Only John 18:6 records Jesus saying, "I AM HE" and the armed mob falling to the ground.

O-n-l-y John 18: records the mob of 200+ soldiers (according to Jewish historian, Josephus) coming to arrest Jesus... and their all falling backward, down on the ground, when Jesus apparently "**flicked His brights!**" and replies: "I AM HE." (John 18:5&6)

O-n-l-y John 19: records Jesus giving the care of His mother to "baby John" at the foot of the cross (John 19:26.27), ...as well as 'Baby John' being the only disciple even there at the cross!

O-n-l-y John 19 as well, records Jesus' last words on the cross, crying out: "It is finished" (John 19:30) ...using the Greek word: "tetelestai" (for it is finished) which in Greek signified: "paid in FULL!"

O-n-l-y John 20: records Jesus' appearing to Mary as "gardener" (20:15). Only John 20 records Thomas' vow of disbelief, subsequent placing his hands into Jesus' nail-wounded palms (& into Jesus' spear-pierced side), and transforming from a "Doubting Thomas to a Sprouting Promise" (John 20:24-29)

O-n-l-y John 21 records: the post-resurrection miracle-catch of 153 large fish & their supernatural Galilee seashore, 'first-breakfast-fish-fry" together!

O-n-l-y the Lamb's "baby lamb", John: records Jesus' vastly, under-taught & extremely crucial words: " If you love Me, feed My l-a-m-b-s" (John 21:15)

Look at exactly what Jesus' closeness and "relation-shipping"...produced in "baby –John's" life:

O-n-l-y "baby John": was there inside the High Priest's Palace, close to Jesus during His "trial" (Jn.18:15), ...when Peter couldn't even stand up to the "campfire girls" and the "rooster-call" 'polygraph!'

O-n-l-y John: was there at the foot of the cross, when all the older disciples cowered elsewhere in depression, disappointment, fear and seeming defeat! (John 19:26)

O-n-l-y John: couldn't be martyred decades later, when the Roman Emperor Nero attempted to martyr and boil John in oil in Rome! Nero had to settle on exiling the aging "baby John" to a life-sentence on the Mediterranean prison island of Patmos. (Intended to be "Club Dead"...not "Club Med"!)

The Roman Emperor Nero... the most powerful person in the world of that day, tried... but not even he... could kill the "Apostle of Love!"

"Long after Jesus' resurrection (& ascension to Heaven),

O-n-l-y "baby John": became known throughout all Church History... as "the Apostle of Love"!

Did listening to Jesus' actual heartbeat make that great of a difference?

Undeniably YES! Jesus' special relationship with "baby John" models for us a deeper, more personal, life-changing, r-e-l-a-t-i-o-n-a-l method of convert-care & its inarguable, world-changing results.

We must devote more time to Jesus' intimate Presence, investing ourselves deeper into heart-throbbing, heart-changing prayer. We must seek out & listen to Jesus' heartbeat of Divine Love! We grow best as we let Jesus' world-changing, Divine love change us...on a "24-7", unending basis!

But Wait! "Baby John" isn't finished "Treat-ing" us yet!

"Baby John's" 3 Epistles provide us e-v-e-n m-o-r-e unique, eternally precious Words of Life!

O-n-l-y in I John Chapter 1 verse 5, do we read: "God is Light and in Him is no darkness at all…"

O-n-l-y 'Baby John's 1st Epistle (1:7) has the freeing Words: "If we walk in the Light, as HE is in (& is) the Light,… we have fellowship one with another, and the blood of Jesus Christ His Son… cleanses us from ALL sin." Again in verse 9: " If we confess our sins, He is faithful and just to forgive us our sins, and to cleanse us from all unrighteousness."

O-n-l-y in 1st John 2 verse 2: we read: "Little children, these things I write to you, that you sin not. And if any man sins, we have an Advocate (Parakletos) with the Father, even Jesus Christ the Righteous: Who is the "At-one-ment" for our sins and for the sin of the whole world!"

O-n-l-y in 1st John Chapter Two do we read three age-specific wordings: "Fathers (2x), young men (2x) & little children(5x)". All through chapter two is a sequenced, gradation of lamb-care: newborns, young sheep & adult sheep: …A-L-L three are to be fed relationally… with age appropriate care!

O-n-l-y I John 3 treats us with these words: "Behold what manner of Love (AGAPE) the Father has bestowed (lavished) on us, that we be called sons of God! Beloved, it does n-o-t yet appear what we will be. When He shall appear, we will be like Him; we shall see Him as He is! (I Jn.3:1&2)

Will the real 'LOVE CHAPTER" please stand up!

John tells us in I John 4 that love is not a concept but a person… …Jesus Christ!

Ask most people: "what is the "Love Chapter"? The usual response is: I Corinthians 13! However, let's take a closer look below as we come to John's 1st Epistle's… Chapter 4! I John Chapter 4 is the t r u e "L-O-V-E (AGAPE) CHAPTER!" (…not I Corinthians 13)

Only in I John 4 do we find the word (Love) Agape… 27 times! (in 21 verses). In 1 Corinthians 13 "AGAPE" is found o-n-l-y… 9x! While 1st Corinthians 13 lists the qualities of God's Love, I John 4 tells us LOVE is n-o-t a thing or mere philosophical, concept. "Baby John" tells us, rather, that Love (AGAPE) is a PERSON in Jesus: the very Love of God! "Baby John" (& John alone)…tells us directly: GOD IS L-O-V-E! (Divine, Agape love!)

O-n-l-y in the 4th chapter of John's 1st Epistle are found the unique words: "Ye are of God, little children, and have overcome them, for greater is He that is in you, that he that is in the world." And again: "This is l-o-v-e, not that we loved God, but that He loved us & sent His Son to be the propitiation (atoning sacrifice) for our sin." "This is (real) Love, not our love for God, ...but in His love... for us" (1 John 4:10) (NIV & Moffat translation)

O-n-l-y 1st John 4 plainly tells us: "God is L o v e" (Agape) (both in 1 John 4 verses 8 &16)

O-n-l-y "Baby John" (1st Epistle chapter 4 tells us: "Perfect love casts out all fear"(4:18) ...and again... "We love Him, because He first loved us." (John 4:19)

O-n-l-y I John 5:11&12 reads: "This is the record, that God has given us Eternal Life & this Life is in His Son. He that has the Son has the Life; he that has not the Son of God has not the Life!"

O-n-l-y John so confidently writes in I John 5:13: that we may K-N-O-W that we have Eternal LIFE! These things I have written to you that believe on the Name of the Son of God, that you may K-N-O-W that you have (now) Eternal Life & that you may keep on believing into the Name of the Son of God!" (John doesn't leave us there! Not hardly!)

O-n-l-y John's 2nd Epistle verse 4 reads: "I rejoice greatly to find your children walking in the Truth."

Finally, in "Baby John's" 3rd Epistle (verse 4) we read: "I have no greater joy than this, than to hear that my children are walking in the Truth (in growing r-e-l-a-t-i-o-n-s-h-i-p w-i-t-h Jesus)! **What about more Words of Life (& jewels) from his "Revelation?"**

O-n-l-y Revelation 1:5 & 6 reads: "From Jesus Christ, Who is the faithful Witness & First-born of the dead. Unto Him Who loved us, and washed us from our sins in His own blood... and has made us kings & priests unto God & His Father."

O-n-l-y Rev. 2:4 warns us: "I have somewhat against thee, because thou has left thy.... first love."

O-n-l-y "Baby John" in Rev. 3:20 tells us: "Behold I stand at the door & knock. If anyone hears My voice & opens the Door, I will come in to Him & will Sup (will feast) w-i-t-h him & he w-i-t-h Me!"

Only in Rev. 4:11 do we read: "Thou art worthy, O Lord, to receive glory and honor and power, for Thou hast created all things, and for Thy pleasure (for Thy will) they were and are created!"

O-n-l-y in John's Revelation: do we read of the Lamb in Whose blood they washed their robes and made them white in the Blood of the Lamb. (Rev. 7:14).

Only 'Baby John' writes: "I beheld a Lamb in the midst of the throne, as it had been slain. And they sang a new song saying: 'Thou art worthy to take the book, and to open the seals thereof. For Thou was slain & hast redeemed us to God by Thy blood out of every kindred, and tongue, and people & nation & have made us unto our God kings & priests." (Rev. 5,6,7,8 &14)

O-n-l-y in John Rev. 12:11 writes; ..."and they overcame him (satan, the accuser)...by the Blood of the Lamb... and by the Word of t-h-e-i-r testimony."

O-n-l-y in Rev. 14:1 are the words: ..."I looked & behold a Lamb stood on the Mt. Zion, and with Him 144,000, having His Father's Name written in (upon: Grk. word `epi')their foreheads".

O-n-l-y John in Revelation 19:7 tells us of the Marriage Supper of the Lamb: "For the Marriage Supper of the Lamb is come, and His wife hath made herself ready. For the fine linen is the Righteousness of the saints! (God's Blood-washed people)!"

O-n-l-y "Baby John" 19:11-14 details Jesus' triumphant return: "His eyes were as a flame of fire, and on His head were many crowns. And He was clothed with a robe dipped (dyed deep) in Blood. And His Name is called The Word (Logos) of God!"

O-n-l-y "Baby John" goes further in Rev. 19:16: "And He hath on His robe & on His thigh a Name written: "King of Kings and Lord of Lords!"

O-n-l-y John tells us of the New Jerusalem: "And I saw a new heaven and a new earth. And I, John, saw the Holy City, new Jerusalem, coming down from God, prepared as a bride adorned for her husband." (Rev. 21:1&2)

O-n-l-y John's Revelation reads: "It is done! I am Alpha & Omega, the Beginning & the End. I will give to him that is a thirst... of the fountain of the Water of Life freely!" (Rev. 21:6)

O-n-l-y "Baby John" in Rev. 22 tells us: "He showed me a pure River of Water of Life, clear(& bright) as crystal, proceeding out of the throne of God...& of the Lamb. In the midst of the street of it, (On either side of the river) was the Tree of Life." (Rev. 22:1-3)

Only "baby John" closes out the Bible with God's final, ultimate, glorious invitation: "and the Spirit & the Bride say "Come!" And let him that hears say: Come! And the thirsting one let him come! And whosoever will...let him come and take of the Water of Life freely!" (Rev. 22:17)

Finally "Baby John" (the Lamb's beloved lamb)
ties it all up with the Bible's final 2 verses:

"And He which testifies these things, says: "Surely I come quickly.
Even so, come Lord Jesus! The Grace of our Lord Jesus Christ be
w-i-t-h you all. Amen!" (Rev. 22:20&21)

Revelation is indeed the "Book of the Lamb": ...It's also: "the lambs' Book!"

Revelation is the "Book of the Lamb". It uses the word Lamb more than the rest of the New Testament.

Only Revelation (in the New Testament) mentions names written in the "Lamb's Book of Life"! (20:15) "Baby John's" Last Book, Revelation... mentions the word "Lamb(s)" 2 9 times! (six times as many times in this one book... as the rest of the entire New Testament combined)! The Greek words for lamb(s): ("arnia" & "amnos") are found in the New Testament 35 times! Three times in John's Gospel (1:29 &36, 21:15)! Once in Luke (10:3), once in Acts (8:32)...& once in 1st Peter (1:19). Six uses so far!

Where do you suppose the other 29 uses of the words "Lamb" & "Lamb's" occur? Take one guess!

Hint! Who's the only one that recorded Jesus' words: "If you love Me, feed My l-a-m-b-s?" Correct! The Lambs 'beloved lamb': ..."Baby John!"

Isn't it appropriate, that in Revelation ("Baby John's" final book)... are found 29 (82+%) of the entire New Testament's 35 uses! (Rev. 5: 6, 8, 12, 13 / 6: 1, 16 / 7: 9, 10, 14, 17 / 12: 11/ 13: 8, 11 /14: 1, 4(2x), 10 / 15: 3 / 17: 14 (2X) / 19: 7, 9 / 21: 9, 14, 22, 23, 27 / & Rev. 22: 1, 3!)

Link John's Revelation of Jesus as the "LAMB" a-n-d John's deep, personal relationship with Jesus!

There just may be more to this whole "relationship" thing... than we've imagined... or been told!

As we close "Baby John:" the Lamb's Beloved Lamb" we see Revelation as the Book of the Lamb! We see Jesus writing the Lamb's Book of Life!

The Holy Spirit is gently whispering in our spirits, that this "Feed My Lambs 1st"& this "relationship thing"... is NOT "the parsley"! It never was & never will be! Rather, it is the Main Course! Relationship is the main dish, God's Program & Jesus' own heartbeat.Our Lord fed His lambs relationally, choosing to keep His 12 w-i-t-h Him, modeling His perfect method for us today!

Look at the results of "feeding a lamb" relationally ...the way Jesus Himself fed "Baby John"!

"Feed My lambs ...FIRST! ...N-O-T LAST! "

We need to invest much more time...listening to Jesus' heartbeat, to connect Jesus' command to feed His lambs FIRST... with Matthew 25:40. Jesus, Who said "lamb's first", also said: "In as much as you did it to the least of these My brethren, you have done it unto Me." (Matthew 25:40).

Who will our own... " Baby John's & "Baby Jane's" be?

Who have our "Baby John's" been? Who have "the least of these" "newborn lambs" been in the past? What have we done (or not done) with...or for them? Who will they be in our future? What "Jesus-style" nurture changes are we willing to set in place... before our Heavenly Father sends one more lamb our way?

How can we re-focus on these "future lambs"... to protect, affirm & nurture each one, in new, special, relationship-powered ways? How shall we put o-u-r lambs f-i-r-s-t, as Jesus said we m-u-s-t... if we truly do love our Lord Jesus?!

Closing Prayer

Lord, we ask You, please, to soften, change and speak to our hearts.

Lord Jesus, breathe into our Convert/lamb-care thinking & methods.

Lord, please show us clearly how to feed Your lambs better!

We promise to listen carefully...

and to do what You say. Enable us to do better & to do it Your way!

Lord, remind us that when "lambs" come our way, Whose lambs they really are!

These are not O-U-R lambs! Instead, they truly are OUR Father's lambs!

They are Y-o-u-r lambs, Lord Jesus! Thank You, Lord, for entrusting their tender care to us.

Lord, help us nurture & love them, as You Yourself, so wonderfully have nurtured and loved us.

Lord, remind us that long ago... we all were lambs!

Even as "Baby John" did, help us to put our head down on Your bosom & to continually listen to Y-o-u-r heartbeat!

Jesus, we ask You to do this. We thank You for Your faithful response & the Holy Spirit's vital help!

Father, we give You all glory... and all the praise... in Jesus' precious Name. Amen!

Chapter 10
"NEW THINKING FOUNDATIONS"

To this point, we've been laying foundation. Pouring the foundation is usually n-o-t the most exciting part of construction. It's the "groundbreaking" ceremony that usually receives a golden shovel & large crowd.

Who Applauds the Pouring of Cement?

Who ever applauds the pouring of cement? Few ever cheer the moving in and operating of heavy-equipment, the excavating of a big hole downward, the pouring of non-descript gray-colored cement.

Foundation:
the "Rodney Dangerfield" of Construction

Each of America's 300,000 evangelical churches had a concrete foundation poured at one time or another. Even if they meet in a rented storefront, office or other structure (unless it's a tent), ...that structure originally needed a concrete foundation poured, to meet construction and building-codes.

Foundation is a bit like comedian Rodney Dangerfield, known for his "famous" one-liner: "I can't get no respect." Foundation (like Rodney), "can't get no respect!"...theologically as well!

Every church foundation, required not just one, but several costly truckloads of cement, running hundreds of dollars ($650 - $850 a truckload).

What a "waste" of God's money...
on foundational cement!

What a tremendous "waste" of God's people's finances: faithfully given, hard-earned, sacrificial finances. How many missionaries could have been financed with those thousands, (literally millions) of "wasted" foundation-pouring, cement-truck emptying foundation dollars?

When did you last consider your own church building's foundation? It sits there beneath your building, getting neither attention or respect. You can't see it, hidden by flooring or carpet. You can easily see and appreciate the walls, ceiling, roof support beams, windows, doors, lighting, multimedia video & sound systems, the platform, Sunday School classes, rest rooms, kitchen, fellowship hall, on and on! Anyone can see, feel and appreciate these "valid" expenditures!

But the "foundation"? Not a very "good investment", not if immediate visibility is the only "value criteria" for expenditures on a well thought-out church structure. How "thoughtless" pastors & church boards have traditionally become, to include this "foundation" expense as a priority and regular component of church buildings.

Quite to the contrary, we know from God's Word (and life itself), that the Foundation I-S ultimately important. Without it, the walls would come tumbling down! Indeed, it is the foundation itself... that d-e-t-e-r-m-i-n-e-s the building!

Jesus prioritizes "the foundation" in Matthew 7:24-27

Read the end of Jesus' famous fifteen minute 3 chapter "quickie sermon" (Matthew 5-7), the Sermon on the Mount. Here Jesus says: "every one who hears these words of Mine & puts them into practice, is like a wise man who built his house & its foundation on the rock. The rains came, the streams rose & the winds blew & beat against that house. Yet it did not fall, because it foundation was on the rock."

The Foundation determines the Building.

A wise man is one who digs d-o-w-n and builds upon the rock. When the wind blows, and the rain and waves beat against it, it does not fall, but rather it stands... because of the Foundation!

A Foundational - Revolution in "New-thinking" about "lamb-care":

We cannot turn around a missing harvest of a half-million converts, if our thinking doesn't change f-i-r-s-t! Just as the foundation d-e-t-e-r-m-i-n-e-s a building, similarly, God designed us so our thinking will determine our actions. If we want a revolutionary transformation, re-"construction" and re-creation of our churches to become "world-class lambery's", our lamb-care thinking must change first!

We need God's Holy Spirit to send us (& our churches) a true revival, ...not just "between our shoulders", but also above our neck-line, a revival "between our ears!"

We need a revival in our "lamb-care" thinking!

We've all heard the statement: "don't just do something, stand there!" In Psalm 46:10, God says: "be still...& know that I am God. I will be exalted; I will be honored among the heathen & among the nations!" Satan hates, more than anything else, the two words that begin Psalm 46:10 , namely... "Be still."

The Hebrew word for "be still" here (at the start of Psalm 46:10) derives from the same Hebrew word in Exodus 15:26. This word in Strong's concordance is related to the "Raphah" in Jehovah Raphah. "Be still" also translates as "be 'Rapha"ed' ... or "Be healed." It is also used elsewhere in Old Testament Hebrew, regarding a sheath of wheat: "being bound up together & thus being made whole or integral".

A "World Class Lamb-ery!"

To build a "world-class lambery", we're also FIRST going to have to come up with world-class, lamb-care understanding.

I believe most readers truly would like their church to be a world class "lambery?". A "lambery" is a lamb-shed: a place for Jesus' newborn lambs to be loved, sheltered, protected and cared for. If we're gonna build up toward this, we first will have to dig "down." If we're gonna change our former "lamb-shed", ...or build a new one, we also are going to have to change and IMPROVE the foundations!

"Be transformed... By the renewing of your mind."

To build a "world-class lambery", we're also FIRST going to have to come up with a world-class, foundational, lamb-care understandings. We must re-prioritize Jesus' clear but vastly ignored and untaught command to "put His lambs... FIRST" ...not last (or otherwise)

We are familiar with
the St. Paul's words in Romans chapter 12, verse 1.
"Therefore, I urge you brothers, in view of God's mercy, to offer your bodies as a living sacrifice, holy and pleasing to God...
for this is your spiritual (& reasonable) act of worship."
(Romans 12:1)

"Do n-o-t be conformed any longer to the pattern of this world, but be t-r-a-n-s-f-o-r-m-e-d, by the renewing of your mind."
(Romans 12:1,2)

Satan hates our thoughts serving God along with our soul, body and spirit. However, when we let the Holy Spirit control our mind, we become thinking "3rd Millennial believers." It is not an oxymoron (like "military intelligence" or "cold-fire") to use the phrase: "t-h-i-n-k-i-n-g Christians"!

The Greek word here for "transformed" is: "METAMORPHOSIS"!

The Greek word "metamorphosis" is used only three times in the entire New Testament. The first occurrence of Metamorphosis is Romans

The Greek word here for "transformed" is: "METAMORPHOSIS"! Only found three times in the New Testament.

12:1-2. Be "transformed" by renewing your mind. This is a clear mandate. As fully surrendered believers, we are to be continually changing, not just spiritually, but also in our "thinking" and foundation as well. God's Word tells us that: "by continually changing o-u-r f-o-u-n-d-a-t-i-o-n...(our "thinking,"), this will automatically change & improve our actions!

The 2nd occurrence is in Matthew 17:2, with Jesus & His "inner 3" on the Mt. of Transfiguration. "And He (Jesus) was transfigured before them: and His face did shine as the sun, and His raiment (garments)... became white as the Light." (Matthew 17:2)

Here we see "Metamorphosis" means not only to "transform", but also "to transfigure", to "shine bright as the sun." How many church's "lamb-care" thinking (& program), need to be transfigured?

The final,
3rd New Testament use of
'Metamorphosis' is in II Corinthians 3:18:
"But we all with open face, beholding as in a mirror the image of our Lord, are being changed into that image, from glory to glory".
II Corinthians 3:18

This verse has the power of the Holy Spirit written all over it! The word "glory" (Greek: Doxa) means splendor and magnificence! To glorify means "to dress with light and honor." We are, in Christ, daily being changed (Metamorphosed) from splendor to splendor by Whom? By the Holy Spirit of God!

We can't change ourselves! Nor does God ask or expect us to. God, however, both can... and will change us, if we but ask and humbly allow Him to. Right now, we are changing the Foundations (our foundational thinking) of our church's lamb-care to become all God wants them to be.

Proverbs 23:7
"As a man thinks in his heart... so is he".

Throughout Scripture, God repeatedly points to the power of our thought-life. In Proverbs 23:7, God tells us, that as a man thinks in his heart, so is he. That's why, in the first and Great Commandment (Deuteronomy 6:5), it is written: "Hear O, Israel, the Lord Thy God is One. And you m-u-s-t worship the Lord your God with (out of) A-L-L your heart, soul , m-i-n-d, and strength."

"If God can change our thinking, He can change our lives & our churches"

If God can change our thinking, He can change our lives! If God can change our thinking, He can change our churches! If God can change our thinking, He can change... and improve... our lamb-care... the vital "life & death" feeding... of His perishable lambs!

What is an acceptable loss-factor of Jesus' precious blood-bought lambs?

What % of our lambs actually remain (or are perennially lost) each year? Is this an acceptable loss factor to Jesus?

Dear reader, I'll let you ask and answer this (in prayer) to yourself! Let's start with 50%. Is a 50% "loss-factor" of His lambs acceptable? Half for us &..? How about a 1/3 loss? We keep twice as many as we lose? How about 25%: we retain 3 lambs, for each one we lose? Not very appealing? Well how about 90%? We keep 9 of 10; we only lose 1 out of 10! Surely that's good enough?

Z-E-R-O... is the O-N-L-Y "Acceptable" loss factor!

We need to honestly answer this question, not as a hypothetical "mental exercise", but humbly in light of our church's actual "fruit". What % of our lambs actually remain (or are perennially lost) each year? Is this an acceptable loss factor of Jesus' lambs to you? What loss % ...will we settle for?

The correct answer is Z-E-R-O-!

The diligent shepherd in Luke 15, had a mere 1% loss factor. He detected & corrected it, thus receiving an eternal praise from our Lord! However, across our nation, we've seen convert loss-factors commonly reported: too often in the 90%+ loss level, and even 100% district-wide losses! Drastic God-honoring, change... is long over-due!

"Lamb-inating"... not merely "lamb-en"-tating.

The time we've spent in Section I, improving our "lamb-care" ...and our John 21:15 foundational thinking ...is not lost! Not if God double-fills our churches with "lasting fruit", with changed-lives, with loved, nurtured and connected lambs. Healthy lambs that are "family"-ed, discipled, (and eventually sent out as missionaries to every part of this world), will spread the Amazing grace and love of Jesus everywhere!

May we never again neglect this truth & place His perishable lambs "second" in care!

Chapter 11
"IMPROVEMENT EQUALS CHANGE"

We now all live in a paradigm of mega-change, a continual, daily, non-stop "change-tsunami", and "24-7" diet of 'toxic change!' If you occasionally feel overwhelmed and "change-challenged", don't feel alone: we are all in this same change-tossed 3rd Millennium boat .... together!

"Working smarter"... or "working harder"?

Most pastors don't need to "work harder." Most are already working as hard as they can. It is more a question of working "harder" at "working smarter", being open to new-thinking; open to change and open to improvement.

Most pastors are "working harder, not "smarter"!

> "Why doesn't what used to work... work the same way that it used to work?"

Too many pastors are working harder, not "smarter!" Too many use socially obsolete methods and generationally-outdated information. Pastors, church boards, and leadership across our nation are scratching their collective heads, wondering collectively: "Why doesn't what used to work... work the same way that it used to work?"

"The Mountain Bike"

Near where I live is a roadway that drops 1,000' in elevation in a two mile stretch, down to the Middle fork of the American River. This incredible hill is (in places) close to a forty-five degree angle going down... and up!

A while back, driving up this road from the river, I saw a couple, on a tandem two-rider bicycle, peddling up it! They were halfway up this two mile merciless, uphill stretch... and amazingly were making progress as I passed!

I thought to myself: "My goodness, do they eat anything else but steroids? My legs cramped just watching them steadily, but slowly, progress up this incredible incline! I was "exhausted", watching them thinking of the energy they must've been putting out... to bicycle up that "monster hill!"

Then the thought came to me: they weren't doing this on an old-style, one-speed Schwin bicycle, like I grew up riding 40 years ago!.

What does a mountain bike do?
I t works "smarter, not harder!"

A mountain bike "thinks smart-er" ...not harder". The mountain bike "re-thinks" the problem:... the challenge of... the h-i-l-l! It doesn't make the incline any less steep! Rather, by "working smarter, not harder", the mountain bike breaks up the uphill challenge into smaller, manageable increments. The effort-ratio/incline uses many more gears and innovatively designed, sequential gear-teeth, creating many more smaller, manageable increments!

A mountain bike helps one
"ride s-m-a-r-t-e-r, not h-a-r-d-e-r!"

I still don't know how to use my son's 15 speed mountain bike. But if I had to ride that hill every day, I'd sure find someone to teach me! I'd be a quick & willing learner, after walking up that hill just one time on a hot summer day!

A "reluctant learner" in Power Point:

I've been learning Microsoft Power Point, a popular visual presentation software. Each time I use it, I get more comfortable with it. At first I clung to the old, overhead projector "technology" and use of overhead trans-parencies. However, to reach this current "visually programmed & video-addicted" generation, I knew we simply cannot "go back!"

I admit I'm a slow learner! My son Christian works in advanced com-puter "tech support", web-design enhancement and computer graphics. His classic line to me is: "Dad, I'd like to teach you computer but I can't keep up with you! You learn too slow!"

We can't turn back the clock !

We can't "turn back the clock", but we can "turn ourselves" and our thinking...forward!

There's not one reader of this book, who wants to return to the days of pumping water from a well...nor to "go back" to the days "B.I.P."(before indoor plumbing)? Now as I travel and present seminars (and in my Sunday services across the nation), I regularly use Power Point with comfort. I use it also as an example of "a reluctant learner". God has called me to continually teach nationally about improvement in the area of feeding His precious lambs! As we've already covered in depth: all improvement...requires change.

Improvement Equals "C-h-a-n-g-e ":

People say: "We like improvement. We're constantly committed to improving and doing better!." However, Mark Twain's famous quote on change is more accurate when he said: "the only one who really likes change ....is a baby with a wet-diaper."

It is not "change" we really like! What we like, is the Improvement that "good-change" brings! This is precisely why each of God's people, must become skilled, ever-improving change-agents. We must learn to spell change continually with an "I" ...for i-m-p-r-o-v-e-m-e-n-t!

Spelling change with an "I" for improvement:

What we, and all people everywhere, really like....is improvement.

I = C Improvement equals change.

All improvement requires change! It sounds like a "no-brainer", namely that improvement equals change. A-L-L improvement requires and produces change! All "I" ("I" standing for improvement) produces & equals change... but not all "C" equals "I".

All I = C... but not all C = I
Not A-L-L change equals improvement:

There is "negative change". Sometimes things do change for the worse, but not when God is in charge. We can be confident that when God changes things, it is always for the better.

Change, however, takes faith. Even if we can't see it at first, God-directed, God-implemented change is ALWAYS for the better! If we ask God for a loaf of bread, He will not give us a stone!(Lk.11:9-13).

Your "I.Q" equals your "C.Q."

What's the "IQ" of y-o-u-r church? We're not talking about Intelligence Quotient, but rather Improvement Quotient.

Our improvement quotient = our change quotient.

Our "I.Q" = our " C.Q." We can't improve any more than we're willing to change.

Are you willing to change whatever God wants to see changed? I pray the Holy Spirit holds our feet, our hearts & our lives, to that fire: the fire of change and improvement... in putting Jesus' lambs first!

There is only 1 nation in the world
where Christianity is not growing... Surprisingly,
...it is the United States!

I would gladly travel at home or abroad with an overhead projector! However, when culture changes, we must seek God's help to use the culture-change to reach, win, nurture & disciple all we can.

God has a strategy for His lambs... for their care, nurture, growth and survival! We must remember the lambs are the future of the flock... and a flock without lambs is a flock without a future!

We desperately must re-evaluate the "success" of non-working methods, and allow our Lord to teach us His methods... and His ways... to produce the fruit He wants to see: fruit that remains (John 15:16).

It's past time to return to the original model.

There is a valid saying: "If it ain't broke, don't fix it." There's another equally valid saying that says: "If the horse is dead... dismount!" You don't need a new saddle, a different feed mixture, new paint on the barn, etc. If the horse is dead it's time for a new horse!

Chapter 12
"TOP 15 MYTHS OF CONVERT-CARE"

Let's now look at some inaccurate, and obsolete thinking that holds too many churches back from becoming a "world class lamb-care center".. or "world-class lamb-ery", a title I prefer..

Definition of a "myth:

A myth, according to Webster, is "making an unproven idea into a fact! One well-known, historic myth, in the days of Christopher Columbus, was the commonly accepted "fact" that the "world was flat".

Since the world was "flat", they reasoned that if one traveled beyond the visible horizon, you would fall off the edge of the world!

Actually, the world is not flat. We all know it's round. The horizon (or line-of-sight & vanishing point) at sea level, is a mere eleven miles. Thus, this myth severely limited their actions, travel, and horizons.

In the realm of convert nurture and "lamb-care", what one believes, also determines (and severely limits) one's actions (or lack thereof). .

"The Circus Elephant, the Stake... and The Chain"

The story is told of a huge three-ton, full-grown Asian elephant, seen at circuses, often staked to the ground by a two foot metal stake it quite obviously could pull out anytime it desired.

The elephant keepers, however, are confident. Through years of pre-programming & reinforced input, when the huge elephant was a baby, the elephant was absolutely "convinced" that it couldn't pull that stake & chain out of the ground.

The elephant's "thinking"...determines...and l-i-m-i-t-s its actions!
In its mind, it is limited by what it believes. It therefore never exerts its independence and never experiences its freedom.

Fifteen All Too-Common Convert-Care Myths:

Allow me to ask you, to challenge yourself, and to challenge your church's convert-care assumptions and thinking, regarding the following wide-spread lamb-care myths!

Our Convert-Care can only improve as much as we're willing to let God change... and improve... it!

To start keeping 96% of our converts (instead of losing 96 %), we need to admit we don't know as much about nurturing New Converts as we thought we did.

The truth of the matter is, ...we don't even know...what we don't know!

Below are 15 Lamb-care Myths that We need to expose and rid ourselves (& our churches) of!

Myth #1) Jesus said: "If you love Me, feed MY SHEEP! We've already irreversibly learned, this is "right" .... but it's W-R-O-N-G! WRONG, both as to Jesus' clear John 21:15 priority & also wrong in sequence! **WRONG!**

Myth #2) That USA "Christianity" is growing (along with most churches) from "widespread revival" in the land! The truth is, the USA is the world's only nation where Christianity is N-O-T growing! **WRONG!**

Myth #3) "We don't need to check on them! We're doing ok & so are our converts Wrong! Ask most pastors specifically who (& where) most of their converts are, and how they're doing. You'll receive a huge surprise! They have somehow been trained... by d-e-f-a-u-l-t... to "not k-n-o-w"! **WRONG!**

Myth #4) "There can't be that much to learn in New Convert Care. That's why it is mentioned so infrequently & taught even less from the pulpit. **WRONG!**

Myth #5) "If it were that crucial, our pastor & God's Word would say more about it!" **WRONG!**

Myth #6) "Our New Converts are very dependable & mature; they pretty much take care of themselves." **WRONG!**

Myth #7) "Someone else in the church will do it (or is already taking care of it!)" **WRONG!**

Myth #8) "We don't know what our convert survival (retention) #'s or % losses are, but I'm sure they're ok" **WRONG!**

Myth #9) "If our baby Christians need our help, they'll let us & the church know!" **WRONG!**

Myth #10) "It was good enough for me when I was saved long ago: it's good enough for them now as well! Things haven't changed that much!" **WRONG!**

Myth #11) "If our new converts don't "make it' and stick with the Lord (& with our church), it's t-h-e-i-r fault : it certainly can't be ours!" **WRONG!**

Myth #12) "There's too many other more important areas than lamb-care that already need attention, ministry help & improvement at our church. **WRONG!**

Myth #13) The Holy Ghost will do it! It's God's job & it is His sovereign responsibility! **WRONG!**

Myth #14) The last thing we need at our church is a "New Convert Task Force." We're as good as we can possibly get! We definitely don't need one more committee, one more meeting to go to, report to gather, or one more way to use our already depleted available supply of congregational ministry man-hours... **WRONG!**

Finally, Have you ever heard this one?
Myth #15) The Myth of the Sower & 75% "Bad Soil" Types:

One final prevalent Convert myth 'mis-uses' Jesus' words in Matthew 13. Here Jesus tells the parable of the Sower. Jesus says: "A sower went forth to sow and as he sowed, some of the seed fell on the wayside (the path or road). Some of it fell on rocky ground. Some of it fell on the thorns and some of it fell on the good soil." Four types of soil.

I've had pastors come to me and say: "Heh! JG! Jesus said the seed falls on four types of soils (souls), right! Since Jesus Himself mentions three of those four soil types are bad, then there's no problem with us losing three-quarters of the harvest. Right?" **WRONG!**

Does this make stupid look smart, or...?

Let's look at this Parable of
the Seed-sowing Farmer a little bit closer.

Soil type #1: "The road" What kind of a farmer would go onto the Interstate Highway & put 25% of his seed out on the 6 lane? Yup! That's "the path" in the parable! No 25% here!

Soil type #2: "Rocky Places" the stony/rocky places. Again, what farmer would plant 25% of his seed in the middle of a rock quarry? Deliberately and on purpose? No 25% here!

Soil type #3: "The Thorn Patch": What farmer would plant 25% of his seed smack-dab in the middle of a briar patch or multi-acre black-berry field? Again, no 25% loss here!

Soil Type #4: "The Good soil": The Good Soil! (Soul soil!) Now, in Matthew 13:8, Jesus tells us that the good seed falls in good soil. It roots & grows there, and brings forth 30, 60 & 100 times as much as that which was planted in it".

The Lighthouse and the Admiral:

A classic story is told of a seasoned American Navy Admiral aboard a world War II battleship off the coast of Europe in a gale-force nighttime storm. Seeing a dim distant light, the ship's radio operator picks up a faint, static-bruised radio frequency from the distant light's direction. The Admiral, directing from the same bridge, commands the radio operator to give the proper maritime "Yield to starboard" warning. He does so, saying:

> "This is the battleship Missouri. Yield and give way to starboard, ...we are coming through!"

The static increased, the storm worsened and the other ship's light drew nearer, with seeming zero response!

> **"I am the South Wales Lighthouse. Admiral, I respectfully advise you to change Y-O-U-R course!"**

Drawing still nearer to this distant faint light, the Admiral stomped over to the radio operator, grabbed the microphone and with his full authoritative, booming voice, commands: "I am Admiral so & so. This is the U.S. Battleship Missouri. As an active 5-star Admiral under the direct command of the United States Commander-in-Chief Dwight Eisenhower, head of the combined Allied Forces, I speak for the entire US Navy North Atlantic 5th fleet: Yield way to us immediately and turn to starboard!"

The Admiral continued ranting: "I command, under penalty of international maritime law... whatever ship you are out there, immediately submit and change your course. Yield immediately: Give way to our battleship!"

Providentially, just for a few brief moments, the storm abated. The heavy radio static cleared up enough for the Admiral (& others nearby) to clearly hear the ongoing response that they had not yet been able to clearly pick up. The message finally coming through was worded like this: "I am the South Wales Lighthouse on the rocky coast of Portsmouth, Great Britain. Admiral, I respectfully request & advise y-o-u...that you change y-o-u-r course!"

The Lord will N-O-T change His course, ...nor His John 21:15 Priority!

The Lord will not change His course or His Word, nor His John 21:15 priority, ...that of putting His lambs first!

We can not win, by either fighting or mis-prioritizing God's Way and His method to build His Kingdom. However, neither can we be defeated i– f we will follow God's simple, Kingdom-wise command... to "put His lambs f-i-r-s-t"!

Section One: Conclusion
New Foundations For a World-Class "Lamb-ery"

We've studied some vastly undertaught, misprioritized, new, scriptural, foundations to change our church's chosen "course" back to Jesus' priorities,

Jesus clearly said through John's writings in John 21:15...
> *"If you love Me... put My Lambs f-i-r-s-t!"*

We've only just begun to change and to improve!.

Just as we had never heard that Jesus put the lambs f-i-r-s-t, we must move on now to learn Jesus' own personal method. Jesus' method is n-o-t a program, but rather what most of us have been actually been theologically programmed against: namely, the power of relationship.

Spelling it with an 'R' ...the life-changing power of relationship... is now, always has been... and always will be... God's quintessential, eternal plan. It is God's heartbeat for mankind , and for His newborn (and older) believers alike. Relationship, indeed, is His blueprint... and His "program"! We may not yet know how to "Spell it with an R" ...but with God's help, we will learn how!

As one District Superintendent said to me over dinner, using so few words to express such a deep, biblically true thought: "Ministry is A–L–L Relationship!"

Section II: Chapter 13
"JESUS' STYLE CONVERT-CARE"

*God in His wisdom brings His genius...
over to... the simple side of complex!*

God in His wisdom brings His genius... over to... the simple side of complex! The simplicity of God's wisdom (and His "all too do-able" plan) is often missed, or misinterpreted within the maze of our over-complicated methodologies, formulas, and convoluted religious programs.

> **The Pharisees "missed God" relationally while teaching about him religiously.**

Jesus elegantly and bluntly put it to the Pharisees and religious authorities of His day! They "missed God" relationally...while "teaching about" Him religiously! Jesus said: "I thank Thee, Father, Lord of Heaven and earth, because You have hidden these things from the wise and prudent, and have revealed them unto babes. Even so, Father, for it seemed good in Your sight." (Matthew 11:25,26)

Man-made, man-centered Theology (often substituted for the study of the pure, Living Word of God), often takes people a totally different direction than that of personally knowing God in an ever more intimate, relational way. Jesus n-e-v-e-r did that!

Jesus never sublimated relationship, or placed it in a subordinate position b-e-l-o-w knowledge!

Jesus' own personal 'method' is neither complicated nor hidden. To reach and teach us, God (in His love and wisdom)... gently brings down His infinite genius.... over to the simple side of complex!

"I never saw it either!"

I've personally read through 22 different New Testament translations Not just the Old King James and New KJV, the NIV, NASV, Living & New Living, Phillips, Amplified and the rest of the basic top dozen other most read versions. I'm not just referring to merely reading the New Testament in one volume, (extracted from 26 Translations). Nevertheless, despite all these various Bibles and New Testament I've read through, I still never saw it!

Neither did I see it in the Berkeley, Barclay, Beck, Williams, Wuest or Weymouth translations, nor the rest of these two dozen New Testament translations. I never saw it! I read the Bible through three times in a year,

73

and still, I never saw it! I learned and studied the original "koinei" /market-place Greek that...the New Testament was written in. Still I never saw it.

I never saw Jesus' "lamb-care" method in John 21:15...that of "putting the lambs F-I-R-S-T until the Holy Spirit pointed it out to me. Once seeing that Jesus did it this way, I was convinced & convicted that I (as we all) should do as Jesus did as well!

Similarly, I never saw this next, major point: Jesus' style of "convert-care".

I also never saw Jesus' style of "convert-care", that is until God's Spirit pointed it out to me as well. This came A-F-T-E-R having preached in 500 churches, after 30 years of full-time ministry, reading the Bible daily, traveling a million miles & teaching thousands of pastors what God had shown me in other areas! There was so much more to learn. Always more...if we stay teachable and "learnable".

"When you really know somebody..."

When you really, really know somebody, more often then not, it is because of a relationship.

The deeper the relationship, the deeper the self-disclosure & "knowing" of the other person. You learn their likes and dislikes, preferences & priorities, and their "hot and cold buttons". Bit by bit, you learn their "psychography": their internal psycho-emotional information, how they think, feel & operate from the "inside out!"

It's said (and true) that a longtime married couple can often sit & comfortably communicate, at times, without saying a word. Sometimes ...often... they just "know" what the other is thinking and feeling.

Here, once again, we see the awesome, under-valued, infinite power of "relationship."

Truth is A P-E-R-S-O-N... N-O-T a Thing... or philosophical concept!

Jesus' own personal method isn't complicated. Jesus' Himself said: "If you continue in My word, you are My disciples indeed. And you shall know the Truth, and the Truth shall set you free."(John 8:32)

> **Truth is A P-E-R-S-O-N... N-O-T a Thing... or philosophical concept!**

What is often totally missed here, is that Truth is not a "thing". Rather, Jesus (Himself)....He... i-s t-h-e T-r-u-t-h. He says this in John 14:6 with the words: I AM the Truth., the Way, and the Life." Truth is a Person, known through a relationship....not a mere cerebral, isolated concept, belief, or mere "factoid". This same relational Jesus said: "if you love Me, feed My lambs... (F-i-r-s-t)! "

An overlooked "n-o-t-h-i-n-g" of a memory verse in Mark 3:14:

As I travel, I ask congregations & seminar attendees nationwide: "Who here today has a Memory verse from John chapter 3?" Knowing I'm referring to John 3:16 (the world's most well known Bible verse), almost every hand is raised! Next, as I ask about Proverbs chapter three, a few less hands go up, for Proverbs 3:5 & 6. If I ask about Revelation chapter 3, I get a few less hands raised for Revelation 3:20. The same with Amos 3:3, or perhaps Genesis 3:15. However, when I ask who present has a memory verse from the Marks 3rd chapter, usually not one hand is raised!

I might be teaching at a District Ministers' Institute, with scores (or 100's) of pastors present, representing literally hundreds of thousands of hours of cumulative Ministry in the room. Present around me are lifetimes spent in ministry, representing 10,000's of verses memorized, and 10,000's of sermons preached! When I ask directly about any memory verse from Mark chapter 3: ...Zippo! Nothing! Nada! Zilch! Not a single hand will be raised.

The reason why is there's obviously nothing truly worthwhile, or anoint-ed in Mark three. Not hardly! Even when I specifically identify by number the verse I'm targeting as Mark 3:14, there is usually a zero-response rate. a Mark 3:14 is an undiscovered treasure and treasure map sitting right there in God's Word!

> **Jesus chose twelve to be W-I-T-H Him.**

Mark 3:14 is an Undiscovered Treasure and Treasure Map

I am presenting a new memory verse for you from Mark 3:14. I urge you to repeat it out loud and memorize it. Its only 7 words! How long can that take! Your staff needs to memorize it. Your entire church board & deacons should learn it. Then, your entire leadership "core" should learn it. Finally, your entire congregation will benefit greatly, learning it by heart! It truly i s t-h- a- t extremely i-m-p-o-r-t-a-n-t!

> *We read in Mark chapter 3 verse 14: "*
> *...Jesus chose 12 to be with Him."*

This one, little known verse clearly unveils Jesus' "lamb-care" strategy!

Is Jesus' personal method hidden and buried very deep? Hardly? It is right here, spelled out right in front of us. We not only haven't seen it... we don't see it, even now! Not really! Jesus' "lamb-care" method: ...in 7 words:

Seven words: "He chose 12 to B-e W-i-t-h Him."

"He chose 12 to be w-i-t-h Him". We can't "see the forest for the trees!" It's right there, right here, right in front of us right now! Our minds are blinded. We still don't see it! It's not esoteric, convoluted or too cerebral for the average mind to grasp.

**The difficulty, is not that it's too complicated...
The difficulty, rather... is that it is too simple!
Too Simple To See!**

Some reading this right now are saying to themselves: "You want me? ...a professional minister. ...or a long-time believer ...to memorize this little "gibbit"...this "nothing" of a verse! What in the world for? Why? How could it possibly be that important?"

As Shakespeare said: "To w-i-t-h or not t o w-i-t-h that is the question!"

It doesn't fit our "Western world-view": our cerebral, program–based, "difficulty-enhanced" theology! Somehow, we deem it as "below" or "beneath"... our "deeper" concepts, beneath our recognized "program-addiction" to facts, cognitivity, empirical data, program, program, program, theology, theology, theology, etc. etc.

Jesus' chosen method (as shown here) is a vital, missing method... and missing element... missing in American Christianity... and missing in our lamb-care thinking!

Jesus program for the 12 was: to "w-i-t-h" Them

Jesus chose them... "to w-i-t-h" them! You may say you can't make a verb out a preposition, but I just did. I did, ...because Jesus did so first! Spelled with an "R", Jesus' program was to "Relationship " them. You may say again: "you can't make a passive noun "relationship" ...into an active verb". Once again I just did, because Jesus did it first!

Jesus chose them to "with" them... to "Relationship" them, and to "family" them! To "family" is a verb as well, a vital "lamb-care" necessity for every single new believer! In Jesus' own personal lamb-care methodology and modeling... to disciple is, at its heart...: "to be w-i-t-h!"

**As Shakespeare is so often quoted... (from Hamlet):
"to W-i-t-h"... or not "to W-i-t-h... that is the question!"**

This is indeed the question not just for every church & its converts, but for your church & y-o-u-r converts.

**Those that Jesus "with"-ed... would g-r-o-w!
Those NOT "with"-ed... would... "w-i-t-h-e-r. "**

Just as there are the "have's" & the "have nots", there are the "with's" and the "with-outs".

Those that are "with"-ed will grow. Those that He would "with', Jesus knew they would grow, develop, be relationally nurtured, become spiritually imprinted, and ever so slowly but surely, mature into healthy, reproducing disciples. Those not "with"-ed will "wither" & perish...& eventually die "with"-out!" All the world's theology, without relationship, will just produce more novels like that famous English work: "With-ering Heights!"

"W" spelled with an " R":

Jesus chose His initial first group of 12... to be "w-i-t-h", not to occasionally see, or intermittently contact in an impersonal, distanced method! Jesus' program was not a program with a "P"... but program spelled w-i-t-h a huge, upper-case, capital "R"! Jesus' "lamb-care" plan for His twelve was a lifetime emphasis on growing a deepening, personal relationship with His chosen disciples. His relational "lamb-care" plan and strategy was a lifestyle commitment.

Spelled with an "R"...
Jesus' program was "relationship."

Jesus' winning "game-plan" was "to relationship" them solidly the next three and a half years. When He said: "Follow Me", He wasn't talking once a week, nor 2 or 3 times a week. Jesus meant "24-7"!

Jesus' program was n-o-t a "Program"!

Precisely what Jesus did w-i-t-h His initial group of 12 disciples: was "to relationship" them. Jesus' own discipleship method was "p-e-r-s-o-n-a-l", not paralytically programmatic, convulsively complicated, doctrine-driven or informationally intoxicated!

Jesus chose His initial first group of 12, to be "with", for this is merely how love connects people: through r-e-l-a-t-i-o-n-s-h-i-p.

"We're using TEFLON...
and expecting it to act like VELCRO!"

The major reason Christianity is growing in every nation around the world, ...except one: the "USA" is plain to see. We are using man's program ("P")... instead of God's program "R"!

We are using "teflon" and expecting it to function like "velcro." Teflon is smooth and designed for "non-stick". Velcro, quite oppositely, is rough, with hooks and loops. It is designed to do just one thing, just like relationship. Both velcro... and relationship... are designed to stick... and hold things (or people) together... through a permanent, non-breaking r-e-l-a-t-i-o-n-s-h-i-p and bond!

"Bear w-i-t-h me... regarding this "W-I-T-H" thing!

Are you still "with" me? What a thrill to know that all day and even while we sleep, our Lord is there... & h-e-r-e w-i-t-h us! He is not only a "w-i-t-h it" God, He is a "with" God! And the God of w-i-t-h!

Jesus' very "NAME" is " W-I-T-H"

Seven hundred years before Jesus' "earth-birth" and incarnation here on earth, the Prophet Isaiah prophetically wrote: "And the virgin shall conceive and shall bear a child, and His Name shall be called Immanuel, which being interpreted means: "God W—I—T—H us!" (Isaiah 7:14)

When the angel Gabriel appeared to Joseph, to announce the coming immaculate Divine conception and birth of Jesus (to and through) Mary, the Archangel himself also repeated Isaiah's prophecy in Mathew 1:23: "And His Name shall be called Immanuel, which being interpreted, means: "God w-i-t-h us". The very concept and meaning of the word "W-i-t-h" is an integral, Eternal part of God's original Divine Design of salvation. Jesus' very own deepest Name, God-hood and nature is "W-I-T-H!"

Jesus chose the 12 to:"be w-i-t-h" Him... right from the very Beginning!

The God of "W-I-T-H" -I-N-G

Our God is a God of "w-i-t-h-i-n-g." Now I've gone and made an "ing" gerund, and "action-verb" out of it. Our Lord Jesus is not only the "Lord... of Lords", ...but He's also the "Lord...of "with"-ing!

Spelling the "W"-word with an "R": Jesus' discipleship program, clearly, was Relationship! You say: "that's not much of a 'heavy-revvy:'...and "JG, you're not a very 'deep sheep!' Some of us are "too deep" for God's plan! God's simple plan is to "w-i-t-h" His lambs. But we come up with something different..."deeper": something "better!" Jesus chose 12 to "be with" Him. We must return to H-i-s plan!

What was it that Jesus did "W-I-T-H" His 12 disciples?

Jesus deliberately chose to "do life" with His 12. For this very reason, He did the Spiritual, He did the Religious, and He also intentionally, did the "Everyday" things with them as well!

Spiritual Things:
Jesus did "spiritual things" W-I-T-H them

Spiritual things like what, you might ask? Well, Jesus prayed w-i-t-h them, He fasted w-i-t-h them, He raised the dead w-i-t-h them & cast out devils w-i-t-h them as well! Jesus walked on the water w-i-t-h Peter (& in front of the rest), He multiplied the bread and fishes w-i-t-h them (twice).

Jesus opened blind eyes w-i-t-h them, healed the deaf w-i-t-h them, touched & cleansed untouchable lepers w-i-t-h them etc.

Almost e-v-e-r-y-t-h-i-n-g Jesus did, He did quite on purpose, for and w-i-t-h them! Just your basic, everyday "garden (of Eden) variety" miracles! Jesus chose them... to "be w-i-t-h Him". They usually (by Jesus' intentional plan), were right there for the majority of those three & half years.They were w-i-t-h Jesus for almost every single one of these wonderful, super-natural miracles!

No wonder "baby John" wrote in the very last verse of his Gospel: "Many other things Jesus did also, which if they were written down every one, even the world itself could not contain the books (Greek word-'Biblia') that would have to be written." (John 21:25)

In the four Gospels, we see Jesus never attended a funeral that He didn't break it up! He attended three and broke up each one with His Resurrection power! Where were the 12 ? They were there w-i-t-h Jesus through each of these resurrections & scores of other miracles as well!

Religious Things
Jesus did religious things "W-I-T-H" His 12

What sort of religious things did Jesus do w-i-t-h His twelve? Well, Jesus went down to Jerusalem w-i-t-h His disciples annually. Like any devout Jew, Jesus attended the three annual Jewish festivals w-i-t-h His disciples. He "festival-ed" w-i-t-h them. Jesus also paid the temple tax w-i-t-h them, studied the Torah and "torah-"ed w-i-t-h them, commemorated Passover w-i-t-h them, etc.

In our Western culture, we do better at emphasizing the Religious and the spiritual things w-i-t-h our converts. The "everyday" has definitely been given a distinct, theological 'back seat.' The one part of these three main areas of "with-ing (Spiritual, Religious & Everyday) that suffers the greatest neglect in our "cocoon-ing" techno-culture, is doing the "everyday" with our lambs. We somehow just don't choose to "be w-i-t-h" them, in the same way that Jesus did the everyday with His original, first twelve disciples!

Everyday Things:
Jesus did "e-v-e-r-y-d-a-y things... "W-I-T-H"... His 12!

Jesus walked w-i-t-h them, He talked w-i-t-h them, He shopped w-i-t-h them, and went to the market w-i-t-h them as well. Jesus traveled w-i-t-h them. They strolled w-i-t-h each other frequently (perhaps daily) in the sun...& in the rain. Jesus shared summer's blazing heat & winter's cold w-i-t-h them as well. Jesus told convicting, humorous stories & continually shared His heart & parables w-i-t-h them!

He even must have, on more than one occasion, done laundry w-i-t-h them! You say: "No way! Not the Lord! Not the disciples!" I dare you, dear reader, to say out loud: "they did laundry!" (at least twice each year!) Much more often, truth be told! They may not have enjoyed it. It may not have been the highlight of the week or month... but nevertheless!

They cooked w-i-t-h, played w-i-t-h, and did everyday things together w-i-t-h their Lord. They attended everyday, as well as special social events, w-i-t-h Him. For example: they attended weddings and funerals w-i-t-h Him, as well as attending parties and both large and smaller dinner meetings (Matthew 8, Luke 5:29 & 7:36). Jesus went fishing and re-created w-i-t-h them. He traveled w-i-t-h them, He played w-i-t-h them. (Matthew 8). Jesus hung out w-i-t-h outcasts (and society's rejects) w-i-t-h His disciples as well. He "did life" "w-i-t-h" them!

TIME: They also spent much t-i-m-e together.

Jesus didn't just spend quality time with His 12 disciples. Jesus also gave them all, His very best 'q-u-a-n-t-i-t-y' time! One minister friend said: "Love is spelled: 'Time w-i-t-h." There's great truth in this! Since God is Love... and God wants to spend all of an never-ending eternity w-i-t-h each of us... most specifically w-i-t-h y-o-u... what does that say about His enormous love for me and y-o-u!

"1.8 million minutes"

Just how much time did Jesus actually spend w-i-t-h His twelve? Do the math and see. that one year equals approximately a half-million minutes (actually 525,600 minutes). Thus, three and a half years together w-i-t-h His twelve... equals one million, eight hundred thousand minutes!

They spent way over a million minutes w-i-t-h Jesus! Jesus made them all "spiritual millionaires" in His Presence. Jesus "got rid of the weakest link." That, of course, was not Peter, but rather, satan!

"Who has the time for Relationships?"

It couldn't be this simple! Only 1,440 minutes a day... 168 hours a week...8,736 hours a year... approximately half million minutes a year. Who has time for relationships? Jesus did... and we must... as well!

The greatest thing Jesus did
W-i-t-h His disciples was... to "w-i-t-h" them!

We , in the Western World, have (by default) been taught that: Jesus would have chosen 12 to n-o-t be w-i-t-h Him!

Contrary to our popular, Western church-culture's ineffective myths (& substitute programs), we see Jesus' program was n-o-t a program.

Jesus' lamb-care method was quite simply to " W" them, to "be with"... and to "relationship" them!

> **God's program has always been relationship... ...but most church's program... is programs!**

Nathaniel asked Jesus where He was living and Jesus replied: "come and see". (John 1:39) Look very carefully at the rest of that verse. "They came and saw where He (Jesus) dwelt, and abode w-i-t-h Him that day: for it was about the tenth hour." Today's methods would have Jesus saying instead: "Don't call me, I'll call you. Let's meet in a week on Sunday!" Anything, but "Come and see; come be with Me."

When Jesus said: "Follow Me", He was n-o-t talking Sunday AM, PM & Weds.night as the "super-saints only" extra-special bonus-time together! Jesus was talking about "24-7". Not just 24-7... but 24-7-31-365!

Our "With-ness" Quotient... or "Without-Ness" quotient:

We need to create a "with-ness" criteria to re-evaluate and re-design our convert-care methods. The "plateau-decline" state of the American Church (as a whole) corresponds to the missing degree (or %) of "with-ness" teaching. "With-ness" is an oasis in the "relational desert" of our disconnected Western world!

We've been taught the exact opposite of what Jesus modeled for us!

While Jesus taught and modeled that "with-ing" (or Relationship)... was His program, we have conversely (& ineffectually) been taught that "programs" are to be o-u-r program, n-o-t relationships.
To change this: ...before we deal with the "how", we must 1st foundationally ask & discover the "WHY?"

God's program has always been relationship... ...but most church's program... is programs!

Due to Protestant, Western-world, post-Enlightenment, Euro-centric knowledge-based modeling the past five centuries (since the early 1500's and the Protestant Reformation), we have breathed in and inhaled "Program" & "Knowledge" ...as our Biblical foundation, much like carbon monoxide. We have it backwards: theologically and sociologically! We've been taught the exact reverse of the life-changing truth Jesus prioritized: namely, the infinite, awesome life-changing power of r-e-l-a-t-i-o-n-s-h-i-p!

"Like driving in reverse on the freeway"

Comparable to "driving in reverse" on the freeway, the car still moves, but so little of the car's potential is tapped. The amount of actual forward progress being made, compared to the vast potential that is present, is abysmal! That which the Information-Age paradigm added to the social "mix" on top of this, is not just self-defeating... but is a toxic, lethal combination and social "high-ball" which we drink daily!

"Relationship" is N-O-T... The Parsley ...It's the 'Steak'!

When we go to a fancy restaurant, and order a nice steak, prime rib, (or whatever fancy, main entrée you relish), there is usually a decorative piece of kale, watercress, or parsley: some tiny piece of "greenery" on the plate. Its usually there for decoration and visual purposes only!

We've been taught: "Oh yes, relationship is nice! We all need it, we certainly do believe in it, ...oh yes, my-oh-my!" Simultaneously, we've been incorrectly taught, that program, information & knowledge are the main dish, and that relationship "is the parsley," ...a decorative, nicety... on the side!

"An 8 Ounce "Parsley... medium-rare"

Have you or I ever ordered an 8 ounce, 12 or 16 ounce medium-rare "parsley?" Of course not! Why? Because we believe the parsley is only peripheral. It is mainly there for decorative purposes.

As long as we have the values reversed... our "relational" progress will also be like driving in reverse... as well!

As long as we have "relationship" and "program"...r-e-v-e-r-s-e-d, we will n-e-v-e-r see the life-change & miraculous results in our Convert-Care that Jesus instituted from the start in His own "lamb-care" method!

Why satan hates the "w" word:

Jesus' "lamb-care" plan is so seemingly simple, yet Divinely profound & productive! His Mark 3:14 method was an incarnational modeling of the "W" word". The word "w-i-t-h" is hated by satan, because "with"-ing, (relationship & love) is God's absolute original and o-n-l-y method of "Life-change," Redemption, and Divine reconnection w-i-t-h "mankind". Salvation in God's plan... is a w-i-t-h thing!

Satan knows the divine, infinite power of relationship, as well as of "non-relationship" & isolation, ever since and he was dis-fellowshiped and dis-relationshipped from God forever! (Luke 10:18-20)(Is.14,Ezk.28)

The Great "Co-Mission":

Contrary to the emaciated, "relationally-starved" western models of evangelism, the Great Co-mission was designed by God to be a relational co-adventure: a "with"- thing... and a "with"-ing' operation!

In Matthew 28:19,20, our Lord Jesus...
in His Great Co-Mission... gave His final instructions:

*"Go and make disciples (Greek word: mathetuesate)...
...out of all of the ethne (Greek for nations/ people groups),
baptizing them in (Greek–eis (into) the Name of the Father,
and of the Son, and of the Holy Spirit, teaching to them to
observe A-L-L things whatsoever I have commanded you...
and... And Yes (lo)... I AM W-I-T H you always,
...even to the ends of the age (eon)& beyond."*

Hebrews 13:5 "Never... Never... Never!"

Jesus strengthens His "to be w-i-t-h" promise...even further, in Hebrews 13:5. Here, Paul, (writing in Hebrews), quotes Jesus' "w-i-t-h you" promise, as a triply-reinforced promise: "I will never, n-e-v-e-r, N-E-V-E-R leave or forsake you."

The Greek words here are not a mere double negative. Instead, there is an intentional t-r-i-p-l-e negative: "I will never... not in any way... N-E-V-E-R... leave or forsake y-o-u!" (Hebrews 13:5)

The end-result and proof of the power of "with"-ing: Mark 3:14 produced Acts 4:13

We clearly can see in the book of Acts, the glorious end-result and ultimate proof of God' plan and Jesus' personal method. Early in the book of Acts, a-f-t-e-r Jesus' ascension and return to Heaven, we find this encouraging and unmistakable proof-text... of the power of "with-ing".

We read in Acts 4:13...
*"And they (that is the Pharisees (self-avowed enemies of
Jesus - His cross & resurrection)... these enemies took knowledge
of these unlearned (non-Bible school/non-seminary trained")...
and ignorant fishermen, ...that they had most unmistakably
and certainly... THEY HAD **BEEN W-I-T-H** JESUS!"*

Jesus had "with"-ed them for 3 years until...

Jesus had "with-ed" them until even after He was gone, Jesus' own personal "markings", His mannerisms, His heart, His Words, His Spirit and His heartbeat, were... w-i-t-h them... in... them, on them... upon them... .and manifesting unmistakably... through them!

Here is the "proof of the pudding"! Even the Unbelievers & "enemies" of Jesus themselves... recognized... the power & effect of being "w-i-t-h-e-d"!

Acts 4:13 is the "fruit" that fully illustrates... what the fruit of Mark: 3:14 & "with-ing!" is designed to produce! Here's the proof of Jesus' own words: "Wisdom is justified by her children (by its results)(Greek: 'ergon': works)." (Mt.11:19) God is a God of results, a God that delights, revels in and is glorified in totally transformed, "changed'" lives!

Jesus' Plan (Mark 3:14)... Produced... Acts 4:13

God is a practical God. Our God is the life-changing, relational God! He is interested & committed, not just to good intentions, best wishes, hopes & dreams, but committed to concrete results. God-changed, transformed lives are the ultimate currency of Heaven, Living-Proof & desired Great Co-Mission end-result!

Agrammatoi... and Idiotai! (Acts 4:13... a much closer look!)

When the enemy Scribes & Pharisees saw the boldness of Peter and John and called them... "Unlearned and ignorant" men, ...we've hardly seen "the half" of what they were saying.

The Greek word for "unlearned" (Acts 4:13 is "A-g-r-a-m-m-a-t-o-i"). It comes from two words: "a" (the negative prefix) for "not", 'un", or 'away from' (as in "a"-gnostic)! The rest of the word "Agrammatoi" ("grammatoi") speaks for itself. You can see most of our English word: "Grammar".

"Grammaeis) (Matthew 23;:2) is the New Testament Greek word for "Scribes"(Used over 58 times in the 4 Gospels). This comes from the word: 'grammati' It also derives from the Greek: 'Grapho"-for learned &/or writing). They were called un-lettered, ignorant & illiterate: ...the "illiterati!"

***Other translations read: "uneducated", "uncultured", "simple men", "with-out schooling", "untrained laymen" &/"untrained in the schools. "(Weymouth) But wait! It gets even better!

"Idiotai" checking In!"

These critics & "enemies" not only called them 'un-learned'! They then finish the 2nd half of Acts 4:13, calling the disciples "ignorant." The 2nd-half descriptive Greek word here is (unbelievably) "Idiotai".

Do you see a close English root-word here? How about "I-d-i-o-t"? How about the English word: "ignorant"? Modern translations "kindly" use the unscriptural word "layman" (New English Bible). Others translations read: "obscure", "mere outsiders" (Moffat), "persons with no advantage", "simple men", "without skill". The Greek here "Idiotns", translates also as: "Ignoramus", "rude", or ... ?

Yes, Peter and John they had no schooling nor seminary background. They had no theological prowess! Instead, and much more importantly, they had the one u-l-t-i-m-a-t-e 'thing' above all other! They had that which counted more than all the Theological degrees in the world.

They had been w-i-t-h JESUS... and had been "w-i-t-h-e-d"... by Jesus!

They had been w-i-t-h JESUS... and had been "w-i-t-h-e-d" by Jesus ...until He (Jesus) could be seen... in them... even after... He was physically long "gone"!

"Illiterati"... and "Idiot–I"... Checking in!

They were recognized as having been w-i-t-h Jesus ....not just by other believers... but more importantly, ...by the enemies and unbelievers in Jesus. U-n-b-e-l-i-e-v-e-r-s recognized Jesus' own Presence, His Spirit, His mannerism. They saw Jesus in their lives, actions... & in the "fruit of their lives!

God's Word is telling us here again: it's not W-H-A-T you know, but rather "W-H-O" you know! "Knowing" here is being scripturally re-defined "relationally": (not gnostically, through cognitive knowledge.

We all, as 21st century leaders, need to continually seek to be constant examples of p-e-r-s-o-n-a-l change, 'Kingdom–Morphing', Life-Change... and systemic change-implementation as well! We say we're comfortable with change; honestly, we're not, that is, not outside our personal comfort zones!

Are we ready to teach that "Relationship" is God's Program?

We have had to learn the 7 new words: "Jesus chose 12 to be with Him" just as we had to learn five new words in Section I, that "Jesus put the lambs f-i-r-s-t." Much improvement will require much change. Our IQ ("Improvement Quotient") can only equal our CQ ("change quotient"), as we previously learned.

If indeed, the most important thing Jesus did "w-i-t-h" His disciples was to commit to "be w-i-t-h" them, we must learn that this is also the greatest thing we can do immediately for each of our new lambs.

Changing from a "Program-based"... ...to a "Relationship-based" Theology:

Changing our churches from a Program-based to a Relationship-based theology (and system) will require our heart and lives to change first. As God leads us in the Way, it will be our privilege to follow!

What was Jesus' curriculum?

What was Jesus' cognitive, theological, basic curriculum. Was it Life of Christ 101, 201, 301 or 401? Was it "Life of Paul"? Hardly! Paul wasn't even been converted yet! Well then, was Jesus' curriculum Old Testament Survey, Hermeneutics or Homiletics? No! It was not linear information nor a "knowledge transfer" that Jesus came to impart. He came rather to give us "Zoe"…Life): Life in all its fullness. (John 10:10B)

Much more importantly and marvelously, Jesus W-A-S His curriculum!

We need to evaluate our own current curriculum by its fruit! If it isn't producing the "lasting fruit" that God wants, maybe it isn't God's method either! The roots & shoots are, after all, that which produces the fruit! If Jesus "with"-ed them, they'd grow. He knew if He didn't "with" them, they would wither.

If our methods are not producing fruit that remains, as Jesus desires in (John 15:16), then the fruit judges the tree.

Jesus said in Matthew 7:16: "you will know a tree by its fruit." Does that also mean we can know a tree (or a method) by its "lack of fruit." Both are equally true.

"In this is My Father glorified (John 15:8 & 15:16), not just that you bear much fruit, but that your fruit r-e-m-a-i-n." If the fruit is not "fruit that remains", then is the strategy which produces "vapor fruit" the strategy God wants either? Yes or no? If it's not producing lasting fruit, then the fruit "judges" the tree!

"Life-Change"… and "changed-lives": the goal God is after!

A disciple is a changed-life…& a constantly changing-life, lived within a saving relationship with Jesus Christ. It is not a "mouthed", memorized, oft -repeated prayer, an evangelism "scalp", nor a number on an annual ministry report. Since changed-lives are what God is after, then this must also be what we are aiming to produce as well! How does "lasting fruit" line up with the convert-care results at your church?

As the aged Apostle John said and wrote in III John verse 4:
"I have no greater joy... than to hear my children are walking in relationship with the Truth (Jesus)"

Chapter 14
"THE POWER OF A MEAL"

*"You have welcomed me as Your guest.
Blessings overflow." (Living Bible Psalm 23:5)*

*"Thou art My Host, spreading a feast before me."
(Moffatt translation)*

*"Envious, my foes have to look on and watch...
while Thou dost spread a banquet for me"*

The "Quality" of Quantity Time

When Jesus chose His twelve "TO BE WITH Him" (as we've studied in depth in Mark 3:14), our Lord provided them both Quality and Quantity Time: ...the Quality of His "Quantity time"... itself!

In giving and committing to them 3 dedicated, uninterrupted years of Himself, Jesus was giving them the best of both worlds: the best of "Quality": (Himself: pure, Holy, Perfect, Loving Eternal God)... and "Quantity": the fullness of His time and Himself (almost 2 million minutes) spread over three & a half years. He w-i-t-h them... and they w-i-t-h Him!

Jesus was not just offering them His uninterrupted time: ...Jesus was offering them Himself. Time is money the old cliché goes, but now even that is obsolete. Time is now even m-o-r-e than money! Time is... as it always has been... .one of the irreplaceable essences of Life itself.

3,800 Meals TOGETHER!

One of the everyday "L-i-f-e" things Jesus did together with His 12 new converts (disciples) was to share meals and to eat with them. We read and take for granted that they had meals together. But stop a minute. Think a bit deeper, as to how many meals they shared.

Take the number 365 (for the number of days in a year) multiplied by three meals a day. That equals 1,095. Now multiply 1,095 by three and a half (the # of years Jesus spent with His disciples). We come up with approximately 3,800 meals. Even settling for three years together, that's 3,285 meals!

Well, maybe they didn't always eat three meals a day!

Above, we see Jesus and His disciples ate close to 4,000 meals together. Immediately someone always asks: "What if they didn't eat 3 meals a day?" OK, take 1,000 meals away... they shared almost 3,000 meals. Even if they skipped some meals, they still shared t-h-o-u-s-a-n-d-s of meals together. Two meals each day... times three years still totals way over 2,000 meals together!

Someone else quips: "What about the meals they fasted?" A good question easily answered in scripture. In Matthew 17, descending from the Mount. of Transfiguration, Jesus heals an epileptic boy whom the disciples had tried to heal, but couldn't. In Matthew 17:19, they asked Jesus why they'd been unable to do this.

In the next verse, Matthew 17:20, Jesus replies to them: "this kind only comes out by prayer and fasting." Apparently, the disciples did not do too terribly much fasting. However, they did apparently like....(and did a lot) of eating! Jesus said: "The friends of the Bridegroom do not fast. As long as they have the Bridegroom with them, they can not fast." (Mark 2:19)

Which of these 1,000's of meals with Jesus was the "most important"?

Would you say the Last Supper (Jesus' third and final Passover meal together with His 12 was His "most important" meal? Most believers would! We read in John 13, that it was here Jesus took a servant's towel, took off His outer garment, knelt down and washed His disciples feet. This is the meal where Jesus gave His one new commandment: "That you love (Gk. Agape) one another, as I have loved you." (John 13:34)

At this meal Jesus identified Himself as the Eternal Passover: that the unleavened Paschal loaf was His body, and the Passover cup (& wine) were His very life-blood, shed for many, for the forgiveness of their sins. No other meal on earth can compare to Jesus' final Passover meal together with His disciples! Without doubt, this was their most important meal together!

Someone might faintly suggest the feedings of the 4,000 and 5000 (Mark 8 & John 6), but the Last Supper certainly eclipses any other as most popular choice for the most important meal. Another might argue, they were a-l-l the m-o-s-t important, being part of an uninterrupted tapestry of time and being "with"-ed by their Master and Lord, before His passion and return back to the Throne in Heaven.

Referring to this one last meal together and its singular, ultimate importance to Himself, Jesus reveals His own heart and deepest, innermost yearnings, when He says:

"With great desire, I have desired to eat this meal (this final Passover) with you before I suffer. For I say to you, I will no longer eat of it, until it is fulfilled in the Kingdom of God." (Luke 22:15, 16)
Again Jesus said:

*"Many will come from the east and west and sit down
at the table with Abraham, Isaac and Jacob, but the children
of the Kingdom will be cast out into outer darkness."*
Matthew 8:11,12 & Luke 22:15,16

Now let's ask: "Which meal w-i-t-h Jesus was l-e-a-s-t important... or a waste of time?

Perhaps just a couple dozen meals were a "waste" of time? Or, maybe, just one really "lousy" meal stood out as the absolute "worst": a charred, sopping "sorry excuse" for a meal on a bitter cold, bone-piercing night, beneath a rain-soaked tree: ...the absolute worst out of all those 3,000 plus meals!

The Important Thing Was n-o-t the food, but the "W-I-T-H"-ing!

Even if... it was a meal cooked in the rain, or in which the fish was not just "blackened' but burned beyond recognition. Even if... there weren't enough for seconds or third portions. Regardless of all else, not even o-n-e meal together w-i-t-h Jesus was a waste of time. Why? Because the very point of the meal itself was not the food: ...it was the "with-ing", the "r-e-l-a-t-i-o-n-s-h-i-p"-ing, the experience-sharing, the "quality and quantity time" together! Even the highly "forgettables," plain old, nothing special means of "left-overs" were still crowned wit Jesus' very Presence!.

What if it was a meal where Jesus didn't teach anything super-spiritual or "heavenly-heavy"?

What if it was a meal where Jesus said nothing at all?

The Important Thing Was n-o-t the food, but the "W-I-T-H!"

No true Christian or devoted follower of Jesus would dare say any of the meals Jesus shared with His disciples was a waste of time. True believers would unanimously agree... that no meal was E-V-E-R a waste of time... if Jesus was there! For He Himself, the Bread of Life, was there W-I-T-H them! The important thing was their being w-i-t-h Him.....and His being w-i-t-h them! This " being with" them was Jesus' very own chosen method of creating life-change in (and discipling) them.

Jesus' favorite meal... "likes" and "dislikes"?

What does a meal shared... reveal to the two persons eating that meal together?

What were Jesus' absolute three top very favorite meals? Who knew? Certainly Mary and Joseph knew Jesus' favorite foods, growing up, as they raised Him to the age of 18 in their Nazareth home!. That would have been nearly 20,000 meals Mary and Joseph would have had with Jesus.

Did Jesus use more salt or more pepper, or neither? Mary, Joseph, and all the disciples knew the answers to these questions: we don't! When you share a meal with someone, like it or not, you can't help but get to know them a little bit more!

The more meals you share with someone, the more you get to know them.

The disciples knew which were Jesus' favorite meal(s) and favorite eating places along the 120 mile road from Galilee to Jerusalem. The disciples knew if Jesus liked lamb, or fish, beef or chicken, boiled in a savory vegetable stew... or roasted over an open fire... baked in a oven, or... flame-broiled in shish-kebab format? Did Jesus prefer His lamb, beef or poultry... well done, medium or rare? Were His favorite meals cooked with mesquite, grilled or broiled? We don't know, but His twelve disciples did!

Which spices did Jesus love? Did He prefer garlic, salsa, onions, cloves, sauce or no sauce? And if sauces: which specific ones best... and in which amounts? Hot, medium or mild?

Which were the top dozen or half-dozen funniest meals the twelve shared with Jesus? Which were their worst... and most "forgettable" meals? Name Jesus' favorite restaurants, inns and taverns... or His favorite homes to stop at for a meal or to stay overnight? Yes, we know Martha and Mary's. But where else?

How many times did they eat in the rain, fog, cold or snow? How many times did they eat shivering under a "rainy day" dripping tree, on their journeys up, down and across Palestine and Galilee?

We don't know, but His twelve knew all this and more... much more!

Let's individualize these questions, asking them about each of the 12?

What were the other 12 disciples' most favorite meals? Which of the disciples loved which meal, or special food... or restaurant best... in which town? Which host home of a disciple's family... (relative or extended family)... did the 12 prefer the best... or consider the absolute 'pits'. Which of the disciples was a great, or a terrible cook?

Which one... of the twelve... was the best (and worst) cook?

Which of the twelve was "always hungry", etc.? Jesus and His twelve learned and knew all these things, as valued elements of their "shared- life". Jesus was w-i-t-h them...as much as they ... by His intentional Divine design, were also w-i-t-h Him...in ever-deepening community & growing relationship!

More of Peter's foibles than we've read about!

> **"Food Equals relationship... and... "Relationship Produces Commitment".**

We can't possibly doubt that the 11 disciples could (& probably in heaven still can) come up with dozens more hilarious things Peter did & said (as well as stories "on" all the other 11!) How many other times did "baby John" put his head on Jesus' breast? We don't know, but they would! Of all the personal signs of intimacy Jesus showed to "Baby-John" (& the others), we have only the slightest clues!

No one on earth can now answer these questions! That's because these things are only learned about someone, by spending considerable time and by "doing life" together w-i-t-h them, at close range.

Any of the 12 Could Answer The above 40 Questions!

We don't know the answers, but the disciples did! Jesus chose them to "be w-i-t-h Him".. and thus make Himself known to them. By doing this, Jesus was modeling for them (and for us) exactly how they (and we) are to disciple new converts, by following in His "with"-ing footsteps!

"Food Equals relationship... and... "Relationship Produces Commitment".

Food is the sharing of life. It is therefore a great, natural relationship & "Memory- maker". Meals develop Relationship! Food equals relationship! And..."R" for (relationship)...produces what God is most after in each of us: "Life Change." It is in being known, in community and through growing, humble, relational transparency, that true vulnerability and accountability develop. It is out of this "heart garden" that true life-change occurs and grows. Life-change takes place in relationship, N-O-T in isolation!

The Power of just one shared-meal... together:

Think of all those you have shared a meal, with in the process of getting to know them. Think of the top 5 people in your life that you've shared the most meals with. What is it that happens when you share that meal? Does it deepen or "thin" the relationship? Other than the family you grew up in, your marriage partner or the lunchroom at work, whom have you had more than 20, 30, or 50 meals with in your life? What happens when you spend that amount of time..."meal-ing" with someone?

God designed Food... as a "relational-sacrament":

Indeed, food is a relational sacrament! When God designed food, He designed it with more in mind than just pleasure and mere biological life-sustainer. Granted, food does "keep us alive" physically! But food transcends a survival purpose. does much more than that! God knew that food it would be a shareable "life intimacy" as well.

It is in the breaking of bread that more than a symbolic life-sharing takes place. Beyond oxygen, food is perhaps the most universally share-able intimacy. Food can be shared between anyone, of any age, with or without words. It is hardly possible for food to be shared, without relationship being developed between the two sharing that life-fuel together.

Universally, in many cultures, sharing a meal together is the committing of a bond or a pledge of a relationship. In some cultures, a covenant, contract or promise can not be properly, officially sealed or consummated, without the sharing of a meal, or the breaking of bread together!

Sharing a Meal with a New Convert Is Helping to Disciple Them

Every meal Jesus had with His 12 disciples was part of His convert–care, "new-believer" nurture. Eating a meal with new converts is something every individual, in every church in America... and entire world...can do! How many people eat? The answer is universally the same: A-L-L!

Since their Lord's one new commandment was to love one another, and love requires a relationship, they knew they had to stay close to each other and remain an ongoing part of each other's lives. "And they (Jesus' twelve) continued steadfastly in the apostles doctrine and fellowship, in breaking the loaf, and in prayers." (Acts 2:42) The Greek word here for "fellowship (in Acts 2:42) is the word Koinonia. However, To the Apostles, Koinonia, (and "church" as a concept... and a word) meant community... and relationship... N-O-T a building or a specific location.

Sharing a Meal with a New Convert Is Helping to Disciple Them

Church was... and still is... a people... not a place!

To the first disciples, church was an "R...a relationship-centered concept. It was not a building or a place, nor was church a place you went to. Rather, church was a gathering of people that "were" together: ...together in Christ, together in Faith, and together in belief! Most importantly, what church was to them, ...was their common r-e-l-a-t-i-o-n-s-h-i-p with Jesus Christ as Lord, Savior, and King! Church meant "family" & "relationship". It meant community, closeness & connection! It still must...and still does!

"The Church in America is 3,000 miles wide... and a sixteenth of an inch deep"!

It's been said that: "the church in America is 3,000 miles wide and 1/16th inch deep!" This is because we've made "programs" our program, instead of God's program, which is r-e-l-a-t-I-o-n-s-h-i-p-s!

It was n-o-t this way at all, with Jesus' first disciples. They had been perfectly taught and modeled before them, the incredible, awesome beauty and power of relationship, by the Master Teacher Himself.

To them, Koinonia was not: "Hi! Goodbye! Hi! Goodbye"!

To them, church meant to live and die together, not mere weekly shallow fellowship, as we've diluted it down to a once a week Sunday AM, "hi-goodbye" in the western world. They were not "strangers in the light, exchanging glances." The early church met in homes until well past year 300 A.D. They had no church buildings, or location focused "edifice complex."

"Breaking Bread"... In their Homes... N-O-T House to House!

In Acts 2:45, we see the apostles continued their habit of having meals together: "And they, continuing daily with one accord in the temple, and breaking bread in their homes (Greek: oikon), did eat their meat with gladness and singleness of heart". We read the word "House", but forget that a house is not necessarily a home. Every house was a h-o-m-e full of warmth, love, acceptance, and RELATIONSHIP!

Meals with your Marriage Partner:

My lovely bride Jeanette and I have now been married 30 PLUS years. At 3 meals a day, that comes to almost 30,000 meals together! Does she know my favorite meals? Not probably, but most certainly! Way beyond that! Of course, vice versa! Reverse the question and the answer is much more than "probably", or "slightly" as well! Sometimes we eat and talk, sometimes we just eat and don't need to say a word.

Fellowship... is spelled with an "F" just like: "food" Food equals relationship!

Food equals relationship. Like all other humans, after our oxygen "addiction", our food "addiction" is ubiquitous. Christians sometimes dog-headedly hang their heads and "admit" that fellowship 'after church' equates to eating together: that meals together amounts to the most common type of easy, comfortable "fellowship". We act as if something in this were wrong!

"All the rivers run into the sea, and yet the sea is never full" (Ecclesiastes 1:7). We can eat to our fill and say "I'll never be hungry again!" It won't be but a few hours until once again, back comes that "hunger thing". Jesus knew (and knows) that food is indeed a "relational sacrament": ...that Life-change flows through relationship!

Sharing Food or a Meal... is Developing R-e-l-a-t-i-o-n-s-h-i-p... and... Building a Relationship... is ministry!

Building a relationship is ministry, but is so vastly under-emphasized in Bible School teaching & theology, that is raises a questions in our mind when we hear these very words relating food to "ministry"!

"I Remember the Chicken"!

As a brand new Christian (over three decades ago), I remember some brand new, loving Christian friends taking me with them to their small country church outside Sacramento. Afterwards, they would take us out w-i-t-h them for lunch to Perry's Smorgy buffet nearby. Amazingly, its still open 30 years later! I don't remember what scriptures they shared with me, or which ones I memorized first back then (many 100's now). But I do "remember the chicken!" These meals together helped bond & confirm their love for me, a new lamb, a former outsider, now a very welcomed part of God's born-again, eternal family!

The Power of "Meal-Sharing" with Church Board Members

John Maxwell frequently states that over 20 years pastoring at Skyline Wesleyan Methodist Church (before becoming internationally known in Christian leadership training), he had a weekly scheduled breakfast meal, (in ongoing sequence) with one board member. The next week, he'd have a breakfast with another board member & friend! This continued in a regular, ongoing, never-ending, weekly cycle.

The point was not the "free meal", or quality of food at whichever restaurant! The obvious point was the development of relationship with these men. As the church grew & more commitment & steps of faith as a team were required, these relationships were growing, to keep up with and fuel the next steps of faith!

Church Board Meals at Board Member's Homes:

After 30 years of ministry, I met a pastor (Pastor Ray Barnett, Amsterdam, NY) who innovatively and w-i-s-e-l-y holds monthly board meetings at board members' homes, specifically to escape the "location trap." These monthly meals together continually re-new the ever-important, vital emphasis on "relationship first", n-o-t program. They avoid the chores of shopping, cooking & clean-up, by having the meal "catered" (inexpensively delivered monthly from a nearby eatery) and using disposable, plastic-ware.

Why is God Almighty called the Lord of Hosts?

Why is God's personal invitation to come to HIS Eternal table, to the Marriage & Wedding Supper of the Lamb in Heaven, ...so incredibly heart-gripping & life-changing?

Robert Maslowe, in his basic hierarchy of needs, wrote that the 1st universal need of all humans is survival: securing & sustaining life itself! Second only to that is food & water: a meal! Thirdly this is followed by: shelter. Fourth is a "purpose for living or reason for being". Fifth is a hunger & need for a higher power: a Divine Destiny! Even from this secular view & matrix, we see food is b-a-s-i-c, even more basic than shelter (a building/or a church building). Food is only superceded in urgency by survival itself!

A Meal Provides the Three Main Ingredients that Relationship requires!

The developing of relationships require three elements: time, smallness, and closeness. In a perfect triangle of relational enclosure, all three of these work perfectly together at the informal sharing of a meal.

This fits perfectly with Jesus' plan (& God's Eternal program) of delivering Life (and life-change) through relationships. We shall explore this in more depth in our next chapter: *Spell it with an "R"*.

Chapter 15
"SPELL IT WITH AN "R"

"The Three Elements of "R":
time... smallness... and closeness

We've seen in Mark 3:14 (and the last few chapters), Jesus' disciple program was "relationship", not program based. It is now imperative for us also to "re-program" ourselves to Jesus' own "non-program" of relationship-based, discipleship and life-transformation.

Re-programming to Jesus'
"non-program" of relationship!

Fire, to exist, requires three components: fuel, oxygen, and heat. Without any of these three elements present, fire can not exist. It is also equally true with relationship's 3 basic components: time, smallness & closeness. Without time together, without the closeness of being w-i-t-h someone, and without smallness, relationships cannot thrive, much less exist. Much in today's society points to a new type of illiteracy, to be educated against, and to be overcome and eliminated.

Relational Illiteracy: the new "4th R"

Today, in our 3rd Millennium Western, Post –Christian American environment, a different, crippling, new illiteracy has developed and gained dominance!

Sunday School was originally designed by Robert Raikes in Great Britain in the mid-1800's, to reach & teach the illiterate, uneducated children in the slums and poorer parts of London. The grammatical literacy lessons delivered by McGuffey's Reader, were designed to teach children the 3 "R's": "Reading, 'Riting &'Rithmatic." (You've noticed 2 of these 3 "R"s'... don't even start with an "R")

Now, however, a new type of "illiteracy" and a 4th "R" needs to be stressed and taught, utilized and enriched. The new 4th "R"... of the new 3rd Millennium Paradigm...is "Relational Illiteracy."

Like deadly and "undetectable" carbon monoxide, it's un-recognized and has similar, drastic consequence. The church, as a whole, is oblivious to the tremendous opportunity this new illiteracy provides.

How to Give Your Church an "M.R.I":

Research shows time & again, that people come to a church for a wide variety of reasons... but they will stay primarily for just one reason: namely, relationship! It is now ultimately important to continually give one's church (& even more specifically the convert-care strategies and program) a thorough internal and external "M.R.I."

Giving Your Church an "M.R.I.": A Magnetic, Relationship Imaging"

I'm not talking about a super expensive hospital "medical science" Magnetic Resonant Imaging. Rather, I am talking about a church-wide, in-depth "M.R.I.," a "Magnetic, Relationship Imaging."

In every situation where there is an currently an established "program", there now also needs to be an renewed, continual re-emphasis of God's Program: not more information, but more of the "R" word: Relationship!

If "relationship" is truly the criterion for God's Program of Life-change and Life-flow, then the richness (or impoverishment) of our relationship dynamics (revealed by a church-wide MRI) is now more ultra-important than ever before. (See 2nd chapter titled: "The Power of The Paradigm," for more detail.)

The Information Age has no heart!" Therefore, ...the Next Paradigm... will focus... on...?

The next paradigm (in this case the one following the Information Age...is always based and built out of the unmet needs of the prior paradigm!

> **Information is the heart of the information age... but the Information age has no heart.**

The Information Age culture has deified Information, technology and program...and has denigrated and hollowed out life's, vital relational aspect and priority! "Cocoon-ing" increasingly limits the relational aspects of daily life and society. Since "the Information Age has no "heart", (much like the Tin Man in the Wizard of Oz), the opportunity to stress relationship and relational values has never been greater!

Hawaiian Airlines 727 Jet Fuselage "peel-back":

In 1979, a phenomenal front-page new story hit the papers nationwide. It centered on a Hawaiian Airlines 727 jet, in flight over the Islands. Suddenly, the 727's roof rivets started to progressively give way (from the front of the aircraft, 80 feet toward the back). The metal roof fuselage consecutively peeled back from the front, caused by aged, extremely weakened rivets and multi-decadal metal fatigue!

The immediate, life-frightening sounds, along with the sudden loss of cabin pressure, alerted every passenger that this indeed was an immediate life & death situation.

The story goes, that not one single passenger who already had their seat-belt fastened perished! However, a few unlucky passengers caught walking the jet's aisle, were immediately swept out of the wide-open jet's rooftop, to their death thousands of feet below!

Most "riveting" (pardon the pun) were stories of middle-seat airline passengers, who did N-O-T have their seat-belts fastened! These frantically being held down and clutched onto by their "neighboring" aisle & window-seat passengers, those already secure with seat belts fastened tight!

These middle seat "unbelted" ones (while being held down by their neighbors) obviously were struggled with all their might to get their own seat belts fastened snug & tight. Meanwhile, a mere 4 or 5 feet above them was the rushing, deafening sound of the deadly howling 400 MPH wind! This story has a miraculous ending. The pilot was somehow able to land the injured, highly unstable craft safely. The only fatalities were the few unfortunate, previously mentioned "unbelted" passengers!

The obvious application here, is that the only people we will hold & keep at our churches, the only converts who will survive, are those relationally connected & "belted in". Only those attached & being fed "God's "un-program": r-e-l-a-t-i-o-n-s-h-i-p... will ultimately survive... and thrive!

A Divine purpose for al l of this... "with–ing time": Jesus planted" R" ...a-n-d Harvested "C"!

Every meal together, (every day, night, week, month and year together) with His twelve disciples, was spent investing in the "with"-ing Principle. It was n-e-v-e-r a gamble. Every meal together with Jesus, whether or not they memorized 10 scriptures, or none, was never a waste of time.

Planting "relationship" to this great a depth and degree, Jesus was ten million percent confident. He knew what His harvest would be: Eternally transformed and changed-lives, men that unbelievers would one day take notice of ..... that these "ignorant & unlearned men" that they had been w-i-t-h J e s u s!

Iron Filings... and a Magnet's "E.M.F"

Way back when, in my High School days, a common science class analogy utilized a thimble full ultra fine iron filings, spilled onto a sheet of paper held between two person's hands. Another helper would come and hold a strong magnet underneath the level sheet with the iron filings spread out all over it.

All of a sudden, with no seeming volition or choice of their own), the iron filings would quickly re-arrange themselves to the previously before-hand invisible electro-magnetic field (EMF) of the powerful magnet being held beneath the paper separating them.

People are drawn to a relationship...
much as the iron shavings are to the magnet!
Love... God's L-O-V-E... is that magnet!

What color is the "Black Box"?:

Prior to the "9-11" USA World Trade Towers tragedy in 2001, few stewardesses knew the above question's "answer!" Frequently on a jet, I've asked stewardesses: "What color is the black box?" At first this seems like a dumb (& dumber)... trick question like: "Who is buried in Grant's tomb?", or "What color were George Washington's four gray horses? The answer is surprising!

The black box is N-O-T black! Rather, the 'black box ' is o-r-a-n-g-e! It is fluorescent orange, to increase its visibility factor! It's reassuring to know the pilots always seemed to know the correct answer.

While we smugly think we can hold people with our programs, build-ings, polish or our religious "got it all together-ness",.... it is n—o—t surprising that the "black box" (God's own relational nature) in our hearts & spirits.... wins out every time.

We, therefore, just as the iron filings, find ourselves magnetized and re-formatted by the EMF of God's love.... and the relationship-pull, mag-netic strength–signal and force of real love and care, being sent out by any given church, group or congregational family!

"Pastor: thanks for calling! What do you need?"

Picture a church board member or deacon, finishing dinner at home, when the phone rings. Screening the call through the kitchen answering machine, the deacon picks up the phone and says: "Thanks for calling, pastor! What do you n-e-e-d ?"

What we see here is a relationally weak "rivet", an overused 'com-mitment & performance' expectation. This would show up, on an "Relational MRI", as a definite negative, and a relational w-a-r-n-i-n-g sign!

Responses (or "subtle hints") like this, should be identified and cor-rected, before it causes either the deacon (or even more importantly, a new convert) to disengage or perish from a lack of contact, caring input, connectivity and being lovingly "with"-ed.

"To with...or not to with..." that is still... the Question!

99

Chapter 16
"THE GOD OF "R"

The Eternal Essence of God.

If I were to ask a room full of evangelical ministers at a large, annual, denominational Conference, to give one-word descriptions of the central, core essence of the God of the Bible, the answers would be totally (theologically) predictable... and also fall short!

Pastors would describe God as: Omnipotent, Omnipresent and Omniscient. They would say, God is Eternal, Immutable & unchangeable, Holy, and Pure. They would surely say: God is Love, God is Merciful, God is Truth, God is Light, and a number of various other adjectives!

True, but tragically lacking one vital, indispensable Essence

Western Eurocentric, enlightenment theology has taught us many parts of God's nature. To an excess, we've been over-instructed in too many linear attributes of the One True, Eternal God Who made us all...in His very image! Chances are slim that anyone would describe God as "relational"! Few would put down on their list: God is a "relational" being. What they would not say, is that: God is r-e-l-a-t-i-o-n-a-l!

Western Theology has failed to teach us that God is "Relational."

Contrary to what we've been taught, "relationality" is at the very central essence of our Heavenly Father's Triune being and essence.

God is a "Relational Being" in His Central Essence as the Trinity

God being the Trinity, is One, as the 'O Shamma, states in Deuteronomy 6:5: This verse, the Greatest of all Commandments, states: "Hear, O Israel, the Lord thy God is One Lord!" Yet there is more than this "Oneness" to the central essence of our Eternal, Almighty God!

Genesis 1:26, in the Bible's very first chapter, reads: "And God (singular) said: "Let US (plural, as the Trinity)....make man in our (plural) image, after our (plural) likeness".

Look at the Community, Fellowship & Intimacy of the Trinity:

Looking deeper at the Trinity and the interaction of the three Persons of the Godhead, we clearly see the central essence and core, relational nature of our God and Creator. We see God's Triune relational being in His central nature... within the Trinity itself... rather, themself!

In the Trinity, we find perfect community, perfect fellowship, and undeniably, perfect RELATIONSHIP! God is relational and He intentionally, irrevocably and eternally made us in His image...as relational beings at our very core as well!

See how God the Father relates and interacts with Jesus the Eternal God-Son, as well as w-i-t-h God the Eternal Holy Spirit! The Trinity models perfect community, perfect fellowship, perfect RELATIONSHIP, and God's Perfect essential relationality.

What a marvelous eternal, "Holy Triad" of perfect interaction. I marvel at the flawless, cooperative interaction between God the Holy Spirit and the rest of the Trinity, perfect in every dimension of relationship. Perfect in deference, respect, communication and cooperation

God as the Trinity, is a totally relational being! God the Father and God the Son, Jesus Christ, do not merely "get along" or merely tolerate one another. They not only get along, but God the Father, God the Son & God the Holy Spirit, (the three Persons of the Divine Trinity & Eternal Godhead) dwell together in perfect, eternal harmony.

The relationality of God... is a core essence

This under-taught "relationality" of God is very much a central and core essence. Without it, theology remains one-dimensional, factual and historical ....but non life-transforming...totally with no power to either give life or to transform lives either!

God is relational, but our theology has bypassed this fact, to our own detriment! Other cultures around world-wide have not surrendered to this theological imbalance, and are infinitely, more relational. They have not received the damage to their churches' health (and growth) that we have in the linear, empirical, Western paradigm we're in.

What made it Heaven on earth?

Adam and Eve were designed for... and destined... to live forever It wasn't just the surroundings. I believe their Perfect relationship with God (more than anything else) was what made Eden a "Heaven on earth"! Because of their Perfect Life-giving Relationship with God, there was no sin, guilt, shame or death. They had nothing to hide or to fear. More than any-thing else, it was not external realities, but a solid, internal reality: The Divine relationship between God and His Creation mankind, that was their "umbilical cord" to the flow of Eternal Life.... and connection with the God of Love! The word Eden, in Hebrew, actually translates as Heaven! Adam had free, "24/7" unlimited, broad-band access to His Creator!

Satan directly attacked man's link with God: the R-e-l-a-t-i-o-n-s-h-i-p!

When Satan brought sin into the world, what was it that he inten-tionally, and directly attacked? Satan knew he could never defeat God. But he also knew he could strike deep sorrow and pain into the heart of God, by tricking mankind to sin. Satan knew that severing mankind's vital, inner, perfect and pure r-e-l-a-t-i-o-n-s-h-i-p with God...would destroy something God Himself so highly and dearly prized!

Genesis chapter three details the breakdown. Satan tricks the first two humans into sacrificing relationship... for knowledge. They had the Tree of Life...eternal, perfect, deathless, sinless, sickness, poverty and curse-free! Tragically, they chose to worship (in disobedience) at the Tree of Knowledge and self-will!

Adam and Eve chose Knowledge... over LIFE!

What did Adam and Eve do? They chose the Tree of Knowledge of Good and Evil, over the Tree of Life. They forfeited Life for knowledge. They traded a Life-giving Eternal relationship.... for mere knowledge! Mankind has replicated that fateful error ever since!

They died Relationally... and the Trust was Broken.

God had said: "In the day that you eat thereof, you shall surely die." Genesis 2:16&17

Instantly, the relational and spiritual intimacy was gone. Physically, of course, Adam didn't die at once. Adam s-t-a-r-t-e-d dying physically at that moment. Genesis 5:5 tells us Adam lived to be 930 years old before he died physically! However, spiritually... r-e-l-a-t-i-o-n-a-l-l-y... he did "die" the very moment they disobeyed and broke r-e-l-a-t-i-o-n-s-h-i-p with God... by their sin!

They died "relationally."

God's Divine design and dream of intimacy died immediately as well. It degenerated quickly into fear, shame, mistrust, disobedience, and death. The prized divine-human relationship and Life-cords were cut in two.

When Adam sinned, he broke relationship with God.

Scripture says: "Adam and his wife heard the voice of the Lord God walking in the garden of Eden in the cool of the day...and they hid themselves from the Presence of the Lord God!" (Gen.3:8)

Sin brought Instant spiritual & r-e-l-a-t-i-o-n-a-l death: ...and with it the 1st murder!

How tragic to think of the impact of Adam and Eve's sin. Spiritual and Relational death spread so far and so fast .... it was like an instant, internal, infernal wild-fire and plague

Genesis 4:2 tells us that their firstborn son Cain was unaccepted by God because of his non-sacrificial heart and "junk-food" offering. We see Cain (the firstborn human being, from Father Adam & Mother Eve)... rise up in the field and murder his brother Able.

When relationship dies, death is never too far behind!

"How should I know? Am I my brother's keeper"

Behold the lethal spread of spiritual death within the human heart. Hear Cain's insolent retort back to God (Genesis 4:9): "How should I know where(my brother Able is? Am I my brother's keeper?" See the hardening of the attitudes breed hatred and jealousy, creating the well-spring of murder, violence & death.

> "God created man to worship and to glorify God...
> ...and to know and to enjoy Him forever."
> Westminister Catechism, 1731

Churches have wrongly mis-prioritized Knowledge above L-I-F-E!

For far too long, countless churches have sublimated relationship, relegating it to a much lower position than the top priority God gives it.

God made us for relationship.

As the Westminster Catechism words it: "Man was created to worship and to glorify God, and to know and to enjoy Him forever!" Nothing else can take its place!

How could this Ultimate Relational Loss ever be restored?

Could Paradise Lost...ever be re-found...and regained?

What could ever be done to restore this monumental, eternal loss?

How would this "relational restoration" ever be accomplished... if not by God Himself!

God Almighty shows His Father-heart of love, voicing His intention to restore mankind to the original, unblemished relationship. As The Solution, He promises a Redeemer and future Redemption!

Genesis 3:15: The First Messianic Promise

In Genesis 3:15, we find the first Messianic Salvation Promise in Scripture. God promised that He would send a Redeemer: "And I will put enmity between you (satan) and the woman. And... HE shall bruise your head: and you shall bruise His heel." (Gen.3:15,NKJV)

God promises the eventual, total defeat of Satan, the Serpent.

To the serpent God said: "And He (the Seed) shall bruise your head, and you shall (only) bruise His (the Descendent, the coming Redeemer/Deliverer's) heel." (Gen.3:15)

The Promise is a "He" ...not an "IT"!

We too easily, miss the key point here.

Genesis 3:15 does not say: "It" will. Rather, God's "Salvation Promise" reads: "H-E w-i-l-l!"

The Promise is a "WHO" ...n-o-t a "w h at"!

Not a thing, but a person! Not an "it"... or a thing, but a Person...a He!

Salvation is a Person... and a relationship, not a thing or mere belief! Salvation is a Promised, Personal R-e-l-a-t-i-o-n-s-h-i-p. Not a religion! Not a set of "do's & don'ts". Not a moral code! Not a ritual, dogma, or tradition of once-a-week exercises in piety at a specific location or building!

Salvation is not just a "relationship" ...Salvation IS A PERSON.

The only thing that could restore a relationship... was a Relationship!

The only One that could restore the "original" plan and relationship was the Original Creator, the One and only (Original Designer) of all "relationship" itself! But a relationship is only a living Relationship, when it connects you with a Person, not a thing! The essence of God's plan is relationship. In all programs that don't hold people, the missing essence is again a simple thing: r-e-l-a-t-i-o-n-s-h-i-p!

God did not create man because He (God) was lonely & needed someone. Likewise, God was not tired when He "rested" on the 7th day Sabbath! God is complete in Himself and didn't need mankind to "make Him complete", or to bring Him happiness.

Rather, God created man... for Fellowship... for Relationship!

> **God promised a "Cure"... a "Salvation"... I-N the form of a Person!**

God originally planned to walk and talk with Adam, His special creation, and to enjoy, deepen and enrich this perfect relationship, throughout all eternity. As in any pure relationship, God built in Life-giving boundaries and parameters to keep it healthy.

God promised a "Cure"... a "Salvation"... I-N the form of a Person!

God promised an Answer, a Solution and a Cure for Sin (for its wages), and the restoration of the Original, broken Relationship. God's Promise of Salvation was to be a Person....n-o-t a religion.

God promised a Person...which requires at heart...a relationship... to bring a-n-d... to b-e Salvation & Redemption. King David prophesied this in Psalm 118:21, when he wrote: "I will praise Thee, Lord, for You have answered me, and have become My Salvation."

Restored Relationship: ...the Ultimate Goal of Redemption

Long before the "Cure", (Who is Jesus Christ) came, God pointed Adam toward Relationship. In His Promise of Salvation, God told Adam to focus on relationships (toward the great Relationship Adam would some-day again enjoy with His loving Heavenly Father.

Relationship would be the path of Redemption.

Satan was so full of hatred, pride and anger, he simply could not recognize (even from the start), Redemption coming in the form of a Person....and a Relationship: rather than a mere religion or moral code.

I Corinthians 2:8 tell us plainly that: Satan did N-O-T know "God's Plan". For had he known, he would never have so fully "cooperated" in God's Redemption plan. Satan, by crucifying the Lord of glory, assured his very own eternal destruction.

This Salvation would be won... attained... and maintained... through an ultimate, personal relationship.

God promised that He would be an intimate, intricate part of this Salvation. This Promised "H e"... this P-E-R-S-O-N... This Seed (capital "S") of the woman... this capital "D" (Descendent of the woman)... He (not "IT") would crush the Serpent, the devil, the enemy of God and of mankind.

To the man (& woman) who had broken relationship through their sin, God sent a future Redeemer! The "Divine Curse-Reverser," would someday fatally crush the serpent's head. Here God was (and is) promising to restore Eternal Life & perfect "Creator-creation Relationship" once again!

The "Redemption-Redeemer" would be...
...The "Relationship-Restorer" as well

*The Cure for sin... the Messiah...
was to be a Person, not a religion. This promised Redemption...
would be a Relationship...not a Program!*

*Through the entire Old Testament, Relationship
remained the 'God of 'R's ... most treasured Goal...
Priority... and the Prize!*

Enoch walked W-I-T-H God

"Enoch lived sixty-five years, and begot Methusaleh.(Gen. 5:21)

"After he begot Methuselah, Enoch walked w-i-t-h God three hundred years, and had sons and daughters." (5:22)

"So all the days of Enoch were three hundred and sixty-five years." (5:23)

"And Enoch walked w-i-t-h God, and he was not, for God took him (5:24)

Enoch in Genesis 5

Four short verses in Genesis chapter five tell us: "Enoch walked w-i-t-h God and he was, not for God took him". What is meant by "walking w-i-t-h God?" Obviously, Enoch must have had quite an intimate, exquisite, awesome relationship with His Creator!

"Walked with God" (as a phrase) is mentioned twice in 4 short verses about Enoch. Great love and trust, obedience, community, all these things add up to one word once again. You guessed it! RELATIONSHIP! This word even way back in Eden, foreshadows Jesus' own strategy (in Mark 3:14) and His new convert-care plan... once again!

One story goes like this: God and Enoch were out "walking" w-i-t-h each other one day. The God of "R" may have whispered to Enoch: "Enoch, my beloved child: you're much closer to My house than yours. Why don't you just come on home to Heaven with Me right now!" And so, he did!"

Friendship With God was Still Possible after
Enoch as well: Abraham was the " F-r-i-e-n-d of God"

Long before Redemption and the advent of the Jesus as the Messiah, friendship with God was still possible and valued by God. We see Abraham 1,200 years before the Ten Commandments came to Moses.

In Genesis 12:1-3, we see Abraham was someone that God was attracted to, because of Abe's heart and r-e-l-a-t-i-o-n-s-h-i-p! God said to

His friend Abraham: "I will bless you and make you a blessing. (Gen.12:1-3) And again: "Because you have placed Me above all others, and not even withheld your own son, in your Seed, shall all the nations of the earth be blessed." (Genesis 22:8)

The 10 Commandments: 10 Ultimate Laws of successful R-e-l-a-t-i-o-n-s-h-i-p-s

The 10 Commandments (Exodus 20 & Deut. 5) are globally venerated and rightly recognized as the ultimate moral code of all time! However, they are not just a mere Moral code. When God gave the 10 Commandments, they were meant to do several things.

Galatians 3:26 also says: "the Law was our schoolmaster (Greek, Pedagogue) to bring us to Christ." This pedagogue ("Schoolmaster" in "King James-ese") was the one household slave responsible for seeing that the younger children "made it to school". The Law of Moses "was our schoolmaster to bring us to Christ". (to Christ-relationally- as a Person, a Savior and as the "Relationship-Restorer" & Redeemer)

The Law... through our "weakness" ...was to bring us to Christ... through relationship!

Thus, the Law was to help do what the Law itself could not do: to bring us back to a Person...back to the "Relationship Restorer" ..back to a Relationship ...to Christ! The Law was designed to bring us back to saving, Life-giving Relationship with God, through Jesus Christ!

Too many preachers over-emphasize the legal side of these 10 Commandments. Too many sermons miss the underlying, promised New Covenant "Relationship". Only this relationship makes Salvation live-able, doable, enjoyable & eternal, by a personal salvation relationship with the Lord Jesus Christ.

THE TWO GREAT COMMANDMENTS: BOTH TOTALLY "R"-elational: What is the One Greatest Commandment?

Jesus referred to Deuteronomy 6 verse 5 (the 'O Shemmai), as the one single Greatest Commandment! (Matthew 22:36). This verse reads: "Hear O Israel: the Lord thy God is one Lord & you must worship and l-o-v-e Him with (out of) A-L-L of your heart and A-L-L of your soul and A-L-L of your mind & A-L-L of your strength."

Can you sense a core "Relationship yearning" in these words? We "calm it down" and make it a mere, moral command. God desires is relationship, not religion! God made us for that, He created us for relationship... for a deep, loving relationship with HIM!

God is commanding
a "full-blown love affair" with Him!

The command: "Thou must l-o-v-e (agape) the Lord thy God with A-L-L your heart, soul, mind and strength," is basically saying: "You m-u-s-t have an ongoing, glowing, ever-growing love affair with the Lord your God. It must burn hot and holy, deeper and higher than any other love in your life! This verse must challenge us to ask the Holy Spirit to search us for an honest answer to the question it evokes. That question is: "How is y-o-u-r Love-affair with the Lord y-o-u-r God?" Is it hotter or cooler, than yesterday?... last week? last year? or ever before in your life?

The 2nd Great Commandment:
Leviticus 19:18... 100 % Relational!

Most of us know the second Great Commandment is: "Love your neighbor as you love yourself." Some reading this book now memorized this verse five or ten, 20, or 30 years ago! Or so they think!

Surprisingly, less than 1% Know
the front end of this: "Love Your Neighbor"

What is the front-end of this verse, Leviticus 19:18? It does have a front half that we simply have never been taught! The front end of Leviticus 19:18 says: "Thou shalt not take vengeance, nor bear any grudge against the children of your people", ...but you must love your neighbor as you love yourself...

Part A of Leviticus 19:18 reads...
"You shall not take Revenge":

Why would God here be forbidding revenge? What does "taking revenge" do to relationship? 'Taking revenge' is a-c-t-i-v-e-l-y destroying relationship. God says: "You shall N-O-T actively destroy or attack relationship!"

Part B of Leviticus 19:18 reads...
"You shall n-o-t bear a Grudge":

What does bearing a grudge do to relationship or to our ability to love o-u-r neighbor? Grudge-bearing is n-o-t actively, but rather p-a-s-s-i-v-e-l-y destroying relationship. God is here specifically, forbidding us to bear any grudges... in our hearts.

Now see how the whole verse of
Leviticus 19:18 reads, when it has Parts A & B in front of...
Part C : "You must love your neighbor"

"You shall not take vengeance...,
nor bear any grudge against the children of your people;

but you shall love your neighbor as yourself: I am the Lord."
Leviticus 19:18

God is unmistakeably saying here in Leviticus 19:18: Thou shalt not "DESTROY "R"... or "RELATIONSHIP"!

The God of "R" is unmistakably saying here (in Parts A & B of the Second Great Commandment): "Thou shall not destroy relationship, neither actively (through revenge) nor passively (bearing a-n-y grudge). Rather, YOU M-U-S-T LOVE... YOU M-U-S-T VALUE RELATIONSHIP ABOVE E-V-E-R-Y-T-H-I-N-G ELSE!"

I've been a born-again Christian now over 30 years. How strange that in preaching in 500 churches, that no one ever taught me, nor have I ever heard taught or mentioned the front end of this verse, the Second Greatest of all commandments, according to Jesus (Matthew 22:39.) The Lord commands us to love our neighbors. We don't have time to even know our neighbors!

What enables us to love our neighbor is the front-end (part A & B) of Leviticus 19:18. O-n-l-y in keeping our hearts clear of interpersonal, relational poisons (like revenge) and the debris of grudge-bearing (and un-forgiveness)... can we ever hope to love our neighbors, as we love ourselves!

James 4:7... Another classic two-part verse:

Leviticus 29:18 works (& doesn't "work") on the same basis as James 4:7! The well known 2nd half (of James 4:7) says: "resist the devil and he will flee from you." Why doesn't the devil flee when we resist him more often?

The first "half" of James 4:7?

The front "half" of James 4:7 reads: "Submit yourself unto God." Then, and only t-h-e-n, will the devil flee from you! Similarly, that which provides power to "love your neighbor as you love yourself" front-end combination of Leviticus 19:18:..... A) n-o-t taking revenge & B) n-o-t bearing a grudge.

The is the Second and Great Inter-Personal commandment from the eternal, God of "R".

We now see... that not only the 1st Great Commandment is totally relational... but that the 2nd Great Commandment is r-e-l-a-t-i-o-n-a-l as well. B-o-t-h of the Two Great Commandments are totally "relationally based!"

Jesus' One N-e-w Commandment in John 13:34 (& John 15:12). 100% R-e-l-a-t-i-o-n-a-l... once again!

After humbly washing His twelve disciples' feet at the Last Supper, Jesus said in John 13:34: "This one new commandment I give you, that you l-o-v-e one another, as I have loved you!"

Love is "R"-elationship... Spelled with an "L":

I Corinthians 13:8 reads: "Love n-e-v-e-r fails." We forget too easily (as 1st John 4:8 & 16 tell us), that: "God is L-O-V-E!"

Did Jesus say in John 13:35: "By this shall all men know you are My disciples... if you have services three times a week?... (or)... by the number of scripture verses you memorize? ...if you quote scripture to each other?"

Not even close! These are theology's & religion's traditions, but n-o-t Jesus' words, nor His one new, relational, commandment! Rather, Jesus said in John 13:35: "By this shall all men know you are My followers, by the Divine, agape love you have ... one to another."

Give us something "deep" ...not this fluffy "love stuff"!

You may say: "it can't be that simple, it's not just that "love stuff." That's too close to the classic Beatles' sixties' song: "All you need is Love" (duh-duh...duh-duh-duh!). Not the "lovey-dovey" stuff. Not the "love thing". We "tried" that! Granted, love is great "in its place". It does have a place. But heh, we're mature believers, give us something deep!"

"The God of R"... is trying to tell us: ...NOTHING is "deeper" than Love!

Nothing is deeper than Relationship! Salvation i-s a relationship, n-o-t a religion. That's precisely why Jesus spent so much time w-i-t-h His disciples. That's also why He is always w-i-t-h... each one of us! We must re-discover the almost untaught relationality of God, and the centrality of relationship as God's "Program": ...for His beloved mankind: past, present... and future!

We need to learn the scriptures of... and the language of... "R"!

We need to find, highlight and memorize the c-o-r-e relational scriptures: ...if we are to live it, model and preach it...out of the Word of God! If relationship is God's program ...(& it so clearly is) then, it is also in...(actually all throughout) God's Holy Word: the Bible! I-F relationship is the crucial missing element in the paradigm of the Information Age, we drastically need to remedy this "Vitamin-R" Deficiency! Let's bring "R" from the "back of the bus" up to the "driver's seat" of our programs. We must put "R" solidly atop our daily emphases: in our churches, personal devotions & our daily walk with God!

Then Jesus will say:
"I never knew you!" (Matthew 7:22)

The God of "R" repeats His key theme over and over to us. We must de-program ourselves from our over-programmed emphasis & return whole-heartedly to God's program of "R".

Jesus is n-o-t talking about knowing; He's talking about... K-N-O-W-I-N-G! Jesus is the God of "R"!

In John 5:39 Jesus said: "You search the scriptures for in them you think ('you Imagine'- Moffatt) that you have life. These are they that testify of Me. And you will not come to Me, that you might have Life." Once again, Jesus stresses Himself as a Person (even above the written Word). Jesus again high-lights His yearning for r-e-l-a-t-i-o-n-s-h-i-p.... not for religious superficiality... and ritualistic busyness!

Then again, in Matthew 7:21-23... (at the end of His Sermon on the Mount), Jesus said: **"Not everyone who says to Me, Lord, Lord, shall enter the Kingdom of Heaven, but he who does the will of My Father in Heaven. Many will say to Me in that day: "Lord, Lord, have we not prophesied in Your Name? and in Thy Name cast out devils? and in Thy Name done many wonderful works. Then will I profess (declare) to them: "Depart from Me, you workers of iniquity. (You who practice law-lessness- Greek 'anomia'.)": "I never k-n-e-w you!"**

"I Never K-N-E-W you:"

What does Jesus mean: " I never k-n-e-w you!"

God is omniscient & all-knowing! Jesus knew the End before the Beginning... before the beginning ever began to be begun. Jesus was (and is) God Pre-existent... Pre-eternal... before Eternity ever began! Our Lord Jesus is both the Beginning & the End, the Alpha & Omega, both the First and the Last!

Jesus is n-o-t talking about knowing,
He's talking about... K-N-O-W-I-N-G!

Once again, he's talking about relationship. He's talking about intimacy, He's talking about closeness, heart-to-heart communication: Life-flow, Connection and Community!

He's talking about "w-i-t-h-i-n-g!" After all, He is the "God of 'R'"!

In this Matthew 7:22 passage, verse, we see 'they' got the "Lord, Lord" part right, at least with their mouths. They got their religious actions right...at least externally... on the outside.

They, however, obviously "missed God" where it counted: ...their hearts!

NOT WHERE IT REALLY COUNTED...
N-O-T R-E-L-A-T-I-O-N-A-L-L-Y!

Our Lord Jesus Christ is saying: "You did the religious things, the Sunday-go-to-meeting" things. But you never did the one thing I wanted most of all...what My heart yearned for, to establish and deepen the one, key, precious, eternal r-e-l-a-t-i-o-n-s-h-i-p that I died and rose again to provide for you... for us... to deepen and to enjoy... together... forever!

The God of "R " is saying to each of us over and over: "All you really have in life... are r-e-l-a-t-i-o-n-s-h-i-p-s!

"All you really have in life are relationships." You may reply: "What do you mean? I'm a pastor, I have a theological degree (or several), I have a building, I have a church family, I have my own family. I have my children, two cars, a deacon board, a budget, I have responsibilities, etc."

Take the relationships out of your life.... and what do truly have? Absolutely nothing!

Take the relationships out of your church, as in when a church splits. When a church's central, key, core relationships "go south", there is nothing left to hold people together.

A church is only as strong as its R-elationships!

A marriage is only as strong as the couple's R-elationship with each other! A Christian is only as strong as his R-elationship... with God!

No wonder they call Him Wonderful...

No wonder they call Him t-h-e Magnificent,
Unsurpassable, Unique, Eternal

Awesome, Splendiferous, Irreplaceable,
Unconquerable, Loving, Merciful, Gracious

God of "R"!

Chapter 17
"THE POWER OF A NAME"

"The sheep hear His voice: He calls His own sheep by name, and leads them forth. The sheep follow Him, for they know His voice. A stranger they will n-o-t follow, for they know not the voice of a stranger."(John 10:3-5)

When God first created mankind, He created Man in His own eternal, relational image (Genesis 1:26). God named the first man Adam, planning to enjoy this relationship forever, on a intimate, first-name basis! Even after Adam sinned, God still called Adam by name. "Adam... where are you?" God foreknew Adam's sin and fall, but His Divine providence provided a Cure for sin. To reverse the curse... and restore the God-to-man relationship, God's 'Solution'... was n-o-t to be a mere belief... but a Person... and a Life-giving, saving Relationship!

The Name above every Name... JESUS!

Space won't permit highlighting all the scriptures extolling the power of Jesus' Name: that one Name above all others!

"God has given Him a Name above every other Name, that at the Name of Jesus... every knee will bow & every tongue confess, that Jesus Christ is Lord." (Philippians. 2:10&11).

"Nor is there salvation in any other, for there is no other n-a-m-e under heaven given among men whereby we must be saved" (Acts 4:12)

"You shall call His Name Jesus, for He shall save His people from their sins." (Matthew 1:19,21)

God... softly... calls our name... throughout our lives... in His Spirit's gentle, loving voice. Because of His everlasting love, God continually calls our name ... in myriad and infinitely diverse ways, throughout our lives. God calls our name... long, long before we ever come to Him! He whispers our name in the silence and roar of our lives, in our calms and tempests as well. He whispers our name in each dawn's first rays! In the beauty of life and in His awesome creation, God continually calls us home... and back to relationship with Him!

How can we teach o-u-r new convert 'lambs' to hear the voice of the Lord... as He calls t-h-e-i-r name?

Many things we now do automatically (as full-grown Christians), we once didn't know. We had to learn our 'God-talk'(and our 'God-walk')... one word & one step at a time. We must help our lambs through this same process.

God called out personally & repeatedly... to finally catch the boy-child Samuel's ear... and spirit!

"Samuel, Samuel", God called to the young boy Samuel. Three times Samuel awoke and said: "Here am I, Lord" (1st Sam. 3:4-8). On each waking, Samuel asks the aged Prophet Eli if he had called him. The 3rd time, Eli realized the Lord was calling Samuel's name! Eli instructed him: "Go back to sleep, Samuel. The next time you hear the voice, say: " Speak Lord, Thy servant listeneth." (I Samuel 3:10)

Eli taught the young boy Samuel to recognize... and respond to... the voice of the Lord!

We must patiently, lovingly... and individually... do the same with each lamb God sends our way!

The power of a name... goes hand in hand developmentally... with establishment & deepening of relationship!

The power of a name...accompanies establishing (and deepening) any relationship! From a 0% brand new, "total stranger" level... to a deep, life-long friendship, the power in a name is involved every step along the way. To get to full term, the name and the relationship develop together.

The Power of a name... & the even G-R-E-A-T-E-R power of a... "NICK-NAME!"

Jesus nicknamed Simon... 'Petros' (little rock)... Not 'pebble'... or "quicksand!" (Matthew 16:17-18)

Our wonderful Lord Jesus (knowing Peter would fail multiple times), nonetheless named "perfect" Simon 'little-rock' or "Rocky"! When Peter replies: "Thou are the Christ," Jesus replies: "...and I call you "Petros" ('little rock', a Greek masculine noun). Then, Jesus switches His "Rock" words ... to 'a large boulder' (a totally different word: 'Petra' (in Greek-a feminine noun, meaning a 'boulder' or immense, foundational rock strata). Here the 'Rock" is n-o-t little 'Rocky', but rather Peter's h-u-g-e recognition of Jesus as God and Savior." (Matthew 16:18)

John: unquestionably was "the disciple whom Jesus l-o-v-e-d!"

It amazes me any 'theologian' can claim "the disciple whom Jesus loved" is unclear, as to its being John. This shows a lack of studying God's Word. The phrase: "the disciple whom Jesus loved" is found 5 times: o-n-l-y in John's Gospel. (John 13:23, 19:26, 20:2, 21:7 & 21:20) John 21 unquestionably locks-in John's authorship! John 21:24 reads: "This is the disciple witnessing concerning these things ...and having written these things", meaning that this ('the disciple whom Jesus loved') is 'me': the writer of t-h-i-s Gospel. Which Gospel? Duh! JOHN's!

We don't know if Jesus literally called John "the disciple He loved". Perhaps it was a private nickname. God's Word doesn't tell us. We do know John's head was on Jesus' chest at the Last Supper & was the "closest" to Jesus!

If you don't know my name... You don't know me... at A-L-L!

If you don't know my name, you don't know me! I'm often asked: "Can I call you John?" I reply: "No, thank you, my name is Jonathan." If they call me Steve or Bill, or "Heh, you!", I k-n-o-w they don't know me. If they mis-pronounce my first or last name (incidentally, unhooked on phonics), I know they also don't know my name... nor me!

If we are going to call our lambs by t-h-e-i-r names... as Jesus did with His... we must learn (& use) our convert's names... (& nicknames) as well!

5 Steps to tap into "The Power in a Name"... with Y-O-U-R lambs!

1.) Launch (& distribute) an ongoing, weekly-updated 1-year name-list of converts:

Most churches have no 'watertight', unified, church-wide system to track their 'lambs' being born. A Convert-Care Task Force can help immensely, with one person in charge of both updating this list... a-n-d also getting the new list regularly to staff, board, deacons, leaders, the Convert-Care Team, sponsors, and entire congregation!

Convert Photo-Name Sheets (& wall boards): One easy way to enhance Name-Face recognition!

2.) Taking photos of converts:

Whether digital, 35mm film (or Polaroid), prayer-photos of your new converts are an extremely helpful & doable idea! Rather than stack photos in an envelope or by rubber band, reduce the photos on a copier platen

> **Launch & create an ongoing, weekly-updated one year name-list of converts.**

(with each name below it). By reducing them to 2" squares (outlined or not), 20 or 30 photos of new-born 'lambs' can be fitted on one page in landscape format: 6 or 7 photos across and 4 or 5 rows down.

A color copier (or color printer) brightens the photo-name sheet, but even a black & white photo-name sheet is a marvelous name-face memory enhancer and help. Distribute these sheets to staff, board and deacons, leaders & lamb-care team members, to pray over, put in their Bibles & study...so converts will feel the delight of being known!

3.) Photo Face(& name) Wall-Boards on an easel (or the church lobby or office wall):

Mounting these photos on a wall-board in the church lobby helps the entire church family recognize, intentionally "love-on," and connect with new believers. A wood-trimmed, lobby bulletin board gives a permanent location for the entire church to remember (& brush up on forgotten names or faces), of these perishable newborns. A newborn lamb-poster can be mounted on portable, low-cost, foam-core & put on an easel in the lobby (or elsewhere).

4.) Pocket/wallet ('purse-size') lists of names of converts...

There is great power in not only knowing someone's name, but also in t-h-e-i-r knowing that you know it... and that the o-n-l-y reason you learned it... was because you care for & love them... and want God's best for them!

5.) A data-base accessible to ALL Lamb-Care Team members (input-able by sponsors.)

There needs to be a centralized, updateable system of input and 'info,' to help compile (and cross-pollinate) the multiple friendships and connections every new lamb needs in his 1st month (& 1st 6 months) at any church.

"Dear Resident:"

Imagine a family... that didn't know each other's names... especially their very youngest children!

We have all received mail addressed to 'resident'. It makes an impact by its stark lack of relationship!

A family that doesn't know each others names:

Here's an early morning family scenario. The dad: "Son, I love you, what's your name again? The son: "Heh, dad, tell me again, what's my Mom's name?"

Aaron (as Old Testament High Priest) bore the Names of the 12 Tribes engraved on Jewels on His Breastplate... to keep them continually over his heart... when going into the Presence of the Lord! (Exodus 28)

In the Old Testament, the priest had a breastplate with 12 stones on it. "You shall take two onyx stones, and engrave on them the names of the 12 tribes of Israel. Put six names on one stone, and six names on the other. Thou shalt put these two stones upon the shoulders of the ephod (Exodus 28:9-11) And Aaron shall bear the names of the children of Israel in the breastplate of judgement upon his heart, when he goes into the holy place before the Lord continually (Ex.28:29).

The Hebrew word for this "Breastplate" (Chushen.. kho'-shen) means to contain or to sparkle. It meant a rich pocket, containing gems, and is o-n-l-y used to refer to this High Priest's breastplate.

As priests of Jesus' and His New Covenant, we must keep the names of our lambs... J-e-s-u-s' lambs... this close to us... continually upon o-u-r hearts: for they... are that close... and dear... to Him!

****

There is a "head- n-a-m-e"... and there is also a "heart-name".

Jesus wants us not only to know His N-a-m-e...but His "heart-Name", heartbeat & Spirit as well!

You can't truly know someone, without knowing their name. You can know someone's name, however, ...and not really know them at all! That is... not i-n-t-i-m-a-t-e-l-y! True to this thought, the main New Testament Greek word for name (`on/-o-ma') derives from the words for authority and character.

THERE IS A N-A-M-E... WITHIN THE 'N-A-M-E'... just as Jesus Himself... is the Living Word... within the written Word! (John 5:39 & 40)

Jesus said it so Masterfully in Matthew 7:22: "Many will say to Me in that day: 'Lord, Lord, have we not prophesied in Thy Name? and in Thy Name cast out devils? and in Thy Name done many wonderful works?

Three times in one verse, they claimed they did it all: "in Jesus' Name"! They knew His 'n-a-m-e"...but didn't know His real NAME...His nature! They knew his 'head-name', not His 'heart-name.' They truly didn't know Him: not His heart, Spirit, soul or heartbeat. That is why Jesus' deep desire is that we know Him in the depth of H-i-s heart!

When Jesus says that He gives to His overcoming, eternal flock a new name upon their foreheads, He is n-o-t speaking of a 'head-name'... but a "heart name!" He will write it in their spirit, in their inner person, in their soul of souls! It is this depth of relationship the Lord wants each of us to enjoy...so we can, in turn, pass it on... to His lambs!

This 'heart-name' relationship... is o-u-r strongest tool of faith... for overcoming!

Jesus said: "To him that overcomes I will give a white stone... with a new name written on it." (Revelation 2:17)

He promises: "To him that overcomes, I will write upon him the Name of My God... and I will write upon him My new name." (Rev. 3:12)

"A Lamb stood on Mt Zion and with Him 144,000... with His Father's Name written upon their foreheads." (Rev. 14:1)

"And they shall see Him face to face, and shall bear His Name upon their foreheads." (Rev. 22:4, NEB)

The Power... love a-n-d intimacy... in a Name... is encapsulated in these words from Song of Solomon Chapter 1&2

"The Song of Songs, which is Solomon's. Let Him kiss me with the kisses of His mouth: for Thy love is better than wine. Because of the savour of Thy good ointments, Thy Name is as ointment poured forth. Therefore do the virgins love Thee. Draw me and we will run after Thee. The King hath brought me into His chambers; we will be glad and rejoice in Thee. We will remember Thy love more than wine. The upright love Thee." (Song 1:1-4)

"I am the Rose of Sharon, and the Lily of the Valleys. As the lily among the thorns, so is my Love among the daughters. As the apple tree among the trees of the wood, so is my Beloved among the sons. I sat down under His shadow with great delight, and His fruit was sweet to my taste.
He brought me to His banqueting house... and His banner over me was love. (Song of Solomon: 2:1-4)

PS. The true Lover of your soul... the God of L-o-v-e... is calling y-o-u-r "heart-name" now! He is calling y-o-u into a deeper, more intimate relationship level than ever before! Don't keep Him waiting... too long!

Chapter 18
"HOW TO SPELL IT WITH AN "R"

Efficient ... or... Effective!

Globally recognized consultant, Peter Drucker, is often quoted as saying: "Efficiency is doing things right!... Effectiveness... is doing the right things!"

Most American churches today are not growing. They are efficient, but not effective: doing many, many things right, but not doing enough of the "right things"! Too many churches today are using teflon, and expecting it to act like velcro!

While there is much activity, there is little actual growth. There are many leaves... but insufficient "full term" grapes at the harvest...too little actual "fruit that remains." (John 15:16)

We excel at finding, instituting and maintaining programs, but are not aware that the crucial missing ingredient in Western Christianity is God's core program: ...relationship!

Becoming "Relational Technologists": T-H-E missing ingredient!

Currently there are dozens of computer languages with many interesting and creative names, such as Cobal, Basic, Pascal, C+, Fortram, Modula 2, ADA, P11 and numerous many others.

However, the language of the heart is none of these, but rather relationships: the language of "R"!

The heart is the ultimate "life computer", and relationships that connect heart to heart are indeed the ultimate, (and ultimately challenging... and rewarding) "software".

Churches, ministers, and effective Christians today must become experts in the language, of "R!" We must become fluent in the language, dimensions and dynamics of "Relationship." In short, we need God's help becoming expert, efficient "relational technologists!" Who can we turn to, better than to God Himself, for help learning to program and write "code" for the language of "R": the language of the heart.

People come to church for a variety of reasons... but they stay for primarily just one... relationships!

Following are several examples of translating church programs into the language of "R"!

I. Put on the front of your church bulletin:
First Church: "Where relationships are #1"

Why not change the slogan on front of your church's weekly bulletin to read: "Where relationships are #1!" In 500+ churches, I've only seen this on front of perhaps two church bulletins.

Imagine a change like this in your church. This one line can give main-street primacy to God's Program: "relationships"... at your church, each week... and year-round!

"Cocoon-itis"... and Inoculating against it

The Information Age has infected us all with "cocoon-itis". We love the "cocoon", its comfort & safety, even if it's killing us relationally! Like carbon monoxide, it kills our church's health & growth.

Affluenza and the Information Age Paradigm

> **The Bible is not only the Book of Life, it is also the ultimate Relationship Book!**

The "R" Factor" has plummeted severely! "Affluenza" (the disease that teaches that the "best things in life are things", has dramatically spread. Divorce has sky-rocketed in the Information Age: from 5% to 50% in one generation. The average annual USA divorce rate the last two decades is 1.5 million!

What does this say about relationships? Down... down... and down! We now live in the midst of a "relational windshear", a relational "Ebolla", also exemplified by widespread, worsening, "relational illiteracy!" Check out Jerry Springer's or Montel's TV guest line-up..and the topics! See Rosie O'Donnell nationally advocating legalizing "lesbian couple" child adoption.

Nonetheless, the Bible is still "T H E B O O K!" The Bible is not only the Book of Life, it is also the ultimate Relationship Book! This book has the answers... to Life... and to Life's greatest challenge and treasure:... relationships!

II. "Put "R" into The 10 Commandments:

Pastor Rick Warren at Saddleback Community Church preached a popular sermon-series and titled it: "Ten Tips for Success In Life." An superlative title. When I first heard it, I didn't even know he was even referring to "The 10 Commandments".

I'd like you now, to improve this same title and "Spell it with an "R"! Add the "R" word to it! Make an "R" sermon series out of it! The new title, translated into "R", would be something like: " 10 Tips (or secrets) of Ultimate Relationships."

Pastors, teachers, and believers, let me challenge you to put "R" both into your Sermon titles, messages, and the targeted "take away" of each message. Bring relationships "from the back of the bus back up front to the driver's seat "where it belongs."

Why has America become the "Dark continent"?

Evangelistic churches & denominations report millions of annual converts, yet few churches are growing. Districts with ten thousands of annual reported converts, are shrinking.

What's missing... once again, is not "a" program, nor evangelistic zeal...but God's program!.

How could America become the "Dark Continent" with 300,000+ non-growing evangelical Bible-based churches? The missing ingredient in American Theology is relationship. Jesus is not a set of beliefs or propositions. Salvation is not the "Four Spiritual Laws": A) God has a wonderful plan for your life, B) You have sinned & the wages of sin is Death C) God's Gift is Eternal Life in Jesus Christ... and D) You must receive this gift & believe in Jesus as your Lord.

God does have a great plan for us to get our sins forgiven... but then what?

God's plan is not just the forgiveness of our sins. His plan is for family restoration: for us to have an eternal, loving salvation relationship with Him! We must teach this to each one of Jesus' baby lambs.

God is foundationally committed to this "r-e-l-a-t-i-o-n-s-h-i-p" concept, which we have unknowingly moved was down low and actually, even off of our "A" list of priorities .

Pastoral Modeling of "R" Development... as "Relational Technologists":

III. Why did John Maxwell meet with His board members 1-on-1 weekly for 15 Years?

We've already covered this concept, but it bears repeating. He was there for one thing and for one thing only: relationship development! As a "relational technologist", Pastor Maxwell knew that if relationship deepened, this would produce life-change. Life-Change in turn, produces commitment!

IV. Re-program Sunday School teachers to put Relationship first!

Sunday School Supts. (and Sunday School teachers) must be re-programmed and taught "the why and "how to", of placing relationship development a-h-e-a-d of Information (& their "Quarterly lesson"). They must be re-programmed to see that "R" is the most important part of their weekly class. We need to d re-program Sunday School's over-emphasis on facts and Bible knowledge. Sunday School Superintendents everywhere must be taught to become "Relational Technologists", to help their teachers (in turn) see the deepening of relationships... in their classes... as the primary agent of "Life-change".

Turning Sunday School Classes... into Sunday Cells:

An encouraging national trend is seeing leading churches like Christian Life Center (Pastor Ted Haggard, Colorado Springs), Victory Christian Center in Tulsa (Pastor Billy Joe Daugherty) and others, progressively turning Sunday School Classes into Sunday Cells. In these Sunday cells, relationship is being re-throned and given its scriptural, proper priority in the teaching, class time, and weekly objectives. The quarterly lesson is still purposeful. We definitely must teach the Word of God.

However, all of this... without relationship... will produce no life change... or spiritual growth!

Relationship Produces commitment... not vice-versa.

Commitment doesn't produce relationship but rather... Relationship produces Commitment!

We've been taught that commitment produces relationship. Actually the reverse is true: commitment doesn't produce relationship.

Rather, relationship produces (and increases) commitment!

Take the analogy of marriage. Gentlemen, before your wife married you, did she first have to meet you? We may have fallen in love with our wives at first sight, but deep down we know that before a lifetime commitment, there first came a beginning... & then a growing relationship!

Commitment doesn't produce relationship but rather... Relationship produces Commitment!

C doesn't equal R
Rather, "R" Produces "C"!

"Pastor: can you just tell me my name?"

I was doing a seminar for a larger church that ran a thousand plus Sunday AM. It was a lively, creative, growing church with many innovative outreaches and ministries. I had presented my "Closing Your Church's 7 Backdoors" Seminar that Saturday to 100's from scores of area churches. On Sunday I'd spoken at their Sunday AM & PM services. Now, I was meeting with their staff that Monday AM and we. were discussing this whole relationship/commitment issue.

The pastor said: "let me illustrate just how true this is." And he proceeded with this story. "We were doing a fundraising for a new facility expansion, asking a $500 dollar commitment, after a first-class dinner, praise time & multi-media presentation."

"Afterward, a gentleman walked up and quietly said: "Pastor, I love the church here. I've been attending a year, have become a new member, have been tithing faithfully, love the worship, love your sermons, and love the church family here." He continued: "I'd be glad to write you out a check for $500. No problem," he said, "just one thing, ...can you tell me my name?"

The pastor thought a moment, looked up & said: "I've seen you and I recognize you. I'm really glad you're part of our church family here. I'm sad and embarrassed to say, I can't recall your name."

The man went on: "I'll still write a check for $500 dollars gladly, if any of your staff (standing round the pastor)...if any of your staff can tell me my name." Sadly, none of them knew his name either!

**The pastor was asking for commitment,
but the man in the pews was asking f-i-r-s-t,
for relationship!**

*The pastor was asking for commitment,
But the man in the pews was asking f-i-r-s-t for relationship!*

Pastors across the land, are asking their people for commitment... for more dedication, and sacrifice. The people in the pews everywhere are asking for more... relationship!

"C" Doesn't produce "R"
Rather "R" Produces "C"

God's plan, is not using the people to get the work done. It is rather, to use the work... to get the people done. Use the work to grow the people... to develop relationship with God, and thus Life-change and discipleship in them.

The Fulcrum of Relationship & Commitment

One can never ask for a higher level of commitment than there exists an equal or commensurate level of relationship. If you want a "C-3" level of Commitment, you can't ask for it with a "R-1" level of relationship.

The problem with the man at the church with the $500 dollar offer... was obvious.

The pastor was asking for a C-3 level of commitment, but the congregation member wanted to be re-assured first, of even an "R-1" level of relationship!

Picture in your mind a play-ground see-saw

Picture in your "minds eye" a playground see-saw, slanting from lower left to upper right, with a triangle as a fulcrum under the middle. The lower left side represents relationship. The upper right side stands for com-

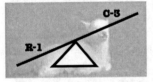

mitment! You can never ask for a higher level of commitment, than exists a equal level of relationship.

Across America, pastors, church staff, Sunday School Superintendents, teachers and nursery workers alike, are repeatedly and invariably telling church members such things such as: "We need more workers", "Would you consider helping us…", etc.

Ask for commitment and you may not get it.

But "plant" relationship f-i-r-s-t, and live out your own deepening, relationship-based level of commitment and love, and you will surely harvest commitment.

Do What Jesus Did!

He intentionally chose 12 to be w-i-t-h Him!

Plant relationship and you can't fail but to create and produce commitment!

When commitment & life-change are produced, the discipleship-quotient goes up automatically as well, even as the wind can't help but move a sailboat, if its sails are raised…& it has raised up its anchor!

Chapter 19
"THE POWER OF THE PARADIGM"

What is a paradigm... &...
What Possible Effect Can it Have?

The word "Paradigm" can be correctly defined multitudinous ways, each of them correct. A paradigm is a set of lenses, or a world view, or a set of understandings that go together, or again, a "map." A paradigm can also be the components of (or a set of) ingredients present in a given environment. A paradigm can also be the rules of a game. Every game is its own paradigm.

However, the details of each paradigm (& its finer points) distinguish effectiveness...and success or failure ... within the paradigm's borders and boundaries!

Take the basic element (or Paradigm) of "f-i-r-e!"

When one is comparing fire with something totally different, for instance with snow or with ice, all "fire" may be considered the same. Some might say: "Well fire is hot, and all fire is alike." In some basic ways, indeed all types of fire are the same: they all do require fuel, heat and oxygen!

Now Let's think more paradigmically here!

However, all "f-i-r-e" is also n-o-t alike! Take a wood fire. If you throw water on a wood fire, enough water will extinguish the fire. However, if we change the "paradigm" to a different type of fire, we may change the components and how they interact. This is what happens when a paradigm shifts.

The same effective strategy, in a different paradigm... can have the opposite effect!

Change the type of fire...from a wood-fire to an oil or grease fire!

Let's change our example from a wood fire...... to a grease fire! It's still fire, but now a "different type of fire." If we assume all "fire" is exactly alike, (& don't understand, the paradigm-change in the components... and how they react together), we're in for a disastrous, rude awakening!

Change the paradigm... and see what happens! Throw water on an oil fire, and the very same previously "effective" strategy... putting water on the fire), which previously put out the fire...now will n-o-t put out the fire... but rather will spread it!

The Information Age is
"Relationally Bankrupt!"... Therefore...

The Information Age has unquestionably overloaded us with both information & technology. The standard of living has risen exponentially. Simultaneously, the quality of relationships has "crashed"! What might be the basis of the next paradigm to "scratch the itch" of our relationally anorexic society?

Let's compare the "R" Factor" to the R-Factor in Construction Insulation.

It is, in few words: a renaissance of new emphasis on "relationships!" Why is the emphasis on relationships more crucial than ever before?

Relationships and the Paradigm

"The Information Age Has no Heart"

The heart of the Information Age is information, but the Information Age has no heart! It has no time for such trivialities.

The Information Age Paradigm is like the Tin Man in the Wizard of Oz. The Scarecrow needed a brain...and the Lion needed courage... but the Tin Man.... had no heart! The Information Age has no heart!

Information is the heart of the Information Age.....
...but the Information Age... has no heart!

The Three Major Paradigms...
and the Diminishing 'R' Factor

In the Agricultural Age, 98 % of Americans lived in smaller towns a-n-d were farmers. Multiple generations lived & died in the same town or area. Most never traveled 50 miles from home in a lifetime. The relational fabric of society (and local, extended family) was rich & thick , an "R-30" at least. This social, relational cohesion & richness held social behavior in check. Divorce was non-existent!

Let's compare the "R" Factor"
to the R-Factor in Construction Insulation

Like an insulation factor, the "R" (Relationship) Factor of the Agricultural Age (paradigm) in the majority of small towns was extremely high: perhaps an "R-30" factor.

My brother-in-law is a custom contractor. His family lives far above the snow line towards Lake Tahoe in the Sierras, at 4,000' elevation. Their winters have frequent 2 and 3 foot snowfalls. He intentionally put R-30 insulation into the ceiling, walls, and floor of his expansive home! His heating bill is less than ours where we live, even though we live b-e-l-o-w the snow line. There is one reason: the intentional installation of heavy insulation! ... and an extremely high "R"-Factor.

Similarly, the R-relational dimension (the "R" factor) was very rich in the Agricultural Paradigm! Perhaps an R-30 (or even a R-40!)

The Industrial Age Paradigm: a dropping "R" Factor

As the Industrial Age developed momentum, urbanization increasingly drew more and more people to the growing, larger cities. Folks desired all the modern amenities and conveniences that city-life provided. The cities were the first to have hot & cold running water, indoor plumbing, larger stores, better hospitals, the latest vaccines, etc. More and more, people "moved in" to town", to take advantage of the better products that the Industrial Age Paradigm kept producing.

As this urbanization took place & increasing numbers of families moved to the cities, Grandma and Grandpa couldn't always follow. Other relatives, extended family and countless, multi-decade friendships got "left behind". In the city, more and more people didn't know each other. Populations sky-rocketed and jumped from 10,000's to the 100,000's... and then to the millions!

The extended family became the dis-tended family... and the relationship fabric of society, progressively weakened and became diluted!

The standard of living increased... but the "R Factor" dropped!

The standard of living increased, but the "R Factor" (for "relationship") dropped drastically! The societal "relationship fabric" plummeted again. The previous paradigm's high, healthy "R factor" had now decreased from an "R-30"... to an "R-20" or "R-15".

Then The Information Age Paradigm came along

Along comes the Information Age, with better and better products! Now there were not just cars, but cars with air-conditioning, power steering, power windows & locks, airbags, more powerful engines, and ever-increasing options, luxuries, and choices!

Higher wages required more frequent moves. IBM now stands for "I've Been Moved!" The average family in America now moves every 3 to 5 years! That "moving factor" used to be almost non-existent in the Agricultural Age. Driven by better products, and a "promised raise" for relocating across country, people and families increasingly acquiesced to the Paradigm's "more and better things" lure!

However, as the standard of living rose, the standard of loving and relationships simultaneously dropped even further. Soon the extended families were left behind a few hours away in the country. Now, people were moving not just hundreds, but thousands of miles away!

As people progressively moved farther and farther from their roots, for a better or higher paying job or education, the standard of living and technology went up and up.

But the standard of "Relationships: (the "R-Factor") dropped further and further.

The R" Factor in the Information Age has dropped from an "R-15" to an "R-10,..to an "R-5"& now finally down to an "R- Zero.

What does the paradigm "stuff" have to do... with relationships?

The Next Paradigm and Drastic need for putting Relationships First!

The next paradigm is based on the unmet needs of the current paradigm, says Joel Barker, in his I book: "Paradigms: the Business of Discovering the Future." The Information Age paradigm is already obsoleting, even as the vast majority of churches struggle to even understand and function in it efficiently. The next paradigm (to follow a-f-t-e-r the Information Age) will be built out of (and based on) meeting the "unmet needs" of this previous paradigm!

"Techno-Care and Human Repair!"... "The N-e-x-t Paradigm"!

Modernists (as Information Age 'natives'), relate to understanding truth and winning others over to it: "propositionally." But Post-Modernists (Third Millennium natives and the new younger techno-pup generation), to the contrary, win others over to the truth relationally...n-o-t propositionally!

An O-L-D Paradigm... is a "50 Year old Map of Chicago"

To tap into the power of a paradigm, one must successfully first understand how it works: its dynamics & borders, its rules and limits, and how one must operate within it... to achieve success.

If you used a 50 year old map to fly into Chicago today, O'Hare International and Mid-Way Airports would just barely be on it. O'Hare was built and opened in 1945.

Since that time, most Chicago super highways and Interstates would have been built. They would not be on that old, Chicago-land metro-map! Exit numbers and locations wouldn't be there! You wouldn't

Most USA churches today are... "playing Tennis on a Racquetball Court" be prepared for the "e-z-pass" and exact change toll booths (with no one there to make change)

It would be a frightening and strange new world! This is the dilemma modern churches, and the Bible schools & seminaries training their pastors... face today!

Most USA Churches Today are Using a 50 Year Old Map... and are "Out of Paradigm!

Many churches are in danger of being a paradigm... (some even "two paradigms") out-of-synch and suffering because of it.

"Playing Tennis on A Racquetball Court"

Many non-growing US churches today are suffering from both "paradigmitis" and "Paradigm blindness". They are "out of synch:" and "out of paradigm." Basically, they are not "winning" in church-health or church-growth, because they are "playing tennis on a racquetball court."

Both Tennis and Racquetball involve two players. The two players in each game use a racket, and they each use one ball at a time. Maybe tennis and racquetball are the same paradigm after all...or are they? Someone has said: "Racquetball is like tennis on steroids!" It's a harder and a faster game than tennis.

Tennis uses one surface. Racquetball uses not just the floor, but both floor & ceiling, both side walls & both front & back wall. Six surfaces! Oh yes, lets not forget the 7th surface:...your opponent's body!

If you play tennis on a racquetball court, you're not only going to lose... you're going to get hurt.

This is the current, painful score-care of 10,000's of American evangelical churches!

Even though tennis and racquetball are both two-player, racket games...

They're really n-o-t the same game... or p-a-r-a-d-i-g-m... at all!

Chapter 20
"5 THINGS CHO'S CHURCH DOES WITH CONVERTS"

Lamb-care at the World's Largest Church

You may be questioning about now: "Who are you to make such a strong "relational" statement and indictment of the Western church. This

Prayer is R-E-L-A-T-I-O-N-S-H-I-P!

"R" concept you're teaching couldn't be that important, universal or successful. There couldn't be that much to learn, or to benefit from. But, say, drop a "big name", some world-famous Christian or Pastor, someone who believes the same way, I just might start to believe this whole thing a bit more!

"How About Yoido Full Gospel Church in Seoul, Korea?

What does Pastor Cho do with converts at his church? I admire and love Pastor David Yongi Cho. He is a worldwide influence in personal prayer commitment, life-change, cell groups…. and Church Growth! With God's blessing and help, Pastor Cho grew the largest church in the history of mankind!

Pastor Cho's Yoido Full Gospel church in Seoul, Korea has 800,000 members, and 80,000 home cell groups. His is an Assembly of God pastor and church. Those who know him, know that the church is built, not even on small groups: it is built on prayer!

Prayer is R-E-L-A-T-I-O-N-S-H-I-P!

What is prayer? Prayer is time spent deepening an intimate, personal relationship with the "God of R-elationship"! Why does satan so virulently hate your (& my) prayer time, even more than our reading of.. or our preaching of… God's Word? It is because prayer is time alone in that quiet place, the "closet of prayer": …relationship-ing, coming closer, getting to know God more intimately…in every dimension.

Relationship requires 3 things:

As we covered already, Relationship requires three things: Time, smallness and closeness. (or proximity). Prayer provides all three of these "relational requisites" in the ultimate, spiritual relationship experience! From Karen Hurston's "must-read", insightful book: "Growing the Worlds Largest Church", let's look now at what Pastor Cho's church does r-e-l-a-t-i-o-n-a-l-l-y with new converts.

FIVE "RELATIONAL ACTIONS IN "LAMB-CARE"...
...AT THE WORLD'S LARGEST CHURCH!

I. "Relational Lamb-Care"
Action Step #1: "Feeding the lambs" is top priority!

Prayer is the actual top priority at Pastor Cho's church. Every Friday evening, 10,000 people pray together til dawn at an all-night prayer meeting at Prayer Mountain tabernacle. They also have 24 hour, 7 day-a-week, continuing prayer is made by individuals in 100's of "prayer grottoes" at their Prayer Mountain Center, an hour's drive outside Seoul!

Cho Puts the lambs f-i-r-s-t!

Lamb-care is made the church's top priority...
that is, after p-r-a-y-e-r itself!
We learned earlier from John 21:15 that:
"Jesus put the lambs first."
Now we see:
...that Cho (& his church)
...put the lambs first. What a coincidence!
If Jesus put the lambs first... and Cho puts the lambs first,
...maybe w-e... should put the lambs first... too!

II. "Relational Lamb-care"
Action Step #2: a Home-visit for e-a-c-h new convert!

Each of Pastor Cho's 600 fulltime pastors are required to make 20 weekly home visits. The flat-lined Western church says: "Come"..(to our program). The growing global church (outside America) realizes it must actively: "Go", as Jesus' Great Co-Mission mandates (Matthew 28:19,20)! We have it backwards! We can't expect the world...or especially the newborn lambs...to c-o-m-e to us. We f-i-r-s-t need to go...to them! The "home visit" to all new converts is relational...to the "max!"

Cho Says: "One Home Visit is worth 10,000 sermons!"

Pastor Cho says: "One home visit is worth 1,000 sermons!"

At 52 sermons a year, 1,000 sermons is the equivalent of 20 years of Sunday morning sermons!

While not denigrating the indispensable preaching of the Word of God to feed men's souls, Cho knows that nurturing responsibility (& pro-active initiative) should n-o-t expect the lambs to come to the church. Rather, it is for us for us...to go, to connect with, and to "relationship" the lambs where they live!

When you take the effort to find and to go visit somebody's home, what does it say to them? It says unmistakably that you want to get to know them. A visit tells them you consider them valuable, and worth investing time and effort in developing a r-e-l-a-t-i-o-n-s-h-i-p!

They visit in two's (Ecclesiastes 4:9,10)

> **It is love that wins hearts. However... it is relationship... that holds them!**

The first thing every week, after someone gets saved, they visit the New Convert f-i-r-s-t! The district pastor and local cell group leader (or men's or women's ministry leader) make a gender/age & life-stage appropriate visit (in two's) to the New Convert's home.

Before I was saved off the streets, my attitude was: "Forget your Bible, forget your church building! I don't want or need you or your Jesus stuff". Nevertheless, God's people found me barefoot on the side of the road. They loved me! In fact, with the love of Jesus, they literally "loved the hell right out of me".

It is love that wins hearts. However... it is relationship... that holds them!

Excuses "Why" We Can't Go To New Convert's Homes:

We can't go to new convert's homes because? We're too busy? We can't buy them a meal because...? Churches spend $50,000 on this item, and $20,000 on that roof, parking lot, multi media or sound system, etc! Yet, we can't seem to budget $10 per New Convert for a church-underwritten meal? Why don't we have $10 budgeted (or personal) to invite them out for a meal the day they get saved? Any church could schedule the next four Sundays a "Friendship-meal dining teams" after somebody gets saved?

We c-a-n build rich relationships where we now have mere "information transfer" and non-relational programs! The #1 problem with New Convert classes is: who's usually not there? Right! The new convert!

It became policy that New Converts were to be visited every week until they became established in the faith:

"Soon visitation grew so that staff pastors prioritized the types of visits to be made, putting visits to new believers at the top of their list. These visits were often done by (so called) "lay leaders" as well. It also became policy visits were made to new believers each week until they were established in the faith: baptized in water, baptized in the Holy Spirit, consistent in church, cell attendance & tithing.

As the church's growth spiraled, more pastors were added, but they never allowed home visitation to slow down! In 1990 over 600 pastoral staff pastors made a recorded total of 600,000+ home ministry visits!"

The visit is Pre-scheduled with both Arrival & Departure times pre-set! About 80 percent of the pastoral staff in the department of Pastoral Care work with cell groups & spend the majority of their days making ministry visits. Most visits are pre-scheduled, so people know in advance when the pastor and lay leader are coming, as well as the time they have to leave.

III. Relational "Lamb-care
Action Step #3: The Personal Testimony:

Next, the visiting team of two each share their personal testimony. The visiting district pastor shares what it was like when they were younger, baby Christians. They don't discuss "deep" concepts like the 7 candlesticks or the plagues in Revelation. Rather, they share a basic, self-revealing, tender, personal story of how they each became born again! This is something a new convert can immediately ...and personally ...relate to!

We forget to remember: we all were lambs!

When we were baby Christians, we didn't know what we know now! We didn't know that when the devil trips you up, we could step in the "shower of Salvation" & the blood of Jesus washes the shame & "garbage" away! We all once were innocent, vulnerable, helpless & unknowledgeable brand new baby lambs.

Often the visiting team has the new convert repeat the Sinner's Prayer again. They invite them to various events. They assess which of the nearest groups would best "fit" the new convert: considering age, educational background, and preferences. The section leader decides which of the five to ten groups in that area the new believer would most likely enjoy and receive the most relevant ministry from.

Often the next cell meeting is held in the new believer's home, when invited to do so. Dr. Cho says of his cell groups' purpose: "Our cell group system is a net for our Christians to cast. Instead of a pastor fishing for one fish at a time, organized believers form nets to gather hundreds and thousands of fish. A pastor should never try to fish with a single rod, but should organize believers into the "nets" of a cell system". The average has been 300 to 500 decisions each & every Sunday at his church!

IV. Relational Lamb-Care
Action Step # 4: A small "Bible-Snack"

Next, the visiting "lamb-care" team shares a brief "Bible snack". In addition to bringing along a gift Bible, they share a brief, meaningful salvation "Word-snack". This is not a long lesson, but a shorter smaller meal. Babies don't eat much at one time,.... but they do eat often... and need to be proactively fed often and regularly as well!

V. Relational "lamb-care" Action Step #5 : "The Pick-up"

Finally, and ever so relationally, they arrange during this initial visit, to pick up the New Convert to bring them, either to the local cell group, or to the men's, women's, youth group, or to the church's next scheduled service or event. Don't ever just invite a new convert to "come back soon" to the church!

If you want a baby to be someplace, you don't just invite him. You pick him up!

Barnabas: care-giver to the "baby-lamb" Paul (Acts 9:27)

In Acts 9:27, after Paul had his "Son-stroke" on the road to Damascus, we see world-class lamb-care in action. In Acts 4:36, we read of a Joseph, a disciple and former Levite priest from Cyprus, whom the Apostles quickly nicknamed Barnabbas (the name we know him by today). "Uncle Barnie", also nicknamed "Barnie the Encourager", was named "the son of consolation or son of encouragement or son of uplift," (Greek word: parakletos). Barnie was a Heaven-sent "germinator" instead of a "terminator",

After Paul, as a brand new baby-Christian was given "the left foot of fellowship" in Jerusalem by the still mistrusting, suspicious church elders, Barnabas took Paul and gave Paul the "right wing" of fellowship & nurture!
The Jerusalem Elders wouldn't even give Paul his "Christian Workers Papers." They were suspicious of Paul, the former "Sanhedrin KGB" "hit-man" and persecutor. of the early church! Their attitude was: "Don't even think about making him one of us!"

In wonderful contrast to this, we read in Acts 9:27 that: "Barnabus (Mr. "Encouragement" and Mr. Nurture) t-o-ok and b-r-o-u-g-h-t Paul with him" .... to slowly, lovingly, develop a growing, nurturing friendship and discipleship-developing relationship with him!

I wonder if (up to that point in time), Barnabas had ever yet heard the young, but growing Apostle John repeating Jesus' words and final John 21:15 instructions (& heart-beat): "If you love Me, f-e-e-d My lambs!"

At Cho's church, Step 5: the offer to "pick up" the new convert, is an offer to spend time with them, bring them home for a meal, or ideally meet with a small cell group. This "pick-up" is spelled with a huge "R"! ...

for ongoing, growing relationship!

This growing relationship with God's people (with friends and "Convert Sponsors") is the umbilical cord through which God's Love and Grace flow...and the atmosphere in which the living out of God's Word...and Kingdom...takes place!

All five of Cho's Convert-Care "actions" are extremely r-e-l-a-t-i-o-n-a-l!

#1: "Putting the lambs first". Prioritizing lambs shows them they matter & must be relationally connected with. If this doesn't occur, the convert won't bond or come back.

#2: "The Home Visit": "The heart is in the home",.... not the church! Cho's lamb-teams where the heart is, visiting the Convert's home. ("1 Home visit is worth 1,000 sermons.")

#3: "Personal Testimony": They each share a self-revealing, personal, relational "re-visit" of what being a "baby Christian" was like for them... when they were a "lamb."

#4: "Bible Snack" They personally share a small Bible-snack, building relationship through a brief, heart-to-heart time together, covering a few simple basics.

#5: "The Pick-Up" The message is sent, by going out of one's way to pick up the convert: "You are very important to us. We really do want to get to know you. We'd like to make you part of our family!"

Chapter 21
"CELL GROUPS & WORLD-CLASS CONVERT CARE"

Smallness... Largeness... and... Relationships:

The church-health dynamic of "largeness" working against "small-ness", happens quite naturally, all by itself. As a church grows, the "weave" (and richness) of relationships (church-wide), will get progressively overwhelmed by growth & largeness! People increasingly can feel they're getting "lost in the crowd", ...or "falling through the cracks."

"Relational Technologists"

As leaders, we need to learn how to be ever-improving "Relational Technologists"! We need to monitor how the overall relationship ("R factor") is either getting stronger or weaker. As the church grows, if we don't "retrofit" the relationship emphasis with "intentionalized smallness", the 'largeness' eventually becomes the enemy of smallness!

Growth becomes the enemy of growth when largeness... ...becomes the enemy of smallness!

Evangelism that Decreases a Church
EV - R = Zero, EV - R = a minus

There are types of Evangelism that actually work against a church growing!

As I go into District Offices, working with District Superintendents and study the growth dynamics (& the individual statistics) of hundreds of churches, I increasingly find that churches with more converts are shrinking. Surprisingly, I find churches with fewer converts... growing!

> **God's program, especially for New Converts... is r-e-l-a-t-i-o-n-s-h-i-p... but most church's program... is programs!**

Why would any church with numerous converts not grow... but instead be reporting a plateau, or even a decline? In the end, it doesn't matter how big a production is put on, or the crowds size are drawn to a church's big events... nor even how many "pray the salvation prayer".

Without the primary focus, and creation of "relationship", n-o ongoing "fruit will remain."

Relationship requires 3 elements...
& smaller Groups... can Provide them Best:

Once again: Time, closeness and smallness. This is exactly what Jesus gives to each of us. How then, can we not offer the same to His baby lambs... as well!

"Food feud" between
Sunday School & Small Groups:

We have been sold a false bill of goods in the USA, namely that Sunday School is the theological, sworn, "blood enemy" of small groups ministry...and vice-versa!.

This has created a longstanding feud like the legendary Appalachian Hatfields & McCoys! The "mentality" of it (or lack thereof) seems to go: "If you're with Sunday School, you have to hate small groups." And vice versa!

The feud tries to force one to answer the question: "Which gang are you with?" Feuding is nothing new! It went on back in New Testament times. Paul wrote in 1 Corinthians chapter 3: "One says: "I am of Peter"; another, "I am of Paul." Another says: "Well, I am of Christ!" Whose team are you on? Which gang are you with and willing to "fight-to-the-death" for? (I Corinthians 3:3-5) This is the same chapter where he called them "infants:" and told them when he should have been able to give them meat, he had to feed them "milk."

Christianity is growing all around the world. Without question or dispute, the largest churches in the world take care of their largeness..... through constant creation of new "smallness"... reproducing small cell groups & leaders on an ongoing basis! Meanwhile, here in America, we "know better" and are plateaued!.

Small Group Basics:
size, location, intention, growth & leadership

Globally recognized small group experts agree that a small group ceases to be "small" above the size of 10 or 12. We've studied Mark 3:14 and know "Jesus chose 12 to be be w-i-t-h Him." World-recognized small group leaders agree: including Lyman Coleman at Serendipity, Carl George, Pastor Cho, Karen Hurston, Ralph Neighbor, Bill Donahue at Willow, Larry Stockstill, Ted Haggard, and others from the largest churches in South America, Africa, and Asia as well!

Above the size of 10 or 12, a group ceases to be small.

It is good "that your women's group has grown." The breakdown occurs when a leader tries to have a group larger than 12, act and function with the same relational results of an actual small group.

Thus, the way to deal with larger is smaller... to break it into a smaller group...or sub-units!

Jesus in feeding the Multitude:

The Feeding of the 5000 is one of the few miracles covered (in depth) in all four Gospels. (Matthew 14, Mark 6, Luke 9, John 6) . However, there are deep teaching points in it, totally & disastrously overlooked by the Western Euro-centric church.

Mark 6:39... and... Luke 9:14

"Make the people sit down in groups of 50's... and... 100's" (Mark 6:39)

In John chapter 6, we find Jesus feeding the five thousand. We know Andrew found a boy with five loaves and two fishes.(Jn.6:7-9). We know the numbers: 5,000 men (plus women & children). (Matthew 14:21) We know the 5 loaves and two fishes they started with, and the 12 baskets of fragments left over and collected at the end! You're thinking: "Been there, done that... nothing to learn here. Next!"

However, Mark chapter 6 verse 39 (& Luke 9:14) tell us something we have not been taught: the important principles contained in Jesus' actions & modeling here. Before Jesus gave the bread to His disciples, to give to the people... we read in Mark 6:39 Jesus' vastly overlooked words. Jesus says: "Make the people sit down in groups of 50's and 100's." (Mark 6:39)

"Make the people sit down in groups of 50's... and... 100's" (Mark 6:39):

First, we haven't even been taught that Jesus did do this! Secondly: why did Jesus do this at all? Thirdly: "Where did Jesus get this "50's" & "100's" teaching concept from?

"And they looked like so many little garden plots"

"They looked like so many little garden plots"...is how the Amplified translation records & describes the scene. (Mk. 6:39&40) In the Lord's eyes, that's exactly what they were! (and what we ourselves are as well!)

Exodus 18 and "The Jethro Principle":

Back in Exodus chapter 18, we read clearly that Jethro, Moses father-in-law, saw Moses standing before a long line of people all day, from early 'til late. Jethro says to Moses: "Why do you do this Moses?" Moses replies: "the people bring me their problems, and I give them wisdom from God." Jethro says in Exodus 18:18: "the t-h-i-n-g that you do is not good. You will surely burn out, and the people will not get their needs met."

138

"The t-h-i-n-g" from the ministerial lagoon':

When ministry becomes "the thing" ...the t-h-i-n-g from the ministerial lagoon, ...it's too often because we're doing too much of one thing... and not enough of another. John Maxwell says of American pastors: "We've been taught to do ministry, but we haven't been taught to equip the saints... for t-h-e-i-r work of ministry."

In Exodus 18:21, Jethro disciples Moses saying: "Moses, pick out for yourself faithful men, and make them captains of thousands, hundreds, fifties and tens."

Obviously, Jethro was not an Amway deale, but he very clearly was into MLM... (not Multi-level Marketing)... but "Multi-Level Ministry!"

A "span-of-care" of "10:1"!

The "span-of-care" of ten-to-one is the most common denominator between Jethro's care-captain delineation of 1,000, 100, 50's and 10's.

A captain of 1,000 would obviously N-O-T care for 1,000 people. Rather, he would care for 10 captains of 100. Likewise, a captain of 100 wouldn't care for 100, but rather for 10 captains over 10. The common thread here is a "span-of-care" of 10:1. One person would care for ten others, not twenty, fifty, seventy-five or more.

"Under-Caring" can Produce "Care-To-Spare."

I puzzled over the number 50 in the ratio sequence for several years. For me, it sort of ruined the 10:1 "span-of-care" ratio. Then the Lord showed me, that it actually enhances it, once understood.

The captain of 100, if only caring for 2 captains of 50, is now not caring for 10 people, but only for 2. Thus, he has a ratio of 1:2, obviously under-caring (... if o-n-l-y caring for two others.) Similarly, the captain over 50 (in only caring for 5 captains of 10), ...would only have a span-of-care ratio & "care-load" of 1:5.

"Spare-Care" or "Care-to-spare"

Both of these, the captains of 100 and 50, unmistakably, now have less than a one-to-ten (1:10) span-of-care load. They each (by intentionality) have "spare-care", or "care-to-spare".

Thus, they're available to coach, to encourage, to step-In and help out when "a captain of 10" is sick, needs replacement or just to "stand in the gap" and help out when needed... wherever immediate help is needed.

How many church systems unintentionally "burn out" fresh volunteers (spelled victim), instead of intentionally building in a reasonable span-of-care... as well as and built-in levels of extra care or "back-up"!

The book: "Prepare Your Church For The Future" by Carl George, (Flemming Revell) is the best book I can point you to, on small group ministry, intentional group replication, new group leader development, and intentionalizing "span-of-care" throughout the entire church (& lamb-care system)

Intentional "care-retrofitting":

What Jethro recommended... and what our Lord Jesus Himself did in feeding the multitude... was "care-retrofitting" the l-a-r-g-e-n-e-s-s (of the multitude of 5,000) into s-m-a-l-l-n-e-s-s! Both dealt with the "large", by breaking it into "small". Jesus was administrating His miracle into smaller groups, so no-one would be by-passed. "God is not a God of confusion, but rather the Author of order." (I Corinthians 14:33)

Why this contradicts our
Western Ideas of Jesus... and His Methods:

One recent Easter, my wife brought home "The Robe", a classic "Life of Christ" video. Once again, just as in the "Jesus Video", "Jesus of Nazareth" or any other Life of Christ video portrayal, we see the same u-n-s-c-r-i-p-t-u-r-a-l thing! Jesus takes the five loaves & two fishes, holds the bread up & blesses it, and feeds the crowd through the disciples. We see the smiling, awestruck faces, the wonderful miracle-time and the Hallelujahs!

Somehow, they never will show Jesus' intentionally commanding His disciples... to break up the huge multitude... into groups of fifties and one hundred's!

**Even now, more than one reader is saying in his mind: Jesus didn't r-e-a-l-l-y do that! Not really! Did He"? Read it again and again... until you both believe it... and will replicate it!

Mark 6:39 & Luke 9:14...:
another "Jesus than we've been taught"

In both Mark 6:39 and Luke 9 verse 14, we read quite clearly that Jesus did exactly what we're saying. In these Mark & Luke passages, Jesus undeniably commanded His disciples to "m-a-k-e" the people sit down in groups. I've had pastors tell me: "we just let people create their own groups." It won't happen unless we I-n-t-e-n-t-i-o-n-a-l-i-z-e it! It wouldn't have happened back then, unless Jesus hadn't intentionalized it. It also won't happen in our churches .... with our new converts... unless we intentionalize it as well!

"Care Retrofitting" ...and California's Freeway Overpasses!:

In California, "Cal. Trans" is our state Highway Dept. They "retrofit" the Freeway overpasses...without totally rebuilding them. Because our freeways are a major religion for us on the "left coast" (California), it would be

Sunday School Classes & Church programs need "care-retrofitting" ...a-l-l across America!

impossible and cost-prohibitive, to tear down and rebuild all tens of thousands of freeway overpasses.

Instead, they "retrofit" them. They leave "the existing structure", and don't totally tear it down. They intentionally "build-in" new strength and capability. They "breathe" new life into the previous structure, to better deal with eventual, future earthquake traumas. They build-in flexibility, to make each overpass earthquake resistant and safe.

Using cranes and massive, power equipment, they raise each end-beam of the overpasses. They then insert huge coils of steel, thicker than a man's arm, placed strategically on each side, under the ends support beams of each overpass. This obviously adds flex into the structural integrity, and a higher sur-vival, functionality into the older overpasses. This "retro-fitting readies them to go through and survive stronger quakes predicted in California's future.

Sunday School Classes & Church programs need "care-retrofitting" ...a-l-l across America!

Sunday School teachers must be re-taught that the Information Age has left their classes, over-programmed, over-programmed, over-information focused.....and under-relationshipped!

"Care-retrofitting"... is... "relationship retro-fitting."

"Care-retrofitting," is "relationship retro-fitting." A-l-l church structures and programs need to be given an "MRI" and to be "care-retrofitted"! Nowhere is this more urgently crying out to be implemented, than in a church's convert-care methodologies, ministries & programs!

"Standing in line to receive care":

Just as in Exodus, chapter 18, where people stood in line all day to receive care from Moses, current church programs, (designed to deliver information & knowledge), need to be retro-fitted and re-designed to put "relational" connectivity f-i-r-s-t... not last!

"Care-retrofitting" will definitely bring more relational-health and con-nectivity to program-based, flailing, non-growing Convert-Care (as well as in Sunday School classes nationwide!)

Example: "Care – retrofitting" a "larger" choir into "small-ness":

I have a choir director friend at a church running 1,400 in three serv-ices. During an annual consulting trip to their church, he shared that he had nearly 40 people in his cutting-edge, growing choir.

He said: "we always pray together in a large circle Wednesday nights. We have a great time sharing prayer requests and praying, before we work on the individual music parts for the upcoming Sunday." I said: "that's great, but do you a-l-l stand in one huge circle?" He replied: "yeah." I asked: "40 people in one circle?" "Yes" he said.

How "largeness" (& growth) can become the enemy of "smallness":

I replied: "Well, that's good, but its also bad. It's good that members can see the choir's 'large-ness' & how God has blessed it with growth!" It's bad, though, because its too big to work as a small group.

I continued: "Most certainly, not e-v-e-r-y-b-o-d-y can share prayer requests... Am I right?" He agreed..

I continued: "there are most certainly numerous people who can't share their prayer requests in that large open circle...not only because of non-confidentiality, but also because of sheer time constraints. Those who "can't" share their prayer requests, are perhaps the very same ones "bleeding" the worst (emotionally, relationally and life-wise)... some perhaps hurting the absolute very worst."

Care-retrofitting a larger choir: Why not break up the larger "choir" prayer-circle into 4 smaller sub-groups?

I said: "why not break up the larger prayer circle of 40 into four groups of 8, 10 12, or so! Why not break them up naturally along the lines of: Soprano, Alto, Tenor & Bass ?

Choose one leader (prayer request facilitator) for each group. Train them to lead and facilitate each weekly smaller prayer-and-care circle. Perhaps train and help each choir, sub-group leader to keep a week-to-week 3-ring notebook, recording prayer requests (& prayer answers). This gives week-to-week continuity to each choir sub-group. Kept in the choir rehearsal room, its always 'there' each week. It also helps document (& remind the group members) of God's faithfulness to the group's ongoing prayers & God's Answers!

I encouraged him to assist these four sub-group leaders each week, providing each sub-group member small, pocket-size, standardized prayer-request fill-in slips (& also pens/pencils). This enables e-a-c-h member of e-a-c-h prayer circle to write down...& thus remember the prayer requests!

Members can keep... (and pray over) these written down ("remembered") prayer requests... during that week, kept safe in their wallets or purses.

The best way to deal with larger... is smaller!

> **Relationship is not the parsley: relationship is the steak.**

We don't have to dismantle Sunday School! However, we can't keep on "pumping" Bible information and quarterly Scripture lessons into church attenders cerebral gray matter, when God's people are starving internally... from a paradigm driven famine and a severe seemingly irreversible societal lack of R-elationship!

Relationship is not the parsley: relationship is the steak:

We've been taught, that relationship is not the main dish, but rather, a nice, peripheral.

We must unlearn this incorrect lesson, and re-learn the absolute, opposite truth of the matter:

> *Relationship is n-o-t the parsley...*
> *...Relationship is n-o-t the watercress.*
>
> *Relationship is n-o-t the kale...*
> *...Relationship is n-o-t the potato... or side dish!*
>
> *Rather, Relationship is the steak...*
> *...the Main dish!*

They met... In their "Homes"... ...n-o-t "House to House."

A house is not a home. It takes love and relationships to turn wood and stone into a loving, warm & relational home. The heart is in the h-o-m-e, not merely a "house"!

In Acts 2:46 we read that: "These all continued in prayer and fellowship, meeting both in the temple daily and in their homes. "Oikos" meant home (not a building). More than home as a building, it meant even more-so a place of acquaintances, friendships and r-e-l-a-t-i-o-n-s-h-i-p-s.

I'm detecting a slight recurring theme here once again!

Chapter 22
"WHAT OTHER CHURCHES WORLDWIDE... DO WITH CONVERTS"

Bayside Covenant Church, Granite Bay, CA. (Sacramento)

I visited the fastest growing church in our Sacramento metro area: Bayside Covenant Church. Led by Sr. Pastor Ray Johnston, Bayside grew from zero... to over 4,000 Sunday AM attendance... in the last four and a half years!

Outside their public High School meeting place for Sunday AM meetings, was a banner atop a table that read: "I raised my hand." This obviously was for new converts who had raised their hand for salvation during the services.

Atop the table (amidst other of new believer literature and information), was a stack of videos, which turned out to be the "Jesus Video." I asked them what they did with the videos. They replied: "these are Jesus Videos. We give one to each person, who gives their heart to the Lord at our church!"

**The Jesus Video...
A great gift for
any new convert
$5 apiece:
(1-800-29-JESUS)**

Jesus Videos: one for each new convert!

I walked away that Sunday morning impressed, but thinking: "Great idea, but probably too expensive for mid-size and smaller churches! Probably just a mega-church idea. However, after making a call or two, I happily discovered ANYONE, any church or any individual can buy a Jesus Video!

I brought the idea (in person) to our Assemblies of God General Supt. Thomas Trask at the AG HQ in Springfield, Mo. I asked him: "You know of the Jesus Video for evangelism. Have you ever heard of giving the Jesus Video as a gift to New Converts?" He said: "No! But that's a great idea! I've never heard of it." Then I brought it to my Northern California Superintendent Glen Cole, who's preached forty years all across the country & around the world." He similarly said: "Never heard of it, but that's a great idea!"

The Jesus Video... $5 apiece: (1-800-29-JESUS)

You can get the Jesus Video for your church by dialing 1-800-29-Jesus, from the Jesus Video Project, through Campus Crusade For Christ. Minimum order is 1. Every church in America (& every reader), can equip themselves to give a Jesus Video to a new baby Christian. It is a great new believer gift!

Reading the Bible takes active energy, but watching a video of the Bible is passive. All a newborn "lamb" has to do, is pop the video into their VCR, press the "play" button, and "s-o-a-k!" (and learn)

You might say: "Well five bucks, I mean, I know our Lord died for them...but $5...that's asking a lot!"

"The Jesus Video For Children"

A great gift for New believers that are themselves: children!

There is a similar, but different "Jesus Video for Children'. At the conclusion of "The Jesus Video for children", the regular salvation/sinner's prayer has a children's version's. Its 3 main narrators (two 10 year-old boys and an 11 year old girl) lead out in a "repeat after me" child's rendition of the closing salvation prayer! What a tremendously, anointed, powerful idea! It costs a bit more ($12.95@, at 1-800-29-JESUS) ...but its well worth the cost!

Any church (regardless of size) could easily have at least one (or a few) "loaner copies" of both the adult and Children's version of the Jesus Video. Other videos as well (age & life-style appropriate testimonies, teaching, Veggie-Tales, marriage and relationship seminars, (etc), would help nurture newborn lambs as well.

Every summer children are led to receive Christ at VBS ("Vacation Bible School ") outreach events. Why not have the whole Veggie Tales set available for your newborn, young "lambs" to borrow!

What is y-o-u-r church (& what are others) doing for New Converts?

I'd love to hear what effective, creative things you (& your church) are doing with Convert Care: especially strategies, actions, gifts, programs, etc. that are working and producing "fruit that remains." (Jn.15:16). Please write or e-mail your ideas to me (to share with others). Address is in the back of this book.

When I was saved off the streets thirty years ago:

When I was saved off the streets, compassionate non-streetwise church folk loved us..... when we truly weren't all that "loveable".

These college age believers were Assembly of God Bible college students. They didn't know marijuana from oregano! They didn't know Jimmy Hendrix from the Hansen brothers! However, they did know Jesus! That makes all the difference: then, now & forever! They knew Jesus' grace & love, not just for themselves, but for A-l-l people, including us as barefoot hitchhiking hippies by the roadside!

Seven years later they saw me on a national "700 Club" broadcast, sharing my salvation testimony. Three thousand miles away (and seven years later), they told me that they jumped out of their living room chairs and said: "Heh, that's Jonathan....that's that hippie that we picked up: that's Jonathan!"

You see, that day in 1969 we were hitch-hiking on an freeway off-ramp outside Sacramento.. We desperately needed some aspirin. We must have looked just like blowing human "space- junk". We were hitch-hiking, heading for Los Angeles, in actuality, headed for hell!

I thank God that young Archie Brooks and Linda Waddell saw us as potential candidates for God's Kingdom...potential recipients of Jesus' life-changing, soul-saving, Amazing grace, mercy, and salvation!

Love lifted me! These Bible School students not only gave us aspirin! They said : "Come with us"!. They fed us and gave us a ride, and a resting place at home for that night. Next morning, they took us to meet Cecil Barns, a Home missionary summer-ing with his family back on the American river. God had broken and targeted Cecil's heart for hippies. As he & his wife Barb loved us into God's Kingdom, he relationally became "Family" to us as well and we ended up spending the summer w-i-t-h him at his family by the edge of the river, 30 miles back from nowhere with no way out, except to get "saved!"

Section III: Chapter 23
Amazing Newborn Analogies
"GOD'S NATURAL SPONSOR PROGRAM"

GOD'S SPONSOR PROGRAM

We've come quite a ways! We learned earlier that: "Jesus put the lambs f-i-r-s-t." (John 21:15)

Next, we learned Jesus' style of New Convert Care was:
"He chose twelve to be w-i-t-h Him!" (Mark 3:14)
Now lets explore God's Sponsor Program and some powerful analogies between newborns and new believers!

"Left - lobe linear": "High-Impact, Low-Maintenance converts"

I still can't believe one well-known American evangelist wrote in his book: "What we need in America, is more high-impact, low-maintenance converts."

Every Mom knows that is as realistic as asking for a glass of "dry water" or trying to warm up beside a "cold fire"! It's like saying to a mother of a newborn: "Your newborn is now six weeks old. You probably only have to change diapers now every week or two?"

"The only High-Impact, low-maintenance baby... is a D-O-L-L!"

Every baby is "high-impact"! Every Mom will vow that there is no such thing as a "high-impact, low-maintenance" baby! The only high-impact, low-maintenance baby... is a doll.

Jesus had a special heart for and attraction to little children. They were (and are now)... divinely, special to Him. Jesus smiled at and played with little children. Children are drawn to smiles and to love! Children are naturally drawn to l-i-f-e and to love. They literally live on relationship, love and care! Can you see little children saying: "Please, mommy, let's go sit on the lap of the grouch again so he can growl & frown at us." Every baby is a high maintenance newborn... living on two things: love & relationship!

Left-Lobe, ludicrous concepts of Newborn nurture and care:

The ludicrous concept of a "Hi-Impact, Low-Maintenance" baby is a male, left-lobe linear concept. In reality, it is an implausible impossibility.

This same reality is true with new converts, their care...and their survival A "low maintenance, high-impact" new convert is a perhaps a "valid" one-time evangelism "statistic", ...but certainly not a day-by-day, relationship-fed, 1st time new believer... with much chance of long-term survival! The only low-maintenance "lasting fruit" ...is a plastic or wooden apple, pear, or orange!

Gary Smalley Story:

In his popular Marriage video series, "Hidden Keys to Loving Relationships", Gary Smalley tells of his family on vacation, years back. They'd be heading out on a four hour drive to a cabin at a lake. His wife Norma would gently ask: "Honey, can we stop at this upcoming rest area." When denied, she would ask for just one good, solid, reason why. Gary says that he just couldn't verbalize what he was feeling!

Years later, he realized, that if he could have honestly verbalized his inner feelings as to why he didn't want to stop, he'd have said: "Honey, if we stop at a rest area, all those cars we passed on the freeway will pass us! Then they're going to get there...before we get there!"

When men get in the car, facing a long drive, they want to put the "pedal to the metal"! They have one thought on their mind: they want to: "get there!" This is left-lobe, linear thinking.

"Corpus collossum:"

The "Corpus Collossum" is a medically well-known, verifiable, "in-utero", pre-birth phenomenon occurring only in males. In the 8th month of pregnancy, a testosterone "wash" occurs that destroys 70+% of the connective tissue between the left and right lobes of the pre-born male brain!

This phenomenon is called "Corpus Collosum." It is a universal occurrence in e-v-e-r-y pre-born male child! Gary Smalley goes on to say, that from time to time, he tells his wife Norma: "Honey, be patient with me, you know I'm brain- damaged." (Many women have suspected this for years!)

The left-lobe of the brain is the stronghold of linear, "bottom-line" thinking. Resultant from this, males are much more left-lobe dominant, focused, and thus 'left-lobe exiled' linear thinkers!

Women are much more " bi-lobal!"

Women, on the other hand (without this Corpus Collossum occurrence), are much more bi-lobal. There is an easy pneumonic device for remembering left and right lobe brain functions. The letter "L" stands for Left lobe, as well as for "linear' thinking! The letter "R", (on the other hand) stands for the brain's "right-lobe", relational functioning. Thus, women are much more bi-lobal & much more relationally oriented and gifted, by God's own perfect Divine design!

God's Sponsor Program: "No Sponsors... No Babies":

God never sends a baby without a committed sponsor first. This is His ideal and perfect sequence: His provision for the survival, nurture and growth of each newborn!

You may have never heard of "God's Sponsor Program." Once it's pointed out, it makes perfect, and extremely scriptural... and practical sense.

For nearly two decades in street ministry, I was leading numerous people to Christ. But if someone were to ask me, where those converts were a month, quarter or year later, I didn't know. I didn't know, because I didn't have any relationship, nor much (if any) emphasis on establishing one with them!

In God's Perfect Sequence & Wisdom: A Sponsor comes B-E-F-O-R-E a baby!

God never sends a baby, without sending and preparing a sponsor first.

The mother & father of every newborn human baby, are the two God-appointed sponsors, ...designated (& in preparation) a long time before a helpless 100% totally-dependent baby arrives.

Why does God take Nine Months to Create a human baby?

God takes nine months (287 days exactly) for the full-term human gestation of a newborn baby... b-e-f-o-r-e... the newborn gets delivered! Why does God take this long? He could easily create a human baby in merely 8, 12, or 16 weeks!

The reason God takes 9 months to create a human baby, is not directly for the sake of the baby!

Rather, God takes that length of time, not for the baby.. but rather... for the parents! The parents need the time: time to change, time to grow, and time to develop their r-e-l-a-t-i-o-n-s-h-i-p with the baby. This developing, pre-birth relationship is used to produce the needed life-time commitment to the baby.

Little do most 1st-time parents know that caring for a baby...is a life-time relationship & commitment!

God's "Sponsor Ratio" ...is ...2 to 1!

God's "sponsor ratio" is two-to-one! In His infinite wisdom, God provides one mom & one dad, long before there's ever a hint of a baby.

What is the "sponsor ratio" at most churches?

The answer to this question (when asked to seminar audiences across the country) ...is far too often ...and sad to say: "z-e-r-o!" The sponsor-ratio in most churches? is too often zero!

What is the "sponsor ratio" for New converts at o-u-r church?

For those with the divine hunger (and intestinal fortitude) for quantum convert-care improvement, the following questions must be honestly prayed over and answered. "What is the sponsor ratio at our church?" What has it been? What is it now? What does Jesus want it to be?

The Scriptural basis for God's Sponsor Program "is easily found:" In Genesis, the Book of Beginnings. We read that God looked at all He had made, and said it was very good." (Gen.1:31) Then God looked at the man, (made in God's very r-e-l-a-t-i-o-n-al image), and God said: "It is n-o-t good that man should dwell alone." (Gen. 2:18). God then graciously, wonderfully created a life-mate: relationship, life-sharer & help meet for him: ...and God created the first woman!

The first mention of marriage in the Bible: As Genesis Chapter Two ends (Genesis 2:24), we read: "For this reason, a man shall leave his father and mother and cleave unto his w-i-f-e... and they two shall become one flesh."

This is the first mention of marriage in the Bible.

In God's sequence, which comes first: relationship or commitment? Is it the relationship... followed by a growing, loving commitment to each other for life in marriage... or is it physical intimacy resulting in procreation and a helpless, newborn baby?

God's sequence & Divine order puts relationship first! First relationship, then commitment. The married couple give a lifetime commitment to join their lives. Only then do their "life-forces" join together. Resultantly, babies... o-n-l-y follow after the relationship and lifetime commitment! Marriage always comes before pro-creation in God's sequence... even as relationship precedes commitment!!

"The American Holocaust: "Babies w-i-t-h-o-u-t a sponsor"

Since the US Supreme Court's infamous 1973 Roe v. Wade decision, every twenty seconds another pre-born child's life has been (and continues to be) snuffed out!

150

"A baby without a sponsor... will die!" What is the precise reason behind this Holocaust...this taking of the life of a pre-born baby? It is none other than this "sponsorship" and parenting/commitment issue. This is the ugly core of abortion. Abortion is the taking of the life... of a pre-born child: a baby without a sponsor!

"A baby without a sponsor... will die!"

God never sends a baby... without a sponsor (actually two sponsors) first! God never sends a baby without a sponsor, because above all others, God knows that "a baby without a sponsor... will die!"

Abortion puts God's sequence... in direct reverse. The gift of life... becomes the curse... of death! Abortion is none other than the reprehensible murder or taking the life of a "baby without a life-time, committed "sponsor" (or God's ideal, a couple... and thus two sponsors)... to nurture it!

What is most church's "Sponsor Problem ?":

Is the problem at most churches: "Too many sponsors and not enough babies?"...or rather, is it: "too many babies and not enough sponsors?" Most churches' sponsor-ratio problem is too many babies... and not enough sponsors!

National convert-loss statistics clearly, repeatedly, and painfully show that this does not work! A baby without a sponsor...will die! Usually sooner, than later!

Large churches with sponsors... can have a high convert survival rate... while smaller churches with few converts and no sponsors... can have a high "convert mortality!"

Some large churches running over 1,000 Sunday AM, keep over 90% of their converts through a "New Convert Sponsor Program." They train & assign a "big brother" or "big sister" to each new lamb. Every sponsor is trained to "relationship" each new believer, to be "w-i-t-h" them, the same exact way that Jesus modeled the same for us, when He "chose 12 to be w-i-t-h Him!"

At some churches, every new believer is given a sponsor. This sponsor concept is strongly modeled in AA, strongly modeled in the Catholic Church, as well as in the military! Jesus said in Luke 16:8: "The children of this world are wiser in their generation, than the children of Light."

Of course, satan, our common enemy, the lamb-destroyer, tells every pastor and believer: "This is way, too much trouble! You could n-e-v-e-r do it!" But God's Word tells us that satan is the father of all lies. Jesus also said in John 8:44 "and there is no truth in him (the devil)". Thus, a-l-l of... and whatever ... the enemy tells us, the exact opposite is the actual truth!

We can do "a-l-l things God asks us to"
...through Christ (Philippians 4:13)

God's Word tells us we c-a-n do it! "It", meaning the nurturing, sponsoring and "w-i-t-h-i-n-g" of the baby lambs Jesus sends our way! Philippians 4:13 tell us: "We can do all things... God asks us to... through Christ Who strengthens us." In reality, we c-a-n-n-o-t d-o a-l-l things! We can't learn all 200 major world languages! We can't "one-on-one" personally witness to all 6 billion people on the earth! We can do all things God asks u-s personally and individually to do!

Within the targeted focus of this book, Jesus says to each of us (and to each of our churches): "if you really love Me, feed My lambs F-I-R-S-T and B-E-S-T!"

THREE LEVELS OF SPONSORSHIP

God provides at least three levels of Sponsorship for all babies, both in the natural (and in the spiritual dimension) as well. These three layers of sponsorship, are not only separate, but also overlap, intentionally designed to provide beneficial "care-system redundancy!"

Level One Sponsors:
Parents... as Primary Care-givers

The parents, the natural mom & dad, are the "primary sponsor" level and its primary caregivers. They are the 24-7, round-the-clock, life-time assigned 1st rank! The Mom and Dad are the God-appointed, committed sponsors, the care-giving "umbilical" for every single, helpless, 100% care-dependent newborn!

Level Two sponsors:
Secondary level Sponsors: the "Extended family ".

Extended family is God's idea. It never was a secondary thought. After more than one child is born in a family, what can increase (and strengthen) the sponsor ratios? If God's Sponsor Ratio is 2: to 1, then when the 2nd child is born, the parents "two-ness" ratio is now reduced to 1:1! Without additional, immediate, sponsor augmentation... the care-ratio would be terribly diluted!

A second level of care is precisely what the "extended family" provides! Here is the "backup" multi-generational, heart, wisdom, prayers, love and help of a grandma and grandpa on both sides of the family. Additionally, on both parents' sides there are brothers and sisters (aunts & uncles), sisters and brothers-in-law, nephews and nieces, cousins, and even more relatives besides!

While parents alone are on call "24-7-365", the "extended family" (as

Sponsors) provides the loving support they can give, as second Level, "on-call", back-up care-givers!

"Honey if you ever get tired of that baby, bring her on over to grandma's!"

Have you ever heard grandmothers saying words like: "honey, if you ever tire of that baby and need a rest, bring her on over to me......cause we'll just "love on her" 'til you pry her out of our arms!" Grandma's are g-o-o-d for both Moms and the "newborn babies!

Level three sponsors:
The entire community (i.e. the Church as whole).

Beyond the 1st two sponsor levels of Parents, and Extended Family, comes the third God-provided level of Sponsorship: the entire community! This holds true in both the natural and spiritual area as well!

The community (this third level of Sponsorship) provides police and fire services, community health-care, medical, welfare, hospital and emergency services etc. The "community" also provides free education, parks and recreation and much, much more!

In the Convert-Care dimension, Level Three Sponsorship is what the entire church provides, as overlapping, simultaneous Third-level care and support.

"What produces a "F-E-R-A-L" Child?... and Adult?

Many have occasionally heard the word "feral" used. What exactly is a "Feral" child.... and what conditions produce "feral" children?

Perhaps you've heard the word used in referring to "feral cats" (wild cats), or else perhaps in the phrase: "feral children". The most common example, is the wild-child main character named Mowgli, taken from Rudyard Kipling's classic novel: "The Jungle Book".

The story is set deep in the jungles of British Colonial India. An infant boy-child is taken from his parents, and is surrogately raised in the wild by a pack of wolves, a bear & a panther!

The word "FERAL" means a child that has not had appropriate parental care and nurture. In a feral infancy and childhood, there is an almost total absence of nurture and protection in its defenseless, infant years! A "feral" child grows up "too fast", in a wild, never-ending "fight-or-flight" survival-mode.

"Street children" by the tens of thousands in third world nations, are tragically born and raised in the streets, slums & barrios of Rio and numerous other nations!

The comparison in passively abandoned lambs (new converts) has ramifications this book could not contain.

"Feral" children must act like an adult... when they're only a child.

"Feral" children have to act like an adult... when they are only a child! In the next chapter, we'll see that "adultification" is the conscious place-ment of age-inappropriate, adult expectations onto a newborn child. In the spiritual dimension, this relates to placing over-expectations onto the shoulders of newborn, "baby lamb" Christians.

Placing Adult Burdens Onto Newborn Lambs:

What does it do to a newborn, toddler or young child, when asked to act and produce like an adult? Does it breed emotional, social and rela-tional health for them...or is it damaging, dysfunctional & destructive?

"Feral Children"... often grow up to be...
"Feral-hearted" adults:

Creating "adult children" can distort and dysfunctionalize a young child up for the rest of his life. When (and if) they do grow up and become elders in a church, they might be overhead saying things like:

"Well, nobody 'babied" me as a new Christian...

or:

..."Nobody had a
"Welcome to the family" meal-team for me, Pastor!"

..."Nobody gave me a Jesus Video.
I had to fight my way into church."

..."Don't baby the new believers! Nobody "babied" me,
and I made it fine!"

..."There wasn't any New Convert budget at the church
I got saved at, and I made it!"

..."If they don't come to New Convert class, let them fall away!"
(actually overheard as quoted from a "feral"-hearted 'pastor'!)

There is an interesting, occasional, surfaced (or subliminal) hostility to the improving convert-care, on the basis of feral-hearted, non-nurtured Board members or occasional church elders. Why el;se would anyone oppose the better feeding of Jesus' lambs?

Matthew 11: 19...

"Results versus Method-ol-atry"

In Matthew 11:19, Jesus said: "Wisdom is justified by her children". By this, Jesus was saying that true wisdom identifies itself as "Godly" wisdom ... by its r-e-s-u-l-t-s! "You shall know a tree by its fruit" (Matthew 7:16)...N-O-T by its sign.

It is the fruit that a tree bears, its actual r-e-s-u-l-t-s, that identifies what type of a tree it truly is. This is merely one more way of saying that God is practical: that God Himself is also interested in results. This then becomes the definition of "sanctified pragmatism!"

The "Sanctified Pragmatism" of our Lord Jesus!

If our evangelism isn't producing "lasting fruit", ...if our Convert Care is not creating "fruit that remains" (as Jesus plainly said He desired in John 15:16), we must once again seek out, and reinstate Jesus' own personal method and plan: ...r-e-l-a-t-i-o-n-s-h-i-p!

This alone will produce the lasting, long-term fruit both we (and Jesus especially)... long to see!

Relationship is the "umbilical cord" to deliver Life... and Life-Change. Information is helpful, Life-giving and life-changing: ...but only... in the midst of Relationship!

As the Apostle John said in III John verse 4:
" I have no greater joy...
than to hear that my children are walking in the Truth."

Chapter 24
"NURTURE: GOD'S SURVIVAL GIFT TO E-V-E-R-Y NEWBORN"

The Nature of Nurture:

Nurslings in a greenhouse (or landscaping "nursery"), are protectively taken care of and tenderly guarded, fed and watered. The greenhouse and nursery exist for one primary purpose: to protect these baby plants... that cannot possibly make it on their own!

> **Nurture is as much the nature of God... as are Holiness, Truth, or His other eternal, core attributes.**

Unfortunately, nurture (in our Western culture), is now perceived as something that, by definition, is not a natural, admirable, or desirable masculine trait.

Nurture, in nature, is predominantly a gender-dominant gift! If it wasn't, none of us would be alive. And yet, the ultimate, purest nature of nurture... is found best... in our Lord Jesus Christ Himself!

Jesus n-u-r-t-u-r-e-d His twelve disciples... & "lambs":

Jesus was the greatest nurturer that ever walked planet earth.

God is Love. Because love meets needs & thinks of the other person before it thinks of itself, love itself is inherent in the nature of nurture. Since God is love, how far does that put Him from having a heart of tender nurture?

Nurture is as much the nature of God... as are Holiness, Truth, or His other eternal, core attributes.

Jesus certainly is the ultimate model for both Convert-Care and nurture. When He "chose (His) 12 to be w-i-t-h Him," Jesus was deliberately choosing to model (& illustrate) what true godly, spiritual nurture would look like for time and eternity. Jesus knew He was modeling the ideal, method of Convert-Care for millions of converts to follow.... after His original f-i-r-s-t dozen!

Jesus personally nurtured His disciples: both spiritually, emotionally, mentally & socially. He also stated unequivocally: "Every disciple, that is perfect (fully trained) shall be as his Master" (Luke 6:40)

Nurture is a "Gender-Dominant" Gift! Let's take a vote:

All we need do is take a vote, to see that nurture is absolutely a female gender-dominant gifting. At seminars, I'll say to the audience "On the count of three, say either Mom or Dad... just one word... as to whom you would rather have care for you the first year of life: ...from the moment of birth, if you could only choose one parent. I'll count out loud: "One, two... three!" The voice vote is unanimous! With a thunderous unanimous response, one word emerges, namely: "MOM"! Here I usually, (tongue-in-cheek), close this it out by saying softly: "Close! Really close!"

Nurture is "Gender-Dominant"... but n-o-t "Gender-exclusive!":

I generally get quite a chuckle from seminar audiences, when I make the tongue-in-cheek statement: "Nurture is, obvious to almost everyone, mainly a male-dominant gifting!" Nurture is indeed a gender-dominant gift... and it is more female, gender-dominant gift!

Re-capturing the power and significance of "Male nurturing":

All pastors... and all of God's people (every believer is part of the Royal Priesthood-I Peter 2:9), must seek and develop this Holy nurture: this tenderness that Jesus had (and has) for His lambs!

"Which baby will live?"

Which baby has a greater chance of living: a weak 4-month premature baby, born weighing just 3 or 4 pounds and receiving perfect, 24-hour, neo-natal care... or a full-term, healthy, 9 pound baby... with no care? Which will live: a weak baby with perfect care, or a perfect baby with no care? We know which will live. The weak baby with perfect care will live... while the "perfect" baby, with no care, will die!

"After-care" is the survival determinant!

We immediately see here that the main thing which determines survival... the "survival determinant" ...is n-o-t the strength (or health) of the baby at birth, but rather... the "care" it is given once it is born! The "after-care" is indeed... the survival determinant!

The McCaughey Septuplets

All seven of the McCaughey septuplets have passed through their "toddler-hood". A great book telling their miraculous, faith-building story, is titled: "7 from Heaven".

All seven of those babies were born two or three pounds and change! The reason they are all alive, is not because of their strength at birth. Rather, it is because 70 people from the McCaughey's "home-church" stepped up to the plate. They volunteered to provide 24-hour help (in continuous shifts) to provide extra "backup" sponsor-care for these out-numbered parents and their 7 precious, preemie-born, pint-size babies

Care is the "survival-determinant"... a-n-d missing ingredient in most convert-nurture programs!

70 Caring Adult Sponsors... For 7 Precious Babies!

How interesting that their span-of-care was set at 10:1... with a team of over 70 volunteers from their home church... caring for 7 babies! These Level Two Care-Sponsors committed themselves to working... in 4 hour and 8 hour shifts, throughout the week, and round the clock, day-in and day-out! They realized that their helping the Level I "over-loaded" Mom & Dad... a-f-t-e-r the birth of the septuplets... would ultimately be the survival and success determinant! These backup support teams had e-v-e-r-y-t-h-i-n-g to do with the ongoing health and success of ALL seven newborn "lambs" (or babies!)

"Nurture" is what P-R-E-C-E-D-E-S... "Crawl, walk and run!".

When asked, most men can't easily sequence the developmental movements and motions of a newborn baby... in the months b-e-f-o-r-e a baby first learns to crawl!

What precedes "Crawl! Walk! Run!?

Crawl, walk & run are easy for a man to identify. But what precedes these initial movements for a newborn?

Before crawl, walk and run, ...in sequence, ...a baby first rocks a tiny bit, then eventually learns to turn over from it back... onto its stomach. The newborn next learns to get up on its hands and knees. It still can't crawl. Next, the infant learns to rock back and forth. Eventually it falls forward. It then learns somehow to scoot forward! Finally the baby learns to crawl!

It is precisely in these beginning stages, where so many converts and lambs... are lost!

They are lost more than in anything else, by our over-emphasis on Bible knowledge instead of relationship.

We lose converts in our totally unrealistic, over-expectations of their development ...and our very inaccurate assuming ... that they will (and do) develop an almost instant "self-sufficiency."

Adultification:

Adultification is the placing of age-inappropriate expectations on "too young" of an infant or child!

This is a vital concept carried over from the realm of child-development theory.

We know the word adulteration means to dilute or pollute something. We know the word "adultery" is the polluting of a marriage and shattering its sacred, monogamous vows!

"Adultification"... is a different word... and totally different meaning! Adultification is the placing of age-inappropriate expectations on "too young" of an infant or child! Adultification is asking an infant to do what only an adolescent, or even worse... only a mature adult... could possibly achieve!

Adultification in the Bible: Genesis 33:13.

In Genesis chapter 33, Jacob is returning from his twenty-year exile! Jake's twin brother, Esau, meets Jacob, and suggests they both travel together back to Esau's dwelling. In Genesis 33:13, Jacob replies:

"My Lord knows the flocks are tender and with young, & if one should drive them too hard (or o-v-e-r-d-r-i-v-e-) them in one day... they would A-L-L perish." Genesis 33:13

Here Jacob is pointing out the tenderness, vulnerability, the pace-ing, and natural limitations, of the flock's most vulnerable element:...their young... the newborns...and the tender lambs.

Ask not what your converts can do for your church... but rather... ask... what your church can do for your (and for Jesus') precious lambs.

The parallel message and analogy is clear: If newborn believers are over-challenged and driven too hard, they will also all die! This occurs, not by intent, but usually by default! It's not a desired result, but rather happens passively, by a lack of intention (& prevention)... to n-o-t adultify, to n-o-t "over-expect", and to n-o-t "over-drive" the new converts and newborn lambs!

King Solomon and the Two Mothers... First Kings Chapter 3: 16-28 ...and the challenge of "method-olatry!"

The story of Solomon and the two mothers is directly applicable to the tendency to cling to old, decrepit methodologies, at the expense of our own lamb-care success. "Methodolatry" ...clings insistently to it's "method", regardless of its irrelevance, its ineffectiveness, and its lack of desired results!

Metholodatry is the surgeon who insists on saying: "The operation was a great success!

The only problem is... the patient died!"

It sort of like the tough-hearted mother who showed King Solomon, that she indeed was n-o-t the real "mother"!

First Kings chapter 3 illustrates the nurture-strength, and the selfless, God-given concern of a mother for the life of her child ...above her own pleasure or her own life itself!

"Two mothers and... one baby!"

A trial case was brought to King Solomon for wisdom and for the King's ultimate judgement!

Two mothers each, on the same night, had both given birth to a new-born. One of their babies had died during the night. The next morning, each mother claimed the living child was h-e-r child, and that the other mother's child had died!

You remember, it was Solomon who, as a younger man in a dream, was told by God: "Ask! What shall I give you,"(I Kings 3:5). Solomon replied: "Lord, give Your servant an understanding heart to judge Your people, that I may discern between good and evil ("Lord, give me Your wisdom!"- I Kings 3:9).

With these two mothers, God gave Solomon this divine, wise answer. Solomon told them: "Well, we will just have to cut the baby in half. I'll give half to each one of you!"

One woman in response to said: "Fine! Go ahead!" The other woman, aghast, said: "No, please! I'd rather let her have the baby and have it live with her...than to have it perish!"

Their actions & words showed clearly who the real mother was!

The "Achilles Heel" of most New Convert Classes?

What stubborn, generational "methodol-atry" allows the continued terribly high mortality rate of precious new converts? We cling to the thought that a Sunday AM New Convert Class will somehow m-o-r-e than meet the entire need. However, ask yourself, is it the teacher who usually fails to show up for a New convert Class... or is it someone else... who is most usually missing in the Convert classes?

The ones most frequently missing in New Convert classes... are the "babes in Christ" themselves! Our expectation is, that if the New Convert is sincerely converted, he will just "show up" faithfully at the New Convert class. However, in real life, if we want a newborn baby to be somewhere, we don't send an invitation. We have to B-R-I-N-G them... if we want a baby... or a newborn... to be anywhere!

Pickett's discovery regarding Convert Survival and motives:

Bishop Waskom Pickett, after studying thousands of New Convert survival and loss factors, discovered that the quality of the "after-care"...of a new convert greatly outweighs the convert's original motive, as to a convert's "survival factor"!

Aftercare (or nurturing) is far more important than motive! Aftercare is "follow-up" that is heart-powered and relational. It is the indispensable life-or-death relationally-driven "feeding and folding" of the baby!

Who is it that most churches blame when a convert fails to "stick" and to grow? Tragically, over and over, too many churches blame the convert ...instead of examining their "aftercare" or lack thereof!

The usual rhetoric goes like this: "If they were truly converted, they would have made it through, would have bonded, and the convert would have become a mature disciple!"

This once again, is overly male-dominant, linear thinking, rather than healthy, bi-lobal balance of linear and relational, process thought!

Nurture : The Missing phase in Left-Lobe Western Discipleship matrix

Lay Literature International, a well known Discipleship equipping ministry, identifies four main, distinct phases in its literature and individually, sequenced, progressive materials.

These four phases, in sequence, from the beginning are: Evangelism, Nurture, Discipleship, and Mobilization into Ministry. Which of these four, is most noticeable by its absence (& damaging effect) in the Western church and its theology?

Correct! The missing, vital and indispensable "N"- word: Nurture!

Chapter 25
"NEWBORN ANIMAL ANALOGIES FROM NATURE"

As previously stated, nurture is indeed a "gender-dominant" gift ...but there are quite a few natural exceptions. Following are a few examples.

The Hyena: "Encouraging Fratricide Among Her Cubs"

From a PBS program, I learned the Hyena is the only mother mammal that allows...(and encourages) fratricide (or murder of the 2nd eldest male) by the firstborn, to establish the "alpha-male's" status in the newborn brood. In the hyena's strictly matriarchal society, this aberration is the "norm."

The Mother Ostrich... and Her Young!

Although nurture is mainly a female gender-dominant gift, it is not universal. In the Book of Job, we find an indictment of the mother ostrich: **"The Ostrich is cruel to her own young. She buries her eggs & forgets where they are & walks on them. She forgets that her foot may crush them, or that the wild beast may break them. She is hardened against her young ones, as though they were not hers."** Job 39: 13-18

"As a hen gathers her chicks under her wings"

Turning back to the nearly universal female gender-dominance of nurture, let's look at a few more of nature's examples from the Word of God. Our Lord Jesus Himself said: **"Oh Jerusalem, Jerusalem, how often would I have gathered your children together, as a hen gathers her chicks under her wings, and you would not."** Matthew 23: 37& 38

Paul wrote: **"When I was among you, I was gentle w-i-t-h you, as a nurse that tenderly cherishes her own children."** iI Thessalonians 2:7

Paul said: **"Let us now go back & visit our brethren in every city where we have preached the Word of the Lord and see how they are doing". Paul was looking back for "lasting fruit". He was doing a "nurture" check & "lamb-check" as well! Paul wanted fruit that remains!** Acts 15:36

Barnabas took Saul "Under his wing":

In Acts 9, we read how Barnabas continually (and r-e-l-a-t-i-o-n-a-l-l-y) nurtured and took the young, new convert (& future global Apostle) Paul "under his wing." Barnabas nurtured Paul as a lamb! Barnabas protected "baby" Paul from widespread, initial and severe rejection from the elders & non-receptive elder brethren, during the early days after Paul's conversion.

162

The Apostles in Jerusalem gave Paul the "left foot" of non-fellowship, but Barnabas took him and gave Paul.conversely, his best, "right wing" of nurture!

Uncle Barnie was "THE Encourager" and THE key "relationship-er." He chose to w-i-t-h Paul!

Barnabas took Paul under his wing... the same way Jesus "with"-ed His original twelve lambs! Barnabas modeled what Jesus referred to as natural for a nurturing mother hen to do, in covering her own chicks with her wings... and with her entire being!

The Mother Eagle's nurture in the scriptures:

There are several wonderful Bible passages, dealing with the maternal nurture, protectiveness & training that a mother eagle provides her eaglets!

"As an eagle stirs up her nest, flutters over her young, spreads abroad her wings, takes them, bears them on her wings, so just like that, the Lord alone did lead him." Deuteronomy 32:11&12

"You saw what I did unto the Egyptians, how I bore you on eagles' wings, and brought you unto Myself." Exodus 19: 3&4

Mother eagles do actually carry their developing young, untrained eaglets upon their wings. At the appropriate time, they teach them to fly by experience. The mother eagle, eventually will even "drop them", activating (by necessity) their eaglet's untested wings. Of course, she will be there to catch them (if necessary)... for their n-e-x-t flying lesson... in the practical benefits of energetic "wing-flapping."

Mother eagles have also been seen showing their fierce protective-ness. They have been documented attacking a helicopter venturing too near to their 10' wide, cliff-top aeries and nests. Mother eagles also have been seen fighting off a 1,000 pound grizzly bear, in defense of their young!

We should be that protective (& even more-so) in our feeding, nurturing and the pro-active protecting of our Lord's precious lambs.

To what lengths a-r-e we willing to go... in defending our "young"? What a-r-e we willing to do to defend our lambs?

"As a she-bear robbed of her whelps, so is a fool caught in his folly." (Proverbs17:12). This scripture also refers to the documented nurture-nature in a mother bear, and her readiness to defend her precious newborn cubs from any... and all invaders, attackers and predators.

We can learn a valuable lesson here as well!

Chapter 26
"NEWBORN HUMAN BABY ANALOGIES"

Newborn human Baby intros:

In my "Feed My lambs" seminars across the nation, I pre-arrange with the local pastor to "rent" a newborn human baby (or two), for the purpose of the following analogies! We forget so quickly that a newborn "can't do"... a whole lot more things... than it can! The one, single main thing a newborn can do well is to: receive! A newborn can and must receive care and love... or die!

> *Newborns can't walk, talk, read, or crawl.*
> *They can do almost "nothing" at all.*

Receiving love & care is their specialty! They will perish, if care is not given and sent them freely and constantly!

Baby "Guest Preacher"
(excerpts taken afrom a 'Live' Seminar)

"Today our special guests here are baby Rebecca and baby Addison, and their moms and dads! These little lambs are beautiful! Amen? Little Rebecca is two months! Wonderful! How old is this big warrior "Addison" is 6 months old! Wow! That's really getting o-l-d!

Asking the infants to give us a Bible Quote:

Baby Addison is "acting up" a little bit. I don't think he's quite ready for Bible College! Let me ask you, Mom, does Rebecca know the Lord's Prayer yet? It's only 6 verses. What's that? She doesn't know the Lord's Prayer! Oh, my!

Now Moms: you a-r-e both teaching your babies God's Word, are you not? They must be learning some scripture. Rebecca, would you please quote me a little bit of Bible? Baby Rebecca, I'm talking to you. Now Rebecca, if I was your pastor, I'd think you might be being disrespectful to me.

Little Baby Addison... is a few months older, a bit more developed at the mature age of six months! Addison, do you know your name? Addison: are you ready to go kick in the gates of hell?

Addison, in John chapter 14 verse 12, Jesus said: "You that believe on Me, the works that I do shall you do, and greater works than these shall you do, because I go to the Father."

Addison, you're not answering me! Do you have a language, Addison? Does Addison have a prayer language? Yes, that's right, Mom!: He doesn't have a prayer language, but I'm sure, he has a "care language!" Am I right?

Let me ask this, Dad. You are a pastor, are you not? Your boy doesn't really seem to have mastered English yet? Am I right? I've studied Latin, Greek, French & Spanish and still working on English! Now Dad, aren't you just a little bit concerned your boy Addison here is a 6 months old & not speaking English fluently yet? I'm quite concerned, even if you're not!

I suppose you're also going to tell me Addison, that you're not even fully potty-trained at 6 months? Folks, I wouldn't say this to the Dad, but as far as linguistic development... this Christian baby is just n-o-t speaking God's Word very well! At least, not yet!

Baby Addison starts saying: "MaMa... mama". Well, ok, Addison, that's more like it! Baby continues: "MaMaMa. DaDadadadada"! Splendid linguistics!

Now folks, this word picture is preaching to all of us, isn't it! We all can see clearly that with these two and six month old infants, neither is developmentally nor linguistically retarded, thank God!

The $10,000 Baby-Preacher "Miracle Bible Memory-Verse" challenge:

"Baby Addison, I'm writing out a check to your parents for $10,000... for your future college fund (probably at least a year or two away)! It's yours... I-F you can just do one little thing for me! All you have to do is quote me five scriptures from the King James translation. Any five verses you like, but one has to be John 3:16. This should be "easy money" for you and your parents! Now, Mom and Dad, you A-R-E teaching your child to memorize God's Word, aren't you?

Just say the Name "J-E-S-U-S" ...for this $10,000 check!

I'm shocked! This newborn baby apparently doesn't know even 5 Bible verses? Wow! Okay! Let's make it even easier. Addison, just quote me one verse, John 3:16. Surely you've learned that! Now Addison, apparently you can't even quote John 3:16. Let me make it totally easy for you to win this $10,000! Just quote me John 11:35, the shortest New Testament verse, two simple words: "Jesus w-e-p-t".

Baby Addison, just say those two simple words, only three syllables, and I'll still give your parents this check for $10,000.

(Dad repeats for child the words several times, slowly: "Jesus wept", ...and everyone laughs!)

What's wrong Dad, you're a minister. How's your prayer life? Don't you believe Philippians 4:13, that: "you can do all things, through Christ Who strengthens you?" Brother, do you and your wife have faith in God, or not! I'm expecting a miracle &...somehow, why is it not happening? Is it unbelief?

The baby girl and infant boy are applauded & released

Now, addressing the baby boy infant. "Addison, you're a lot older, well mannered & mature! Everybody, let's say together: "Addison, ...you 'de'man!.'" This here baby is "John Rambo," I mean, he is a stud, ladies. This guy Addison is pure 'warrior material'! He is ready to kick "devil-pew!"

Well, we'll let you go, baby Addison. You are still "the man". You are a conquering king and a priest. Right now, you just want your mommy and dad.

Just say the Name "J-E-S-U-S" ...for the $10,000 check!

All you have to say is the Name above all other Names: ..."Jesus," and the check for ten grand is yours! A long, long but light, humorous silence! Well, Ok, I guess not today: ...and probably not tomorrow either! But thanks for being here with us also, with your mom and dad. Let's give both these beautiful families here a big round of applause for being with us today & letting two month old Rebecca and six month old baby Addison "preach" so loudly to us... without... even... saying a word!

Right on schedule... not a bit developmentally "slow"!

These beautiful newborn babies (& lambs) are right on schedule!

Maybe not on o-u-r schedule! Not right on our sometimes "adultified" convert-development schedule and frequent "over-expectations!" But they are right on God's newborn developmental time-table and schedule. We need to remember JFK (President John F. Kennedy's) famous quote and apply it to lamb-care:

"Ask not what your converts can do for your church.
Rather: ask what can your churches do for its converts!"

"RE-CALIBRATION"

One pastor, perhaps feeling some heat, but not yet seeing the light, asked me in front of a larger seminar setting of many ministers: "So what's the big difference between a lamb & a sheep?" I let everyone there join in with me in answering! In unison we all replied: "A lamb is a B-A-B-Y SHEEP!"

We need to re-calibrate our expectations, delivery systems and

166

understandings of a new convert. Continuing the analogies of a newborn will be helpful with this, in these next few pages & examples.

"As a newborn baby", ... the Bible says... "desire the sincere milk of the Word....that you may grow thereby! " I Peter 2 :2

How does a newborn desire the "sincere milk" ?

It may seem overly-simplification to ask: "How does a newborn baby desire the sincere milk" ...from its Mom? Let's answer and see!

A newborn can not desire the "sincere prime-rib", or "sincere sirloin"! It knows nothing of "grown-up adult food" ...neither is it capable of even chewing or digesting it!

If anything, a newborn can only desire the milk that God specifically created for it's initial food and growth. This is the finest, God-created "mother's-milk." The perfect match for the newborn's needs is created from the best of the mother's own body system. This milk... and this alone... is what the newborn requires for its maximal newborn survival, health and growth!

Babies don't have to cry... or do they?

Perhaps babies really don't have to cry! Right!! Newborns probably have numerous ways to communicate. Maybe they could send a fax, or an e-mail, beam a message with their Palm Pilot, use their cell phone, write a letter or send a Fed-Ex or Airborne overnight! Newborn lambs don't have to cry....or do they? Could baby Addison (in front of us today) just say: "Hey, Dad, how 'bout some milk?"

No! He can't use the language like that... for one major reason.

Fascinating Etymology of the Word: "Infant! "

A baby can't talk, because a baby's use of language is totally undeveloped. It is not "behind schedule!" It's "right on" schedule! God's schedule! It's just that language at this stage is N-O-T a part of God's perfect developmental plan! Newborns are 100% un-developed in verbal ability! Infants are "pre-verbal"!

Looking up the word "infant" in a larger dictionary, I discovered the etymology of our English word "infant", comes from the old French wording. The Latin prefix "in" (seen "in" such words as incurable, etc) means "not, or unable to"! The second half of the word "I-n-f-a-n-t," ...is "fanse", ...from the Ancient French, meaning: "to speak"! Thus the root meaning of the word "infant" comes from this meaning: that a newborn "infant": ...is one: ...who is incapable or unable to speak!

> **The Etymology of the Word: "Infant!" comes from two words, "unable" and "to speak".**

167

A newborn has no language skills whatsoever!

A newborn infant has absolutely no articulate, acquired language. They can n-o-t speak! They can only cry! Every good mother and father learns, and responds accordingly, to the different cries their baby communicates with!

All a newborn can do is cry and be heard and live,
...or cry and n-o-t be heard, ...and die!

"If a newborn baby cries... why don't we hear them?"

During one meeting with a pastor and his church board, a board member sincerely asked: "If a newborn cries, then... as a church family... why don 't we hear him?

The Lord gave me the answer. He whispered to me: "do the math", then slowly explained to me which "math."

The Lord said: "How many hours would a new Christian be in church, if he actually attended all "big three" weekly church services: Sunday AM, Sunday PM, and Wednesday Night?"

"All together, they make up about six hours, Lord" I replied"!

Six hours a week... out of 168... equals... 4%?

The Lord then said to me: "What percentage is 6 hours... out of the 168 hours in a week? If a new convert (improbable as it might be) were even to be in church, at all 3 weekly services... that would still be only be 6 hours a week!

What % is six hours... compared to the hundred and sixty-eight hours in a week? The shocking answer mathematically, is less than 4 % of the week (3.7 %).

96% of the week... "a-l-o-n-e!"

Leave a newborn baby alone 96% of 1 week: ...what will happen?

Three church services a week leaves the New Convert all a-l-o-n-e, (totally un-connected, un-protected and un-touched)... 96% percent of the week!

What about the other 96% of the week that the New Convert is a-l-l alone! "Oh well, I'm sure he'll get along and be just fine! The devil won't lie to him that much, tempt him that much, or send that many former 'sin-life' friends to call up & invite him/her out to 'party'! I'm sure the new lamb will be just fine all a-l-o-n-e!"

If we were to leave a newborn baby alone for even half of a week, even only 24, 36 or 48 hours... what would result? The baby would be d-e-a-d! Its would d-i-e before we return! A newborn can N-O-T be left alone for any length of time... or it will perish!

A Newborn needs a Person: ...n-o-t a Program!

God's program is N-O-T the information we ask the newborn to "learn", Rather, it is the relationship God intends: that is, for us to be "W-I-T-H" (and to give to the infant!) It is only through loving "Relationship"... that God's love and care will flow... to cause any infant to live & not perish!

Newborns don't need information. They do continually (& increasingly) needs a loving r-e-l-a-t-i-o-n-s-h-i-p! By God's own design, every newborn needs a person... not a program!

Other newborn baby verses include:

Paul wrote to his newborn church in Thessaloniki:
"But we were gentle among you, even as a nurse loves and cherishes (and nourishes-Greek word Thalpei) her children."
I Thessalonians 2:7

Paul wrote to the Corinthian believers and church:

"And I brethren, could not speak unto you, as unto spiritual, but as unto carnal, even as unto babes (infants) in Christ. I have fed you with milk ("Milk I gave you to 'd-r-i-n-k'...") (Greek literal) I couldn't give you meat because you were babes (babies, Greek 'napios). I had to feed you milk, because you were spiritual babies, newborns, carnal, fleshly (mere earthlings / 'worldings') ...mere worldly people."
1st Corinthians 3: 1 & 2

In Hebrews 5 we also read:

"For everyone that uses (partakes of) milk is unskilled in the Word of righteousness... for he is a babe! But strong meat belongs to them that are of full age, even those who by reason of use, have their senses exercised to discern both good & evil."
Hebrews 5:13-14

God's program for a newborn... is not a program... but a person... Not something... but someone!

Indeed, God's program for a newborn, is not a program, but rather, something much warmer,.....something alive...someone breathing, touchable, living and relational!

Actually, God's program, plan, and provision for a newborn is more than 1 person: it is two persons! God's program, R-e-l-a-t-i-o-n-s-h-i-p, is a lifelong, committed "Sponsor team" of two persons: the mother and the father!

ISAIAH 49:15

Following is another marvelous "lamb-care" promise and verse we can all tremendously benefit from by committing it to memory! God promises each of us:

> " A nursing mother may forget her child,
> but I will never forget thee. ...I have engraved your name
> on the palms of My hands." Isaiah 49:15

This improved, maximal care and nurture of Jesus' lambs is not "one-coat paint!"

We are not going to learn and develop all of our lamb-care improvements, in one seminar, nor from one reading of this, or any single book! We're not going to be able to teach it all in a one or two week of emphasis. Nonetheless, we can be sure, any church can turn their convert-care around, if they will start!

IF we increase the Intention... to increase our Attention...
we'll definitely increase our Retention!

"A Newborn Baby and its Meals":

What actually is a newborn's diet? What about quantity, consistency, taste, appearance, temperature, spoon-feeding, flavor, etc.

"Meat will K-I-L-L a baby"

Meat will kill a baby! These five short, brief words are brutal... but true! While milk is tremendously inadequate as a diet for an adult... conversely, adult food is totally inappropriate for a baby? Adult food will not n-o-u-r-i-s-h or help a baby. Rather adult food... will take the very fragile life of a baby... from them... and leave them lifeless.

"Baby food" is R-E-P-U-L-S-I-V-E to an adult

Baby food is repulsive to adults! In the fully equipped diaper bag I travel with for these seminars, I carry a little jar of Gerbers or Beechnut Turkey and Noodles. Someone say "Yummy!

If what you (at your church) are currently feeding your new converts is attractive, and appetizing to you (as an adult believer), it's probably not appropriate for a newborn! Even from a distance, baby food in a jar, called "Turkey & Noodles" doesn't look like turkey, and it certainly doesn't have the consistency, (or texture) of noodles!

The consistency of baby food, in one word, is "yuck"! Sometimes in seminars I'll offer $5 or $10 to a youth pastor, to come up and ingest that little, delicious, nutritional container of "food!" I don't get that many eager-beavers to take me upon on that deal. Baby Food is N-O-T a treat to adults! Many adults actually, are afraid they would "gag" on it, in front of their peers.

A Newborn's "Eating" Quantity:

How much does a newborn infant "eat"? Well, a standard little rounded jar of Gerber's (or Beechnut baby food) is approximately 3-4 ounces.

The Lord has blessed us with 4 wonderful children! My wife Jeanette has studied in great depth with La Leche League, towards becoming a lactation consultant. She is very "into" nursing and breast-feeding. I am also a bit familiar and conversant with those realities. Can you believe that God could possibly have been part of the original "Divine design" of nursing a newborn baby?

Newborns can't "e-a-t" anything! They must "drink"!

When we ask how much will a brand new infant "eat", the answer of course is: z-e-r-o!

A newborn doesn't eat at all, ...but rather must d-r-i-n-k A-L-L of its "food" ...pronounced m-i-l-k! A newborn's drinking quantity is included below, when we look at frequency and quantity together, as a tandem concept of ingestion (and needed nutrition) for a newborn.

A newborn will "eat" 2.5 times (in ounces) its weight (in pounds)!

A newborn will eat (pronounced "drink") approximately 2 1/2 times (in liquid ounces) its weight in pounds! Lactation consultants and pediatricians state a general rule for the drinking (nursing) input of a newborn. The formula roughly states: "Take the weight of the baby in pounds and multiply it by 2 to 2 1/2 times. That total (in ounces) is, roughly, the 24-hour period drinking intake of a newborn.

Thus an eight pound baby's 24 hour intake (8 times 2.5) is roughly twenty ounces per day!

A New-born baby's Drinking Intake:

A newborn will eat or drink (especially in its first six months) approximately 6-8 times round-the- clock. When you divide 6 or 8 (even 10) daily "feedings" into twenty ounces, this comes out to roughly 2 to 2 1/2 fluid ounces of Mom's milk... per serving! Babies don't eat much at a time, but they do eat frequently.

We must re-calibrate the Convert-Care at our churches,
to make the most of these realities!

Picture 1/4th of an 8 Ounce Glass of milk

Picture with me, an eight-ounce glass of milk. Now divide its height into fourths! Imagine if you only had the bottom fourth to drink, and you simultaneously had a giant, chocolate brownie. If someone asked: "got milk?"

...what would your answer be?

If you had a half-gallon container, or a full gallon milk container, but in the bottom only had this same 2 ounces of milk (only 1/4 inch depth spread out accordingly), what would you say to "Got milk?"?

"Got milk" or "no Got"? You wouldn't say "got milk", would you? That small inch and a half of milk in the glass, is a full meal for a newborn! However, it's only 1/4 inch (or less) of liquid spread across the bottom of the "huge" gallon container! We wouldn't consider it worth pouring into a glass!

"GOT MILK"?
I Peter 2:2 ...and Other " Word Milk" Scriptures

I Peter 2:2 states: "As a newborn babe, desire the sincere milk of the Word." What are some of other "m-i-l-k" scriptures from God's Word?

Of course, there's John 3:16, certainly a key, faith-producing "milk verse" for brand new believers. How about John 3:17: "For God sent not His Son into the world to condemn the world, but that the world through Him should be saved." What else?

How about Revelation 3:20: "Behold I stand at the door and knock. If any man hear My voice & open the door, I will come in to him and will feast with him...and he with Me."

How about John 10:10 and yes, the 23rd Psalm: "The Lord is my Shepherd". Jeremiah 29:11, Psalm 37:4, Hebrews 13:5: "I will never, Never, NEVER LEAVE OR FORSAKE YOU!..&scores more!

Identify them! Write them down! Use them! Do this as an exercise with your leadership, altar teams, and church's "Convert-Care Task Force!" These scriptures can be collected, put into snack-packs, onto laminated wallet-size memory cards ...to help your newborn believers feed regularly round-the-clock. Help them learn God's "delicious", Life-giving Word & Words of Life...a little sip at a time!

Oxytosin: The enzyme that creates "Mother's Milk" in Moms of Newborns

When a full-term pregnant woman goes into the final process of labor and giving birth, not only does the water break in her placenta, but Oxytosin is developed through the Pituitary gland. The Oxytosin flows from the pituitary... to the milk ducts... making the "milk drop" ... in the new Mom after labor.

Application: "The Milk" and Nurture-Gift... of the Holy Spirit

It's the Holy Spirit, the Comforter, the Guide, the Helper & "Labor-Coach" of the New Birth, Who births new lambs into God's Kingdom & Flock! The New Birth's Heaven-sent mid-wife is the Holy Spirit!

The same Holy Spirit Who creates the desire to birth new "spiritual babies.. and lambs!"

Again, the same Holy Spirit brings (just as Oxytosin) the "m-i-l-k" of nurture into a church body, an unending, ever-growing desire to love, cherish, nurse and care for e-a-c-h precious newborn lamb!

Chapter 27
"FAILURE TO THRIVE: (MARASMUS)"

Most ladies are familiar with this "Failure to Thrive" concept, especially Moms!

Below follows an intriguing article
(excerpted form Allan Loy McGinnis' "must-read" book
on relationships: "The Friendship Factor." (p.86,87)

"British Foundling hospitals in the early 1800's discovered repeatedly, that abandoned, orphan newborns (even when warm, clean, well fed & in a "perfect" environment) would still start to fade & die!

During the 19th century, over half of the infants died in their first year of life, from a disease called marasmus... a Greek word meaning "wasting away." As late as the 1920's, according to Montagu, the death rate for infants under one-year in U.S. foundling Institutions approached 100%!

A distinguished New York pediatrician, Dr. Chapin noted that the infants were kept in sterile, neat, tidy wards, but rarely picked up. Chapin brought in women to hold the babies, to coo to them, and to stroke them...and the mortality rate dropped drastically.

Who was responsible for all those babies who had died unnecessarily? Not the foundling home directors. They were operating on the best "scientific" information available at that time.

The real villain was one Emmett Holt Sr., a professor of pediatrics at Columbia University. He authored the booklet: "The Care & Feeding of Children", first published in 1894 & in its 15th edition in 1935. This book was the "Dr. Spock" of its time.

In his book, Holt urged mothers to abolish the cradle & refuse to pick up the baby when it cried, for fear of spoiling it by too much handling. Tender loving care was considered unscientific.

We now know small children become irritable and hyperactive without adequate body contact. In various experiments with normal & subnormal youngsters, those given the most physical contact with parents learned to walk & talk earliest, and had the highest IQ's. The young desperately crave physical affection."

"Daddy I know! ...But I can't..."

A father was reading his four year old daughter Melinda the "Three Little Pigs" nightly. He tape-recorded the story that he had read to her night after night! When Melinda next asked for it, he simply switched on the recorder's playback!

This worked a couple of nights. Then one night Melinda pushed the storybook at her father.

"Now, honey," he said, "you know how to turn on the tape recorder."
"Yes" said Melinda" ..."but I can't sit on its lap."

Jesus reached out and T-O-U-C-H-E-D the children

When mothers brought their little children to Him, "Jesus took them in His arms & blessed them, laying His hands upon them."(Mk.10:16). Here we see Jesus saying the wonderful child-affirming words: "Don't ever hold back little children from coming to Me, for only of such is the Kingdom of Heaven!"

Follow Jesus in His contacts with the peasant people of Palestine. See Him touching people again & again. Jesus "stretched out his hand, reached out & actually t-o-u-c-h-e-d the l-e-p-e-r. " (Matthew 8:3) When Peter's mother-in-law was sick, Jesus "t-o-u-c-h-e-d her hand & the fever left her." (Mt 8:15)

How many of our converts suffered... or perished from "Failure to Thrive"?

Do we dare ask ourselves the haunting and piercing question: "Which converts from the past year (or past several years) have suffered from "Marasmus" (Failure to Thrive) from a non-intentional, but just as deadly lack of touch, and lack of being made to feel "wanted" and "loved".

How can we connect them to care, attention, relationship and friendship ...that not one perishes?

Allow me to bring this issue of "Failure of Thrive" across directly into the arena of Convert Care... ...and the "feeding of Jesus' lambs."

A new convert at your church may traditionally be given a New Testament, or a Gospel of John, a New Convert class, a short Bible study, this or that program of Bible training. However, most converts will not thrive with merely this. What's missing, once again is God's Program of r-e-l-a-t-i-o-n-s-h-i-p!

Without relationship, they will all die. Love (and relationship) are the "milk"! It is "the meal", it is God's program, and it is "t-h-e mainline connection" for Life-flow and Life-Change!

God is Love! Love flows through relationship(s). As the chorus puts it so well: "Love wasn't put into your heart to stay; love isn't love until you give it away." Give it away to yourself?

Increase the I-N-T-E-N-T-I-O-N, ...to Increase the personal A-T-T-E-N-T-I-O-N, & we'll increase the R-E-T-E-N-T-I-O-N!

No! Until we give it away to someone else, its isn't really "l-o-v-e"!

Even so, "Marasmus" here, was only discovered and cured when Dr. Chapin brought to the Foundling Hospitals women to "coo" to newborns. Then the mortality rate dropped from 90%... amazingly... to nearly nothing!

**From ninety percent mortality...
to almost zero! Wow!**

*Increase the I-N-T-E-N-T-I-O-N,
...to Increase the personal A-T-T-E-N-T-I-O-N, &...
we will increase the R-E-T-E-N-T-I-O-N!*

At a District Council dinner, a District Superintendent capped off our conversation on this topic, stating, in a quiet but elegant "grand-slam" home-run statement: "Ministry is A-L-L R-E-L-A-T-I-O-N-S-H-I-P!"

*God tells us in Isaiah 55: 8&9:
"My thoughts are not your thoughts, neither are My ways
your ways. But as the heavens are higher than the earth,
so are My ways higher than your ways."*

Our God... is teaching us... His ways & teaching us to think... His better thoughts! We're slowly, steadily learning: that even as Jesus chose 12 to "be with" them...

*He's teaching us...
what following Jesus closel... truly means :
We also must choose... "to be w-i-t-h...
each of His precious lambs... as well!*

Chapter 28
"ONE PAGE PER NEW CONVERT CARE-GIVING SHEET"

When you are a patient in the hospital, the surgeon (attending physician or nurse) comes by your hospital bed. There is always a clipboard at the end of your bed which is regularly monitored and updated. There's only one clipboard at the end of every bed. Why are there not a half-dozen names on that clipboard at the end of your bed?

Whose name is it at that the top of that single clipboard?... and why?

Your name is on it! Specifically, and only: y-o-u-r name! On the clipboard are included the patient's individual statistics and v-i-t-a-l-s: the case-history, progress, feedings, a record of medications & comments, observations, record of contacts made, when & by whom, etc.

There's only one name on it, intentionally, to focus the attention and care on just one person: you!

Y-o-u-r healing... y-o-u-r welfare... and y-o-u-r recovery are the total focus, intent and purpose of that single, focused clipboard.

Focused Attention = Increased Care
Increased (& focused) Care = Accelerated Healing & Health

If we will increase our attention... we will increase our retention.

I strongly suggest a one-page-per-convert follow-up lamb-feeding care-chart and sheet modeled somewhat as follows.

To increase the retention,
we must increase the specific individual attention!

Old-style follow-up card information:

Old style Convert Follow-up cards, would of course have asked for: name, address, phone, date, etc... but precious little else. What else could and should be added? Yes, of course, "please print". Some had a space for the prayer counselor's name.

Some had "check-boxes" for: salvation, rededication, need baptism, __ prayed with for ____, etc. Others would perhaps add: religious background, and a few other areas: Names of children, birthday(s), prayer requests, etc.

What was missing on old-style
New Convert follow-up sheets or cards?:

In one word, the "relational" element.

THE R-E-L-A-T-I-O-N-A-L ELEMENT WAS MISSING

Far too obvious... by its absence... was the relational aspect of the New Convert's life : both covering b-e-f-o-r-e their salvation prayer... and experience... and even more importantly... a-f-t-e-r!

The "a-f-t-e-r" is even more important, the on-going relational and connecting plans and intentional dimensions were lacking: the intentionalized activities...times & activities planned together... are usually totally missing!

Jesus chose His twelve... to be w-i-t-h Him:
Do we choose our 1, 5, 12, or 20 to be w-i-t-h us...?

The Pre-Conversion & After-Conversion
Relational Elements are "V-I-T-A-L" & "V-I-T-A-L-S"

Since 85% of visitors to a church are invited to church by a friend or acquaintance, the relational pre-connection and after-connection with the inviting (or other close Christian friends) is absolutely vital for follow-up. This is a God-designed, nurturing connection (and pre-connection) with the New Believer, to be utilized by believers... by definite intention.

Too many churches, among the few that are aware of this fact, proactively utilize this "relationship-connection", much less maximize it on purpose w-i-t-h e-v-e-r-y single convert.

It can n-o-t be expected to happen "organically" all by itself!

A Prayer List of new Converts in the
Church Lobby for the Church Family to Pray for

It would also be a great idea in caring and gathering specific prayer support, for each of the church's new converts (& new members) to be listed on a weekly updated prayer sheet & list going back at least for one year from the most recent convert.

ONE PAGE PER NEW CONVERT CARE-GIVING SHEET

INDIVIDUAL NEW BELIEVER CARE & FOLLOW-UP SHEET: PLEASE P-R-I-N-T

***Name of person/altar worker filling out this form: _____

Day: _____ Date: _____

Year: _____ Name of Convert: _____

Prefers to be called: _____ Date prayed with: ____ Service: _____

Convert's Local Address: _____

City: _____ Zip: _____ E-mail: _____ Age: _____ Birthday: _____

Phone #'s: (H): _____ (W) _____ (Ok to call at work ? _Y _ N)

If ok, best times to call _____ Days: _____ (other than Sunday)

Prayed with what time: ____day: ____date: ____After service: ____Before: _____During: _____

Other: _____

DETAILS OF THIS SALVATION/ALTAR EXPERIENCE: (check all that apply) Photo (below at right:) _____

__ 1st time salvation prayer: _ Prayed to be made "ready" for salvation

__ re-dedication " __ other:_____ Prayed for salvation __ nth time

__ prayed for healing: _____ received Baptism in the Holy Spirit _____

__ prayed for healing (details) _____ Other specific prayer request:: _____

FORMER CHURCH EXPERIENCE: PREVIOUS SPIRITUAL EXPERIENCE(S) & RELIGIOUS BACKGROUND

TO BE ASKED BY ALTAR WORKER (BUT ANSWERED BY NEW BELIEVER):

Can the altar worker call you? _____ Would you like a Bible with your name engraved on it? _____

Like a 30-minute, weekly __ 3 or __ 6 week Bible study? __ At your home? __ At Church? Other: _____

Can someone __ call __ visit you at home this week to start this extremely helpful new Bible study?_____

Family Members: If married: Spouse's Name: _____ Attending church here? _____

Attending elsewhere? _____

Is spouse a believer? _Y _N Details: _____Other: __Name of church & city: _____

***Name of Father & Mother (if new believer is under 18)

Dad's name : _____Attends this church: _ Y _N __ Elsewhere? Church name & city: _____

Believer: _Y _ N _Other: _____

Mom's name: _____Attends this church: _ Y _N __ Elsewhere: Church name & city_____

Believer: _ Y _ N _ Elsewhere: Church name & city_____

**If convert is an adult with family & children: ***Children's names at home (if applicable)
Name Age (Birth date (optional) Misc. Inf.. Name Age(& Birthday optionals) Misc.Inf.
(use back of sheet if necessary for additional children)

HOW ARE YOU CONGRATULATING (& CONNECTING WITH) THE NEW CONVERT?

1st Week Actions & Get-togethers: What activities & contacts are scheduled for convert's 1st week?:

Day 1: _____ Day 2: _____

Day 3: _____ Day 4: _____

Day 5: _____ Day 6: _____

Day 7: _____

1st Month: What specific Convert-care is scheduled for Week One through Week 4 ?

Week 1: _____ Week 2: _____

Week 3: _____ Week 4: _____

Altar Counselor: Name: _____ Home ph #: _____ (best time to call) _____

Convert Sponsor: Assigned Person as ongoing Sponsor? _____ Ph#: _____ Date assigned: ____

Who does the altar Worker/Convert Sponsor report to on the staff? _____

Is there a system to develop more convert sponsors? _____

Christian Friends at our Church: Names(details)_____ Invited to church by:_____

Finances: How much finances have been committed to the care & gift-ing of this new convert? _____

Convert invited to: _____ meal out with sponsor _____ meal at sponsor's home _____ meal with pastor

_____ offered ride to church _____ taken to Christian bookstore to buy them a CD? Date done: _____

_____ invited to small group _____ taken to a small group

Gifts given to New Convert: _____ Bible (which translation___/___when) _____ New Birth Certificate

____ "Welcome to the Family" tape by pastor ____ The Jesus Video ___(Date) ___Local Resource List for

Converts ____ New Convert study materials? ____Which? When? ____Other tapes? ____other: ? ____

other? ____other:____? Meals Shared with New Convert: with whom?____ when: _____

Chapter 29
"BABIES, BUDGETS AND DOLLARS"

YOUR CHURCH'S BUDGET... A-N-D... GOD'S PRICELESS LAMBS!

The Apostle Paul, writing to his beloved Corinthian church, penned the following words:

"Anyway, you are my children, and little children don't pay or their father and mother's food: ...it's the other way around. Parents supply food for their children... I am glad to give my life for you and your good." (2 Corinthians 12:14 Living Bible)

"Babies are... EXPENSIVE!!":

If we took time to survey a seminar audience, church congregation (or each reader) and asked them to write down four words describing newborn babies... we would come up with words like: adorable, self-centered, care-dependent, vulnerable, needy, work-intensive, center of attention, odiferous, helpless, etc. Babies are: loveable, cute, perishable, precious, spectacular, gorgeous and miraculous!

However, what I'm 'fishing for' here, is that babies are not just adorable, lots of work and 24 hour needy... but babies... are also... very expensive!

Budgets and Babies:

Billy Graham has said,:
"Money is just a person's life in the form of currency."

If money is just a person's life in the form of currency, then what is money to a church? It follows, that money in a church... is just a church's life... in the form of currency as well.

What is in most church's budget for Convert-Care?

If babies are not just miraculous,
100% care-dependent, and work-intensive, but also expensive...
let's dare to ask the corollary question:
...what is in most church budgets for convert care?

Can you guess the most common response to this question at conferences across America, when I ask the above (and following) "Convert Budget" question to scores of ministers at a time: "What is in most church's budgets for Convert Care? "

The tragic (and revealing answer) is chilling. The most common answer is a softly pronounced "zero"... or "Nothing!"... followed in second place by: "next to nothing"... or "far too little!

Is it any wonder that we have a mortality rate so high, running commonly in the 90% range ?

"Where your treasure is... there your heart will be also!"

Jesus Himself said in His immortal Sermon On The Mount: "For where your treasure is, there your heart will be also" (Matthew 6:21).

I want to see your church budget change, because that W-I-L-L change the survival and the "thrival" rates of Jesus' lambs... at y-o-u-r church!

This will also, all by itself, change the heart-beat and priority of the church, when considerably... and measurably... more dollars are being funneled directly to lamb-care and for the benefit and singular, specific purpose of Feeding Jesus' lambs...and putting His lambs f-i-r-s-t!

> **Jesus said: "Where your treasure is, there your heart will be also."**
> **Matthew 6:21**

I'd like to see the Women's Ministries in your church really maximally "flex" that divine gender-dominant "nurture gift" that God has given them. Let your "WM"(Women's Ministries) focus their nurture gifting church-wide on the "lambs" that God gives you! Translate that nurture-heartbeat into new, overlapping, redundant "caring-systems" for our converts: to be relationally connected and "family"-ed by your entire congregation!

What would any church spend $'s on for its new converts?:

Since Jesus put the lambs f-i-r-s-t, shouldn't our church budget show this priority as well?

What things would have to change, for our church budgets to show that we are indeed putting the lambs first. What budget shifts would Jesus Himself make in your church budget, if He were t-o-t-a-l-l-y in charge of shifting a—n—y amount from any account, to create and fund a new (& growing) Convert-Care love-budget ?

JG: ..." if you had $150 budgeted per convert... what would you spend it on?"

One East Coast Executive Presbyter actually asked me, during a consulting session: "JG! If you had $150 budgeted to spend per convert: what would you spend it on?"

Perhaps $150 is too high per convert, but what is a reasonable amount to budget "per convert" for the lambs, that Jesus' entrusts your church with? Start somewhere! Is $5 or $10 too high to project, budget & spend per convert per year? Doubtful! Start out at some level next Board meeting. "Get the boat in the water!"

Both the momentum... and inertia... are almost terminally stacked in churches a-g-a-i-n-s-t budgetary change toward... Jesus' lambs. However, the improved results of "lasting fruit" will be infinitely more than worth the extra effort... and minimal expense!

I spoke with one mega-church pastor running thousands and shared the idea to provide a $5 copy of the Jesus Video for their church's converts. This huge church has several hundred converts yearly. This "Jesus Video gift for New Converts idea" (& investment for feeding Jesus' lambs) would perhaps have cost them $1,200 (if that) a year! They spend more than that on paper towels, tissue and restroom soap.

Yet this simple, "miniscule" convert expenditure was never y-e-t approved! That same mega-church has reported a decline: a church with thousands of people in it. Our priorities must change!

It is not a matter of finance, it is a matter of heart... and putting Jesus' priorities above our own!

We need to let God 'cut the deck', shuffle and re-deal the cards... as to our church prioritie... and church expenditures... exactly as He wants to deal them out.

If Jesus put His lambs first, and since He told us to follow Him and do the same... how can we effectively do any less?

Below are partial samples of:
Primary, 2nd & 3rd level Convert-Care Budgets

I. A primary 1st $ Level lamb-care Gift-budget ($10-$25/per lamb /per year):
(Below are a few ideas for a primary first level budget for New Converts)

    A) A copy of the Jesus video$5@ o-r the "Jesus Video for Children" $12.95(800-29-JESUS)

    B) A New Testament (&/or Bible) with each converts name imprinted on it ($5-15/or more)

    C) A "New Birth Certificate" framed (8x11")with their name on it, signed by the pastor. ($2-$4)

II. A secondary $ $ Level lamb-care Gift-budget: ($25-$75 per lamb /year):

    A) A "Meals-Out Budget" for New Converts with Pastors, board members, Lamb Care Task Force & sponsors, New Convert Meal-Team, etc.

    B) A Lending Library for "lambs": life-stage, age & gender-specific tape series, videos, books, CD's

    C) A Special, New Convert's Retreat-Weekend with Pastors, staff members, Sunday School teachers, Care-Group leaders, sponsors and Church Board, or deacons

III. Third Level $ $ $ lamb-care Gift-budget ($75-$150 per-lamb/ year):

    A) A _, half-time or full-time staff person SOLELY in charge of "Feeding Jesus' lambs" properly, a Convert-Care Pastor at larger churches (or part of a Pastoral Care portfolio position.

    B) A $250-$500 annual budget solely to expand the "New Convert Lending Library"

    C) Emergency benevolence funds for those converts with special needs".

Dozens of other Lamb-Care Budget (& gift ideas and items) for New Converts are available to our Lamb-Care Network partner churches. Monthly missions partner-churches receive these items (and more) to help equip their church, entire Leadership and Convert-Care Task Force.

Chapter 30
"THE BASEPATH OF SEQUENTIAL LAMB-CARE"

The Power of Sequential Intentionality!

How important to the survival of a newborn is the sequence of "First things FIRST!" The classic tongue-in-cheek mis-sequence of "Ready! Fire! Aim!" is nowhere more apparent, than in the tremendous convert losses regularly sustained in American mainline, evangelical churches! We must decrease & eliminate the infant-mortality rate of our New Converts, by increasing our intentional care!

*"Follow-Up" (as a mechanical, obligatory, "have to do it" thing)
...must once again re-gain God's tender heartbeat...
for "Feeding and Folding His precious lambs!"*

We have clearly established that the "after-care" of new believers (by God-ordained, caring, relational, trained Sponsors) and emphasizing God's program ("Relationships") ...i-s the survival determinant of a newborn. Too often the newborn believer gets wrongly blamed for his own lack of survival... when the responsibility for survival of a newborn belongs to the parents! Where are the gaps (and the linkages) in our follow-up and Convert-Care systems? If we will just honestly ask... and answer this type of question, we can build better bridges and links... and eliminate fall-through gaps, where we lose the precious, perishable lambs we work so hard to "birth"!

If they don't survive the 1st day... they won't survive the 1st week;
If they don't survive the 1st week... they won't survive the 1st month;
If they don't survive the 1st month... they won't survive the 1st quarter;
& If they don't survive the 1st quarter... they won't survive the 1st year!

*A "Baseball Base-path" of Lamb-care,
starting from "Day One" ...to the end of "Year One"!*

Below are some ideas for sequencing lamb-care at your church, from the initial moment of birthing a New Convert at the altar (or elsewhere from the moment of "new birth") ...through the end of Year One!

There are some ideas you can implement immediately, others can be customized, adapted and worked into the environment, "mix":... and "specific needs" of your individual, specific, local church and ministry!

HOME PLATE : At the Altar & Counseling Room:

A) The Altar a-n-d a nearby Prayer Room**: Increasingly, churches are finding benefit in separating Altar responders, asking "1st time decision for Christ" responders to follow a staff person into a nearby prayer room. Thus worship & other prayer ministry continue, while giving intentional specific care to N-e-w lambs!

A1) If possible, take them for a meal to celebrate their very 1st day in Christ! Food is a "relational sacrament" & bonding/ "friendship-creating" element. Try to have a "Welcome to the Family" ongoing "meal- team" that are signed up & ready to invite out a new convert...for the n-e-x-t four Sundays!

No theology is required, except... LOVE! The church should underwrite these meals with part of the church's lamb-care budget. Important:**New Convert Sponsors shouldn't have to... nor be asked to... bear the costs alone!

A2) Give the New believer a "new gift Bible" with their name written in it & congratulations written inside the) front cover. If possible, get Pastor (& staff) to greet them & sign it as well that very Sunday!

A3) Introduce them to Convert Task Force members & if a specific Sponsor available to bond with them that day!

A4) Definitely set up the next time to get together: either that evening or next day if possible! *Do n-o-t say: "Let's get together next Sunday". You'll lose 90%+! A baby can't survive a week a-l-o-n-e! God didn't design new converts to... either!

A5) Why not have "Welcome to the Family" packets (pre-assembled)? Not just a small pocket-size New Testament. How about a "Re-Birthday Present-Pack" with a "Welcome to the Family" greeting card, a Jesus Video enclosed (with packet of microwave popcorn attached), perhaps a chocolate bar, (one church uses a '100 Grand' candy bar), a literature piece with some brief, written testimonies of those saved at the church, etc.

What are some specific, unique, creative things you do at your church for brand new Believers at the moment of their salvation & at the altar? Make this a matter of ongoing prayer, brain-storming & "think-tank"-ing. You'll be surprised at the additional g-r-e-a-t ideas the Holy Spirit gives you & your New Convert Team!

1ST BASE: 1ST WEEK:
"From Day 1 to Day 7": ...where we lose 75%!

B1) Arrange to pick them up for Wednesday evening service (or to go with them to a home group or class). Merely inviting them is N-O-T effective! Inviting is ineffectual & fails more than it succeeds. The reverse is true also!

B2) Call on Monday (or the day after) for a brief hello, encouragement & 30-second prayer just to say: "We're thinking of you and praying for you! You are on our hearts!.. and you are going to make it!"

B3) E-mail them a congratulations and a short verse or two. Also mail them a small "new believer" 1st-week snack-pack. More than anything else, pursue establishing a relationship! Make clear the church wants to make this convert a close, ongoing, valued part of the church family.

B4) "Changed-Lives Testimonies brochure, tape or mini- books: Why not write down(or audio/video record) the extract of some testimonies in your church. For each, edit a one or two paragraph written extract of how their life changed since coming to Christ. Part of it can describe their "BC" (how 'bad' life was before coming to Christ!) Put this all into a nice little brochure of "baby food." Make this literature piece (or small bundle) an ongoing part of one of your "snack-packs" for your new "lambs". (*Also great in Visitor-Packs!)

B5) Invite (& take) them to the nearest Christian Bookstore. Tell them their church family's given funding to buy them a Christian CD of their choice... of their type of music! If they're teenagers, they may prefer Sonic Flood, DC Talk, the Newsboys, Delirious, rather than a Gaither Homecoming Video!

When you spend money on somebody, what does it say to them? Of course, it says: "We value you! You're important!... and "we care!" When an entire church family sponsors (& underwrites) a free CD gift like this, what does it say to the New Convert... and to their circle of unsaved friends.

*What do y-o-u do for a new convert... in the first week at your church? Phone call? Good. Take them to lunch, or Starbucks! Perfect! A short, sweet encouraging personal follow-up letter is great! Send a note & a special Bible Bookstore Dayspring quality Congratulations card! Excellent! (Computer generated, full-color cards can be just as meaningful!) Make a basket of "snack goodies" & baked goods" (Krispie Crunch? Yeah!) & drop them off for them to snack on. As they eat them, they will remember who thoughtfully dropped off these delicious chocolate chip cookies(etc.). A Follow-up visit? Good! Call 1st!

2ND BASE: THEIR 1ST MONTH:
What's intentionally done for lambs in month 1?

C1) Get them involved in a smaller group (Sunday school class, home group, Alpha Group, dinner-group, etc) more for relationships... than for Information & Bible study.)

C2) Take them to the group; don't expect them to take themselves... or to just "be there"!.

C3) Send a sequenced series of weekly "snack-paks" of spiritual goodies, small booklets (babies eat little, but often)

C4) Teach Convert-Sponsors (& Task Force) to invite converts to do "everyday things" w-i-t-h them (Mk.3:14)

3RD BASE: 1st Quarter (1st 3 Months In Christ)

D1) Celebrate by letter, phone, church bulletin (& pulpit) their completion of their "at home" 3 week "START - UP" Bible Study, ("101" class), or a-n-y other New Christian starter-unit they complete!

D2) Run the "Alpha Course" (1-800-836-ALPHA) for their 1st "learning set" & group-involvement with the church.

D3) Start & re-start new Groups & the class for New Believers, with the emphasis on the building of relationships (not the primary acquirement of Bible knowledge)

1ST YEAR HOMERUN:
Completing Their Very First Year...
& Celebrating their very 1st anniversary in Christ!
Proud parents celebrate their children's achievements!

E1) Be sure to note & celebrate t-h-e-i-r one-year anniversary & "re-birth-day"! This can influence an entire church culture, and promote better lamb-care church-wide, as we conscientiously and responsibly celebrate the successful feeding, nurture, survival and growth of each of Jesus' lambs.

As the elderly Apostle John wrote in his 3rd Epistle verse 4:
"I have no greater joy, than to hear that my children are continuing to walk & live in the Truth"

E2) Celebrate their 1st year in Christ Birthday in the pulpit Sunday AM for the whole church, with an interview, balloons & celebration. Make it an wide-open, unabashed celebration for the entire church celebrating the successful feeding & "1-year parenting" of this specific, precious, unique single one of Jesus' lambs!

*This is a g-r-e-a-t time to recruit more, n-e-w Convert-Care Sponsors & Convert-Care Team-members. Also a great time to "hero-ize" your Lamb-care Meal-Team members as well!.
E3) Why not videotape testimonies of these 1 year anniversaries. Use them to "feed" and encourage other converts in their first week, 1t month, 1st quarter, and 1st year.

*Many more ideas are available on the full-sheet in the "Feed My Lambs Implementation Workbook"

Section IV: Chapter 31
"IMPLEMENTATION INTRODUCTION"

How will this massive, ongoing lamb-care improvement take place?

*More than any other method's response,
our heart-answer needs to be Zechariah 4:6 which reads:
"Not by might, not by power, but by My Spirit... says the Lord!"*

The spiritual opposition that the Apostle Paul writes of in Ephesians 6 certainly will be marshaled against any efficient, continued improvements in lamb-care. After all, these lambs are the very future of the flock of God!

Paul writes: "For we wrestle, not against flesh & blood, but against principalities and powers, against rulers of darkness, & spiritual wickedness in High Places." (Eph. 6:12 & 13).

We can n-o-t pray too much... Especially in this vital area!

We simply can N-O-T pray too much; we certainly can pray far, far too little, especially in such a vital, previously under-prioritized arena and area. Only through Prayer... Prayer and more Prayer... will these changes take place! However, at the same time, to change our thinking as well as our spirit, we must intentionalize the implementation process.

Without a continuing foundation of intercessory prayer (for each new lamb), it is doubtful any permanent significant, change and improvement will actually occur and remain.

*To change our actions... we must f-i-r-s-t change our thinking...
To change our programs... we must first change our values!*

Creating a Convert-Care Task Force will be resisted & attacked as nothing else!

In the next chapter, the details and rationale behind creating a Convert-Care Task Force will be spelled out. Many readers will attempt improved lamb-care in a "Ready! Fire! Aim" style w-i-t-h-o-u-t this crucial, foundational Convert-Care Task Force being formed first! Remember: the foundation determines the building!

It is vital to establish a Convert-Care Task Force... F-I-R-S-T!

Unless the foundation is first changed: what we try to change and build upwards...will n-o-t end up any different! Remember: This is satan's favorite, "stocked fishing pool" you are now setting out to protect and reclaim.

Chapter 32
"A CONVERT CARE TASK FORCE (& TEAM) AT YOUR CHURCH"

Any Church Will Benefit From A Convert-Care Task Force idea: Every church needs a Task Force (as a separate committee) focused on Convert-Care!

Committees focus on everything else... except... Lamb-care!

A-l-l churches have church boards, deacon boards, building committees, special & annual event groups, and myriad other committees. Strangely, almost A-l-l churches do N-O-T have a "Convert-Care Committee" or Task Force. Called by a-n-y name, lamb-care is far too conspicuous by its absence, across our nation's church landscape.

Jesus so clearly said: "If you love ME, feed MY lambs" (Jn.21:15), b-e-f-o-r-e you "Feed My sheep"! Too many assumptions are made regarding the nurture and care supposedly being given Converts! No wonder more converts don't survive, and our new believer mortality rate (in USA churches) is so high!

Immediate Benefits of Having a "Convert-Care Task Force":

A1) It creates a continuing presence (& focusing) of church leadership (& church-wide) resources on the vital needs of New Convert Care, nurture & their survival.

A2) It creates a separate "team" to work on Convert Care issues & lamb-care (to then report to pastor & board.)

A3) This entirely new, separate group can cross-pollinate church-wide across all departments on Lamb-Care.

A4) The Convert Task Force is a "landing place"/funnel for Jesus' special loving concern to Feed His lambs. It makes sure that what we want to see done...actually gets done!

People don't always do what's expected: they're more prone to get done what will be i-n-s-p-e-c-t-e-d!

A Few Benefits of the "Feed My Lambs" Implementation Workbook

B1) 6 immediate Tasks your Convert-Care Task Force should begin & complete.

B2) Why: you need b–o–t–h a Convert Care T-a-s-k F-o-r-c-e... A-N-D... a Convert Care T-e-a-m?

B3) 5 common mistakes in launching a Convert Care-Team (...and how to a-v-o-i-d them)

B4) Who to select (& not select) to be on your Convert Task Force (...and why)

B5) Why (& how to find & process) last year's Convert numbers and losses.

It will be very profitable to create a New-Convert Task Force at your home church.

It will be very profitable to create a New Convert Task Force at your home church. It takes humility and honesty to truly evaluate one's own church's Convert-Care, and to humbly pray as to what room there is for real improvement in Lamb-Care... at y-o-u-r church!

This is especially true when figuring out and looking at any church's one-year retention rates.

Who is it at y-o-u-r church, that focuses the church's attention onto newborn lambs? A New-Convert Task Force and a New-Convert Care-Team will get this d-o-n-e... and get it done right!.

Items the Convert-Care TASK-FORCE can work on right away:

1. Assign a Task Force member to round up convert # totals for this year (and previous years.)

2. Track the total # of converts for the last entire year (and the # of those still "in" the church)

3. Track the total # of converts this current year (by month) & the # still "in" the church (or "not").

4. Assign one Task Force member to create a one-page Local-Area New Convert Christian Resource Info sheet (AM/FM radio-dial call #'s, phone #' & contact inf. of local Christian radio & TV stations, Christian bookstores, Christian singles papers, magazines, events etc. (Send us a S.A.S.E. for a sample.)

5. Assign one member to help head up (or oversee) filling out the one-page per New Convert follow-up lamb-Care sheet.

6. Assign a Task Force Member to oversee recruiting (& coordinating) New Convert meals: joining new converts with Church members: aiming at similar age, life-stage, etc.) to have a meal (or several) with the New Convert (invite them over to their home, or out with them).. as well as to church meals and special events, etc.;

7. Assign a Task Force member to order Jesus Videos & make sure every new (& past year's convert) receives one.

8. Assign one Task Force member... to be in charge of "Snack Packs": (ordering materials, assembling & mailing weekly "snack-packs". I encourage churches to send all new converts packs their first 6 weeks!

9. As you, (or other as the Sr. Pastor), see things that need "done" or "begun" (researched, etc) in Convert Care, your Convert Task Force is there to serve (the church, their Lord, and His wonderful, vulnerable newborn lambs.

SHORT TERM:
"Convert-Care Task-Force" Goals

A) Research what other 'growing' churches in your area are doing that is commendable & reproducible in Convert-Care. ID actions & resources (videos, books, tape series, etc.)to buy for a Convert Lending Library.

B) Research your converts themselves that "stuck" with the church. Ask and discover the reasons why?

C) Research those converts who didn't stick with the church. Ask & find out "Why not" (if they're willing to share that information either by phone (or perhaps by an anonymous postage-prepaid mail-back survey)

Who should... (and shouldn't)...
be on the church "Convert-Care Task-Force?:

1. The Pastor is the head, but should N-O-T be expected to attend every meeting beyond for 1st 3 - 6 months.

2. At least one Convert Task Force member should be a staff member.

3. At least one should be a Board Member with a passion & heart for Convert Care Improvement, and a heart... and mind... (and time)... for the details that involvement will bring with it.

4. At least one should be a lady, Women's Ministry head, Pastor's wife or lady chosen for a heart for "lambs."

5. A Task Force member needs responsibility to write up the 'minutes'(often the Church secretary helps here).

6. Other posts include: Snack Pack Coordinator, Meal Team Coordinator, Materials re-orderer & coordinator, Bible-study Team coordinator, Transportation & misc. needs Coordinator, etc.

Further Thoughts on
the Convert-Care Task Force:

1) **Serve how long?** It does not need to be a "life sentence" for multiple years. Perhaps ask for a 1 year "renewable" (and decline-able) commitment.

2) **Meet how often?** Meet monthly for at least the start-up first 3 or 4 months, to get "launch-momentum" going! "Who is it that's responsible for

the care of a newborn? The baby itself, or the parents? The initial meetings will help break "inertia", get start up momentum going, to help focus the energy, heart, love and resources of the e-n-t-i-r-e church... specifically on converts!

3) Please write down & share with me your process & discoveries in forming your church's Convert-Care
Task Force... and Convert-Care Team.

4) A Convert Care Task Force...start-up booklet with more details, tips, errors to avoid, (etc.) is automatically sent to all National JGM Lamb-Care Network monthly missions partner pastors and churches

What's the Difference between... your Convert Care "T-E-A-M... and the pastor-appointed... Convert-Care "T-A-S-K F-O-R-C-E!"

The Convert Task-Force is 'Pastor-chosen' and appointed, especially for leadership, influence, administrative skills, spiritual & relational maturity levels...& proven team-building ability and track-record.

The Convert "C-A-R-E-T-E-A-M" is Different:

Unlike the Convert Care "Task Force", ...anyone can be on the Convert Care Team. The Care Team is a place that anyone walking with the Lord in a godly, loving way, can serve where their talents (as well as inabilities or limitations), will not negatively influence the entire operation... or the newborn lamb itself.

Example: The "pastor-chosen "Task Force" person in charge of the "New-Convert Sponsor" Training Program... would be on the Task Force. Many, many others (the actual Convert Sponsors themselves) would... be on the Care T-e-a-m as members of the Convert-Care Sponsor t-e-a-m. (NOT the Task Force!)

A crucial difference that must be respected... and treated accordingly:

The differences between the Task Force choices, and the Team Member opportunities, are crucial! These must be respected, recognized and rewarded, as well as treated with different levels of confidentiality and responsibility! It's better to be slower appointing someone to the Task Force, than regretting it down the line. Anyone immature enough to take offense NOT being chosen for the Task Force isn't Task Force material.

More materials on this are automatically provided to all Lamb-care Network, JGM monthly-missions partners in a Implementation Workbook & partners-only on-line materials at our: FeedmyLambsnetwork.Org web site.

Chapter 33
"LOCAL-AREA NEW-CONVERT RESOURCE SHEET"

A "New-Convert Resource Sheet"
(An 8 1/2 x 11 sheet & laminated wallet-size card)
is a simple, practical, universally applicable idea
e-v-e-r-y church can benefit from.

Ask any Senior Pastor, staff member, or church leader to identify local Christian radio stations. They usually, immediately know a few... and a good part of the overall, local Christian Media resource picture.

Ask a brand New Convert the same question...
and you will receive a blank stare...
and silent answer!

In my frequent cross-country travels, I'm often can't find a Christian radio station on the hotel rooms' AM/FM radio. Theoretically, I know there are probably several on both AM & FM! When I ask my local Christian hosts, they tell me there are 4 or 5 at least... and rattle off the call letters & radio-dial frequencies! (**as if everyone knew them by heart!).

A wallet-size version of this... if also laminated...
will last a long while... &... really help...
"feed your new lambs"

What Christian Resources (such as Christian radio)...
are instantly available in your local Christian community...
to minister to all new believers?

Every believer reading this can instantly see, a-n-y church can easily write down on paper their local Christian radio stations, local Christian TV stations, plus assorted other information of help to a new believer.

Also keep copies of these local resource sheets (& identical, twin wallet-size cards) with your New Convert packets at the altar. We should give this information at the moment of the "new birth". Let them benefit from tuning in their car radio, right away, Day One, ...on their way home from church... that very day! (These cards are also useful as evangelism handouts as well!).

How much better this is, than expecting them to stumble upon these "refueling" stations by chance.

What toll-free national ministry 1-800 phone #'s are there to benefit a New Believer?

How about the established, national number for new believers: 1-800 NEEDHIM, or Focus on the Family at (1-800-A-FAMILY); Dennis Rainey (Family Life Today Ministry's) at 1-800-FL-TODAY; Cloud, Townsend & Steve Arterburn (Minerth-Meyer) 1-800-NEW-LIFE. Billy Graham Evangelistic Assoiciation 1-800-2GRAHAM, What others can you add to this list, especially of quality, established national radio & media ministries?

What web sites could be listed... or can your church create and provide:

Start with your church's own web-site. What if there were a special page of resources and daily hope (interactive Bible study, place for questions, chat-box) for converts? Your Convert-Care Task Force folks (who are "web-footed" & proficient) can do this easily. How about Christianbook.com, the Christian Book Distributors 24-hour web site listing more Christian items for sale than any other site. (Christianbook.com. or 1-800-Christian) Or Christian Research Institutes www.equip.org. There are countless, specialized web sites dealing with micro-"targeted" interest, gender, life-stage areas, life-controlling problems, etc. This paragraph is mere sketch of what you & your church can provide & "feed" your "lambs" with on (& off) the Internet.

Portions from a sample Placerville (Sacramento) area "New Christian" Resource/Contact sheet:

(Following is a sample introductory paragraph before Resource listings):

Dearest new believer:

We are so excited FOR YOU (as your friends & new church family) about your recent decision to become a follower of our wonderful Lord Jesus Christ. This will become your life's richest relationship! Walking with and growing spiritually in Jesus daily (in your Christian experience) is life's highest privilege & joy!

Your salvation is now y-o-u-r personal relationship with God through... and with God's Son, Jesus Christ!

As you learn to love, know & trust Jesus, this loving, vital relationship will deepen & grow! You will begin to see Jesus more & more in His people. Jesus loves y-o-u- just as you are, so very, very much!

For you, the greatest & most satisfying adventure in life has only just begun! God has many wonderful surprises for you: many miracles just up ahead with your name on them!

In I Corinthians 2:9 God promises y-o-u: "Eye has not seen, nor ear heard, nor has ANY HEART imagined the w-o-n-d-e-r-f-u-l things God has prepared for those who love Him!"

Below are a few resources to help feed & build-up your spirit and your faith!

1) Local Area Christian radio stations (with their contact inf., favorite shows & days & times you recommend. (Enclose a copy of the station's weekly programming sheet, plus web-site info in your New Convert "Welcome to The Family" packets!)

2) Local area (& cable accessible) Christian TV: contact Info. for local & available national media.

3) Local Christian Bookstores & regional Christian publications, such as Christian Yellow Pages, etc.

4) Local area meetings specific to gender, life-stage or life-controlling problems, hobbies, etc.

5) Web sites and contact inf. for proven, strong national Christian media ministries: such as Christian Research Institute, Women's Ministries, like Christian Women for America, national Women's Aglow, Christian Business Men's Committee, Gideons & others.

Chapter 34
"IMPROVING Y-O-U-R CHANGE-AGENT SKILLS"

A "leader-of-change" must himself be ever 'morphing" and working at personal change, (as well as working with institutional and methodological changes) around him. Becoming a better "Change-Agent" (as a leader is where the "rubber meets the road". Successfully leading...and personally "modeling change", "separates the men from the boys".

John Maxwell's says: "he that thinketh he leadeth... & no one followeth... only taketh a walketh." Mega-church leader Pastor Tommy Barnett, First Assembly Phoenix, puts it so well in this 'silver-bullet' saying of his: "Motivation without implementation... produces frustration."

Bringing The Church Board "on Board" F-I-R-S-T!

Pastors must make sure the church board is ..."on board" ...so we don't go "overboard" alone. We must consciously desire, work at, and make sure our church board is eagerly going through these lamb-care changes (and improvement steps) with the pastor as leader!

Change-Management and Leading "Change"

A) #1 is Prayer, P-r-a-y-e-r & more PRAYER! In real estate the saying is: "Location, location, location!" Prayer alone is God's anaesthetic (& fuel) for the Holy Spirit's "heart-change" & improvement "surgery."

B) Work from the foundation that: Relationship... Produces... Commitment... but: ...commitment does N-O-T necessarily produce relationship! Deepen the relationships and it will naturally produce commitment. Change involves risk. Risk requires Trust. Trust requires faith and relationship.

C) Spell the word "change" with an "I" for Improvement.

D) Re-cast The Vision Often! "Where there is no vision, the people (& "follower-ship") perish" (Prov.29:18). As the leader, the Sr. Pastor is uniquely responsible to be the "Vision-Caster". Pastor Cho puts it so eloquently: "Dreams & visions are the language of the Holy Spirit."(Joel 2:28)

E) Work on developing your Leadership skills & qualities as a true "change-agent" leader: Transparency (Let people see under the surface) Team Building Vision casting Vulnerability: (Share your fears) Personal areas for improvement Innovativity

F) "Find Clyde": Influence the "influencers" & others will follow! Maxwell says: "Leadership is Influence!"

Chapter 35
"GAINING CHURCH-BOARD AND CHURCH-WIDE INVOLVEMENT"

Discipling Y-O-U-R Board:

We have previously well-established that: "Life-change takes place in Relationships, not in isolation." The following idea is applicable for every church and every pastor reading this, both at home and abroad.

Remember how John Maxwell pre-scheduled a weekly breakfast with one church board member, on a rotating basis. Maxwell made it clear to his board, that just as Jesus chose 12 to be w-i-t-h Him, John had chosen his church board, to be w-i-t-h him... and they with him... as well.

Often board decisions require a step of faith: a step of commitment and trust. "Food equals relationship", ...and "relationship produces commitment". This weekly "relational technology" proved to be a tremendous, bonding, commitment producing habit and disciple-making tool!

> **Following is a sample letter to a "church board" to break ground for better Lamb-Care and a Convert-Care Task Force.**

Getting Church-wide Involvement and Agreement

B1) Go slowly, prayerfully and carefully.

B2) Let the Lord's Holy Spirit change hearts, from the "inside out!" (Jn 15:5)

B3) Lead the way personally in openness, humility and always love.

B4) Use sermon "anecdotes" on "change" (and past resistance)... to help current resistance crumble.

B5) Recognize "early" adapters (as well as "middle", "late" and "never" adapter.").

B6) Seek to let the history & tradition of the church work "with" you

B7) Research, locate and "dig out" past resistance issues, especially former resistance by key board member's to past issues, that they will now openly share about. They may be willing to share this with the congregation to help "win over" the church to the new "improvements" requiring some "change." This can be done either (or both) in written, audio, video, or live Sunday AM formats!

**If they will share how they moved from being adversaries of a former change, to acceptance of the former "change", this will greatly help to disarm (and win over) "change-opponents."

"DEAR CHURCH BOARD": A SAMPLE LETTER

*(below is a sample letter to the church board to
help break ground for better Convert Care
...and establishing a Convert-Care Task Force)*

(Pastors: Feel free to change & personalize the following letter as being directly from you to your church board (or from you as a board member to your pastor, to others, etc.)

Memo: To the Church Board & Deacons
Subject: Improved Convert-Care at Our Church!

Dear valued Church Board member:

This letter is sent as an encouragement to help your church model & our Lord's heart for better Convert-Care in His church. Other churches will see your innovative, successful changes and will change for the better as well!

As board members, I salute your leadership & sacrificial efforts assisting your pastor, staff & congregation, in growing God's Church & Kingdom there. My prayer is that you will make this letter a matter of prayer, and action.

In John 21:15, in His miraculous post resurrection, seaside appearance in Galilee, our Lord Jesus asked Peter: "Peter do you love Me? " Peter replied: "Yes". Jesus then replied: "Peter... If you love Me, feed My _____".

Right here most pastors, boards & believers wrongly answer with the word "Sheep." But here Jesus does n-o-t say sheep.

Instead, Jesus first aid: "if you love Me, feed My l-a-m-b-s!"

The Greek word for lambs here (Jn.21:15) is "a r n i a ". It's different from the word sheep ("Probata") used in verses 21:16&17. Jesus did say: "feed My sheep" twice.

However, f-i-r-s-t Jesus said: "Feed My lambs."

Theirs is great significance here that Jesus said 1st: "Feed My lambs!" Jesus puts the lambs first... intentionally!

Why did... Jesus put the feeding of the lambs f-i-r-s-t?

Why feed & nurture the lambs 1st b-e-f-o-r-e feeding the rest of the flock: before feeding the sheep?

The majority of a flock are sheep, not lambs. Why not care for the majority first?

Jesus knows... that to wipe out a flock, a predator does not have to attack the shepherd, sheep dog, or big daddy ram! All a predator need do is to destroy, one-by-one... the defenseless, baby lambs!

Jesus knew: The grown sheep are the "N-O-W" of the flock...
...but the lambs are the "future" of the flock.
...and a flock without lambs ...is a flock w-i-t-h-o-u-t a future!

Church Growth and Church Health experts say that the last 20 years, USA evangelical churches have not grown in number nor influence. No growth... despite millions of annual, reported conversions and salvations!

As A Board Member, I ask you to consider things... to make a major difference!

Please support your pastor in the changes he may want to implement in this better Convert Care regard.

1) Please be open to and read whatever books (& other literature) he may ask the board to read.

2) Please help him create (& use) a Convert-Care Task Force at y-o-u-r church, if he asks.

3) Please help your Pastor change the church budget to have many more specific 'line items'. approved for converts. Babies are not just miraculous and a lot of work. Babies are also expensive!

When ministers , by the roomful, are asked: "If babies are expensive... then what is in most church budgets for Convert Care?..."Z-e-r-o" is the most common reply!

Jesus said: "Where your treasure is, there your heart will be also."
(Matthew 6:21)

Since Jesus put the lambs first, we also need to obey Him and do that as well. Someday there will be a Great Commission Audit.

Someday we all hope to hear our Lord Jesus Christ say: "Well done, good & faithful servant. You have been faithful over the few. I will make you master over much. Enter the joy of your Lord." (Mt.25:21)

Thank y-o-u for taking time to read this. Thanks for your listening heart & Kingdom-attention to this request. Thanks, for your willingness to do whatever our Lord Jesus....leads you (and the church) to do in prioritizing His John 21:15 heartbeat when He said: "If you...really...love Me, Feed MY lambs!" f-i-r-s-t!

Devotedly His and yours... in Jesus' heartbeat... and John 21:15 priority,

Chapter 36
"24 UNIQUE... AND CREATIVE... 'LAMB-CARE' IDEAS"

 Few more creative Lamb-care ideas.

A1) Day One: New Convert Friendship-Meal "Dining Teams" linked to each convert for their 1st first 4 Sundays! Because "Food = Relationship", eating a meal with a New Convert (just by the establishing of a relationship).... is helping to disciple them.

A2) Day One: "Happy Re-birthday Packs" (of gifts at the altar.... for New Converts)

A3) Day One: "New-Birth Certificate" handed-out with a 8x11 Frame ($2@ at Walmart) for each New Convert, signed by the pastor

A4) Day One: Take a Polaroid (or digital) photo of each New Convert for pastor, staff & prayer team to pray for.

A5) Day One: A "Jesus Video" as a gift for every new believer at the church (1-800-29JESUS)(only $5 @) *Use the "Jesus Video for Children", as gift for all your 'children's age' converts as well.

A6) Day One:: Audio-Tape copy of same Service at which they got saved (especially Sunday AM services) A powerful gift because it is that very service God used to speak into their heart and save them!

B1) Week One: take them for a "Free Gift" visit to the Local Christian Bookstore, to get a free, "paid" Gospel music CD (or audio tape) of their choice, paid for by their church family .

B2) Week One: F-r-e-e monthly national Christian ministry-magazines: Call national ministries that are gender, Life-stage (age or interest-area specific and relevant to the convert). Ask them to send their monthly ministry mailings to that convert. Example: For a newly saved married couple, contact: Focus On the Family, Family Life Today (Dennis Rainey), Billy Graham's ministry (1-800-2GRAHAM), Norman Wright's Ministry: Marriage Keepers, Promise Keepers, Women of Faith. Ask each to send t-h-e-m their free monthly, ministry magazine.

B3) Week One: Create (& keep an up-dated) prayer list of recent Converts in the Church lobby: Put a sign above these, asking church members to take one & pray for new members of the church family (& God's Kingdom): to invite them for a meal...and to "family" them the way they would want to be "family'd".

B4) Week One: Assign a "Praying Grandma" to each New Convert with a Photo: Tell each new convert that the photo you take of them, is going right onto a "praying grandma" (saint's) icebox door! *Also provide a picture of the praying grandma (for them to pray for & to put on their icebox) to know they are loved, & prayed for daily by a seasoned saint, who will be praying for him/her (the new "lamb") every day.

B5) Week One: Free "paid" monthly Christian magazine Subscription sign up & choice! Raise (budget) funds and allow each Convert to choose a paid-by-the-church subscription to a Christian magazine (one-year subscription) from an approved list given them.

B6) Keep an updated prayer list (updated every week) of all converts for the past year. Bring the list monthly to the Church Board meeting. Have the Church Board pray over it and use it, as well, to invite & get to know the converts. Combined with a church lobby prayer list, pray for all converts for at least one year.

C1) Month One: Six Weekly "Snack-Packs" sent to each new 'lamb" Packs of small materials & Gospel booklets, short, easy "baby food" for "lambs" to nibble for their 1st 6 weeks, mail different weekly packets!

C2) Month One: Create a photo-page of New Converts . Reduce convert photos to stamp-size with their names written below each. Now you can pray on one page (by face & name) for 30+ of your church's newest lambs. This greatly improves name-face recognition and "lamb" memory for all staff, board, Convert-Care Team, Sponsors & prayer team as well! (Whether color printer or black & white, both help)

C3) Month One: Church "Convert-Meal Team" Reimbursement Budget: Designate part of the church's Convert-Care budget, to reimburse "Friendship Convert-Care Meal-Team" members, who take a convert for a meal, (up to a $20 reimbursement, or some reasonable amount for your area & people). The Lamb-Care "meal team" shouldn't repeatedly bear the burden of buying the meal. The entire church family should share & bear that weight, responsibility & privilege of helping f-e-e-d Jesus' lambs!

C4) Month One: Ongoing Referral Department (& growing a Database) of local referrals & Resources for Specific areas & Life-controlling problems,etc.*Many more great ideas in the Lamb-Network Workbook

C5) Month One: Arrange & actualize a "Pick-up" ride, meal and visit to an Alpha Group (or local small group ministry cell meeting). Keep the purpose and "heart" of this...relationship: not knowledge!

C6) Month One: A New-Convert Lending Library, full of videos & tape series and new Christian materials

D1) 1st Quarter: Create a sheet (&audio or video) of 1 or 2 Line comments of now 1 year-old "lambs!"

D2) 1st Quarter: Produce (edit & regularly update) a composite testimony video of your church's solid believers made of t-h-e-i-r 60-90 second individual "When I was a lamb" flash-back testimonies. "When I was a lamb", somebody really blessed me by ...i.e:

For a sample of the "When I was a Lamb" lamb-care Testimonials Video, send $25 to JGM Ministries.

"The church sent me the nicest Bible with my name engraved in gold letters on it. Or.. "I remember when the church helped me move out of my apartment. The day was pouring rain. Nobody else would help me." Or, perhaps a lady saying the Pastor and his wife unexpectedly sent her flowers, just to say how much the Lord loved & thought of her & how much they loved her as well.

*For a sample of the "When I was a Lamb" lamb-care Testimonial Video, send $25 to JGM Ministries.

E1) End of Year One: 1st Year Birthday Party & testimony Sun. AM in the pulpit. (or on video, or slides!)

E2) End of Year One: Video Testimony of New Converts (other former New Converts) reviewing & thanking the entire church for their 1st year, And for being so wonderfully "family"-ed by the church.

F1) During the 1st year (& ongoing): Compile a file-cabinet on different areas & common questions (& Answers) asked by New Converts at y-o-u-r church. Create (& compile) a file of areas they ask for help in, with an up-dated referral list. Also put on-line on church's web site (or special site just for 'lambs.')

F2) Do create a New-Convert Web Page: everything from humor, book reviews, testimonies, to a chat room etc.

Share your great ideas! Please mail them (or e-mail)to:
FeedMyLambsnetwork.org or jg@Gainsbrugh.org

Chapter 37
"IMPLEMENTATION TIPS TO REMEMBER"
(& mistakes to avoid)
Implementation Introductories:

More than any other single major start–up mistake to avoid is:

"Ready! Fire! Aim!"

Avoid the 'READY! FIRE! AIM!' Syndrome:

It is better to pray first, pray early... and often... than to "run people over with the ambulance..." then have to rush them to the Hospital or to a Doctor. We don't want the operation to be a success, but the "patient" die! There's the proverbial story in a Charlie Brown Peanuts cartoon strip. He fires a bullet into the wall, then draws circles around the bullet hole. When he's done, he proudly proclaims: "Bulls-eye!"

Pray first! Allow the Lord to sequence your implementation process.. with His perfect, "Ready!... A-I-M!...F-I-R-E!... rather than the rushed, haphazard "Ready! Fire! Aim!"... sequence!"

The Process of Implementation is:
Prayer!... More Prayer... and then... Sequencing!

A) Create an ongoing 'New-Convert Care Task Force... within the next 30 days!

B) Actualizing new concepts, ideas & strategies from "The Feed My Lambs" seminar will necessitate becoming a JGM Lamb-Care Network partner, acquiring the tapes (CDs, videos & training manuals) and other ongoing support materials to see your church excellently implement! this and become a "World-Class Lambery"

C) Why not order 10 or 20 copies of "The Lamb's Book" to get your board & leaders off to a great start!

D) Hold an "Administrative Party": You will need to identify God's people with spiritual maturity, love, Administrative giftings and the "planning muscle" first, to help plan out the Implementation process & path... of becoming a "world class lamb-ery". Do this one-by-one, chosen by Pastor & staff.

E) To Change our actions in Convert-Care... we must first change our thinking!

F) To change programs, we must 1st change values. This will be a slow, steady process!

G) Cast the Vision first (& repeatedly) in different creative ways. Pray, ask & let the Holy Spirit implant a new vision first deep into the hearts of your staff, board & elders: only then to committed, core leadership. *Finally, move concentrically outward to the entire congregation!*

H) Set "S.M.A.R.T" Goals for your improved Convert Care. Be willing to adjust, monitor & change them!

Specific **M**easurable **A**ttainable **R**e-viseable **T**ime-defined

I) Incrementalize: Realize that many, sequential, slow, small, "wins" will eventually carry the day at the church, and win over the majority... and eventually, the whole congregation!

J) Partner with Gainsbrugh Ministries & NAtional Lamb-Care Network. We're here to help your church become a world-class lambery! Monthly ministry partner churches receive all resources & ongoing help!

Evaluation Intros:

Here's a few one-line, silver-bullet rhyming, summaries of basic principles we've studied so far.

You can n-o-t Correct... what you first don't... Detect!

The only way to correct more... is to "detect" more!

The less you track, the more fall through the "Backdoor crack"

As we increase the A-ttention... we also increase R-etention!

We need to "re-train"... to "re-tain"!

The "Retention Dimension"...
requires (& deserves) our full attention!

Let's look at a few final points... to help implement what we have learned in this book:

A) Accept the "process" of improvement & the importance of "Process."

Jesus said: "The earth brings forth of itself: 1st the blade, then the ear, then the full kernel in the ear" (Mk.4:28)

B) Set some "time–lines" for evaluation, to see what progress has been made. Learn to enjoy gradual progress!

C) Have an "administrative/statistics-gifted" team gather the #'s, to get the cold, hard, true "mortality rate."

D) Jesus said: "Blessed are you, if you know these things... if you DO them": (John 13:17)

E) Willow Creek has a Ministry Management Team "over" every ministry...
   a. To help them achieve their goals (the goals each ministry itself had set).
   b. To ask the hard questions.
F) Have your Convert Care Task Force report to a management Team
G) Get the Information coming to leadership, in practical, objective and ongoing ways.
H) Set up "focus groups:" ...targeted to listen to both converts that stuck...and converts that didn't!
I) "Kaisan": is a management principle of daily seeking even the smallest amount of improvement... in one area.
J) Keep Track of the Numbers. Don't tolerate the "Paralysis of Non-Analysis!":

The only way the diligent Luke 15 shepherd with the 100 sheep (missing one) could have had any idea of who was missing, was to be "spiritual enough to "count"! Be prepared for critics to say that the new systems are "non-spiritual," showing lack of faith, prayer, or "t-r-u-e spirituality!"

These same critics would have criticized Jesus when He systematically, told His disciples to:

"Make the people sit down in groups of 50's and 100's".
(Mark 6:39,40)

K) Remember, the "cold", ('negative') information... feeds the improvement curve. The "negative" information tells us where we have the greatest need (and potential)...for immediate improvement. Admit, accept and correct your BLIND SPOTS & the weakest areas in your Convert Care process.

As you do, continued improvement... and World-Class Lamb-Care excellence... will be yours!

Chapter 38
"100+ 'SNACK PACK' CONVERT GIFT-LIST HERE"

Different Types of Convert-Gift Materials listed include (…but are not limited to): Bibles, Bible Catalogues, Books(100+ pages), Booklets & Mini-Books (15-100 pages), Catalogs, Curriculum, Devotionals, Greeting Cards (see Misc.), Miscellaneous, (artwork, cards, bumper stickers, T-shirts, etc), Tracts, and Videos, For the largest Christian materials site on the Internet, go to Christian Book Distributors: www.christianbook.com or 1-800-Christian (24 hours). Give them a topic and they'll supply you with resources.

BIBLES:
Of course the ultimate gift for any new believer, is a new Bible &/or New Testament. There are now so many scores of life-stage, gender-specific, specially-targeted Bibles. Many have built in theme-targeted devotionals, Bible Studies, concordance & commentary features added. Contact your local Christian Bookstore & major Bible distributors, as well as christianbook.com to see the amazing, ever growing variety of differentiated, targeted Bibles: from Seniors to toddlers, Childrens' Bibles, cartoon-illustrated Bibles, Women of Faith Bible's, expectant moms, wives & widow's Bibles, men as husbands, dads', widowers, Promise Keepers or as singles (and more). There are Jewish New Testaments & Bibles, 12 step & Counseling Bibles, Bibles for seekers & New Believers, Teen & Pre-teen Bibles, Military, etc. etc.

"Seekers Bible", from Tyndale Press, Wheaton, Illinois (through any Christian bookstore)

"Life Recovery Bible:" (Based on the Christian 12 Steps) (Living Bible version), Tyndale House, Wheaton, Il. 60189

BOOKS:
"Basic Christianity" "an introduction to personal faith" (paperback book, 142 pages) by John R. W. Stott, Inter-Varsity Press, PO Box 1400, Downers Grove, IL 60515

"Basics for Believers" Foundational Truths to Guide Your Life (book: 183 pages) by William L. Thrasher, Jr., Tyndale House Publishers, Inc., Wheaton, Illinois 60189.

"The Bible Promise Book: One Thousand Promises from God's Word" (Book. 171 pages) Excerpts from New International Version of the Bible. Handy collected Bible references for various categories and topics, i.e., faith, death, gossip, etc. $4.95. Pub.: Barbour Publishing, PO Box 719, Ulrichsville, Ohio 44683 ISBN 1-55748-235-7

"Building Your Self-Image (216 page, paperback book, 4x7"), by Josh McDowell, world famous author & veteran college campus debater. Author of "Evidence That Demands a Verdict". Excellent new believer scriptural & personal-example material, to build up any believer, especially a new "lamb" ISBN # 0- 8423-1395-8

"Confessions of a Contemporary Jew" (Paperback book, 142 pages) by Zola Levitt. Tyndale House, Wheaton, IL.60187.

Counseling Books targeted to specific life-experiences, crises, and problem areas: there are 1,000's of topically-targeted books, sub-categorized in the Christian Book Stores, under every area of life: Marriage, parenting, children, youth, teens, etc. addictions, interests, hobbies, life-controlling problems, etc.

"Disciplemakers Handbook": helping people grow in Christ, (Paperback book, 204 pages) by Alice Fryling, InterVarsity Press, Box 1400, Downers Grove, IL 60515

"Disciples are Made-not born" (Paperback,160 pg.) by Walter Henrichsen, Victor Books, Box 1825, Wheaton, IL. 60187

"Experiencing God" - Knowing and Doing The Will of God (Book, Workbook (8x11") full curriculum) by Henry T. Blackaby & Claude V. King, LifeWay Press, 127 Ninth Ave., North Nashville, TN 37234, (800)-458-2772.

"A Faith To Grow On: Important Things You Should Know, ... Now that You Believe" (book,191 pages, full color) by John McArthur, Published by Tommy Nelson (Thomas Nelson childrens' division) Nashville, TN. www.tommynelson.com ISBN 0-8499-7512-3

"From Milk to Meat: A Guide to Christian Growth": (94 pages, 5"x8" book), by John Laughrey, Leathers Publishing, 4500 College Blvd., Leawood, KS. 1-888-888-7696

"Getting a Grip on the Basics: Building a Firm Foundation for the Victorious Christian Life" (book 8 1/2 x 11, 123 pages) by Pastor Jeff & Beth Jones. Excellent, large-print workbook for New Converts. Harrison House, Box 35055 Tulsa, OK. 74153. ISBN 0-89274-62 or contact Kalamazoo Valley Family Church, Kalamazoo, Mich. Phone: 616-324-5599. Web: www.kvfc.org Email: kvfc@kvfc.org Address: 995 Romence Road, Portage, MI 49024.

"The Life You Always Wanted", by John Ortberg (Available through any Christian Bookstore)

"The Life Worth Living" (Here's How It Can Happen To You) by G. Raymond Carlson, Radiant Books, Gospel Publishing House, Springfield, MO 65802

"Light for the Darkened Heart" (Book 5x81/2", 92 pages) by Steve Eutsler, Christian solutions for (and ministry to) homosexuals. From: Teen Challenge Int'l, Box 1015, Springfield, MO 65801(color cover & a teacher's guide).

"New Born" (mini-book 3x5",80 pages) by Pastor Jack Hayford, Living Way Ministries, 14820 Sherman Way, Van Nuys, Ca. 1-800-776-8180 www.LivingWay.org

"New Christian's Handbook-Everything New Believers Need to Know" (Book 5" x 8") (301 pages) by Max Anders; "discover new ways to grow in Christian faith". Thomas Nelson Publishers, Nashville, Tennessee

"New Covenant Prophecy Edition"(book) International Bible Society. 489 pages. Selections from New Testament designed to reach saved/searching Jews. 1820 Jet Stream Dr. Colorado Springs. CO 80921-3696.

"Now That I Believe" (paperback book, 112 pages) by Robert A. Cook, Moody Press, Chicago, IL.

"The Purpose Driven Life", by Pastor Rick Warren (300 pages) from Zondervan Publishing, 31 excellent devotional teachings, good for new believers and the most seasoned believers as well.

"A Shepherd Looks at PSALM 23" (book 5" x 8", 142 pages) by Phillip Keller. Lively, classic devotional on Psalm 23, one of the best-loved Bible passages, published by Zondervan Publishing, Grand Rapids, MI 49506.

Search for Significance, by Robert S. McGee, from Rapha Publications, Box 6580355, Houston, TX. 77258, ISBN #: 0-945276-01-X Counseling classic on seeing oneself as God sees you & as God's Word describes you.

"Touch-Points for Couples" (God's Answers for Your Daily Needs) (book, 3" x 5", 326 pages) Scripture quotations taken from Holy Bible, New Living Translation, published by Tyndale House Publishers, Inc., Wheaton, Illisnois.

"What Every Christian Should Know About Growing" Basic Steps to Discipleship.(Book, 5x8"168 pg) by Leroy Eims Covers basic concepts: prayer, intercession, Lordship of Christ. $1.95 Victor Books,1976, Wheaton, IL. 60187.

BOOKLETS & MINI-BOOKS:
"The Bible Incorporated: In Your Life, Job and Business". (book 3"x5", 305 pages.) Compiled and written by Michael Q. Pink. Hidden Mannah, Inc. Box 807 Mt. Juliet, TN. 37122. (615)754-0937. Extracts the wisdom & counsel of God and His Word (from Genesis to Revelation) on a wide variety of business & work related topics.

"The Book of Hope"(booklet, 5" x 8", 104 pages) 3 month devotional from Sunday School Curriculum. Published: Assemblies of God & Tyndale House Publishers. Wheaton III. ISSN I01904299. Order from God's Word for Today. 1445 Boonville Avenue. Springfield MO. 65802-1894

"Campus Crusade for Christ, Ten Basic Steps Toward Christian Maturity" "The Life & Teachings of Jesus" (booklet, 77 pages) by Bill Bright. Published by New Life Publications, 100 Sunport Lane, Orlando, FLA 32809.

"Devotions" (booklet, 5"x7") 3 month devotional. Standard Publishing Co., 8121 Hamilton Ave., Cincinatti, OH 45231.

"Encouraging New Christians" (Booklet, 3"x54", 29 pages) by Michael Griffiths. Topics based on Home daily Bible & International Sunday School lessons. Publisher: Inter Varsity Christian Flshp Press, Downers Grove IL 60515.

"Eternal Life Abundantly Yours: A Handbook for the Christian Life" (booklet, 3"x6" 32 pages), by Mark A. Hinman. Discipleship Dynamics, Box 127, San Bruno, CA 94066.

"Faith" (booklet, 3"x5") by Sarah Farascio, full color booklet of short poems of faith, beautiful pictures behind the poems, Salesian Missions, 2 Lefevres Lane, New Rochelle, NY, 10801

"The Gifts and Fruit of the Holy Spirit." (Booklet. 4"x10") Scripture based introduction to the Gifts of the Holy Spirit. Written by Dr. Stanley M. Horton. Published by the Assemblies of God Gospel Publishing House. 800-641-4310.

"God's Word For Today" (booklet, 4"x6"104 pages) Daily devotional month by month. Publisher: Radiant Life Press, Assemblies of God. $2.75per quarter. $12/year. 1445 N. Boonville Ave. Springfield, MO 65802-1894.

"The Great News". (booklet, 3"x2" 64 pages) The Gospel of John. Excerpts from the New International Version. Published by International Bible Society. 144 Tices Lane, East Brunswick NJ 08816.

"Growing in Christ". 5x8. Lessons on assurance of Salvation. 16 page Booklet/workbook published by NavPress. P.O. Box 35001, Colorado Springs, Colorado 80935.

"Growing In Christ: A Thirteen Week Follow-up Course for New and Growing Christians". (booklet 5"x 8", 71 pages) Get started & keep going in your Christian walk with Life-changing Bible Study & Memory Materials. The Navigators: NavPress. Box 35001. Colorado Springs, CO. 80935. 71 pages. ISBN 0-89109-1571-2

"Growing in Christ: Lessons on Assurance", (booklet 5"x 8", 32 pages) Five Life-changing Bible Studies and Memory Verses For New Christians. Navpress Books, PO Box 35001, Colorado Springs, CO 80935. 1-800-366-7788.

"Growing In Christ: Lessons on Christian Living", (booklet 5" x 8", 45 pages) One of 5 life-changing Bible Studies & Memory Verses For New Christians. NavPress Books, Box 35001, Colorado Springs, CO80935 800-366-7788

"He Did This Just for You: What God Did to Win Your Heart." (booklet, 3x6" 64 pages) Max Lucado, Word Publishing.. Box 141000 Nashville, TN 37214. WWW. Wordpublishing.com. ISBN 0-8499-1683-6. $2.99.

"How to Live Forever"(booklet,27 pg./4"x5").By Greg Laurie.Tyndale Publishing www.tyndale.com. ISBN 0-8423-3344-

"Men of Integrity: Your daily guide to the Bible and prayer". (booklet 4"x6", 60 pages) Monthly Devotionals by Promise Keepers. Covers two months. 1-800-756-8509.

"Living In Christ & Beginning your Walk".(4 x 6 booklet, 43 pages). 30 day devotional from Billy Graham Evangelistic Association, P.O. Box 779, Minneapolis, Minnesota 55440-0779. (1-800-2GRAHAM)

"Our Daily Bread". (5"x4"). Devotionals from Genesis to Revelation in one year. Available from Radio Bible Class Ministries, Grand Rapids, MI 49555-0001. www.gospelcom.net/rbc

"The Power of Kindness" (booklet 3"x5", 32 pages) by HM Tippet. A teaching on kindness for the least of these and pity for the less fortunate. Publisher: Pacific Press Publishing Association, Boise, Idaho.(1955) ISBN 0-8163-0076-3.

"Recovery: A Guide for Body and Spirit". (booklet 5'x8", 35 pages) Editor Rick Griepp. Published by General Council of Assemblies of God. Sold only in units of 50. Gospel Pub. House call: (1-800-641 4310). Item #739503.

"Start Up Studies: Discipleship for the New Believer. (booklet 5"x8", 21 pages) by James Hall. 6 devotional Bible lessons for new believers. James Hall. Printed by Decade of Discipling 1411 East `Stoneridge, Springfield, MO 65803. Phone (417)833-9052. E-mail JHHalls@aol.com. and other resources.

"Tell Them I Love Them: Receiving a Revelation of God's Love for You".(minibook 3"x 6", 64 pages) by Joyce Meyer. Sample Chapter titles: Am I good enough?, Love is Relationship, Tell them I Love Them, Harrison House. Joyce Meyer, Life in the Word, Inc. Box 655 Fenton, MO 63026 (314)349-0303 or Harrison House

"Ten First Steps for the New Christian" (booklet, 3"x11, 30 pages) by Woodrow Kroll, glossy full-cover cover, Back to the Bible Ministries. Box 82808, Lincoln, NE. 68501.

"What Must I Do To Be Saved? How may I know I am Saved? (booklet 4"x6", 95 pages) Chaplain Ray and Leola. International Prison Ministry. Acclaimed Books. PO Box 180399. Dallas, TX. 75218-0399. Www.ipm.org.

"Victory & Success are Yours". (booklet, 4x6" 31 pages) by Jerry Savelle. Thoughts on success and winning, in a Christian frame. Box 748. Crowley, TX. 76036. Or call (817)297-3155

CASSETTE TAPES:
"Funniest Jokes And Stories" (cassette tape) by Pastor Craig Andrus, Christian Heights AG, 13711 Joshua Way, Sonora, CA 95370 (209)532-7305; Fax (209) 532-4374.

Pastor David Jeremiah's annual funniest Stories Cassette series, from Pastor David Jeremiah, Shadow Mountain Community Church, El Cajon (San Diego)CA www.Turningpoint.org (done annually the last 8 years & available)

CATALOGS:
Christian Book Distributors Catalogue (& online website). Largest distributor of Christian Materials in the USA. Send, call or e-mail for their monthly free catalogue of Christian Materials. 1-800-Christian

Gospel Publishing House. Books, Bibles & Gifts for new members converts & visitors. 1445 Boonville Ave., Springfield, MO 65802-1894

Group - Helping Church Leaders Change Lives Resource catalog. (Group's Mission: To Encourage Christian Growth in Children, Youth and Adults. 1-800-747-6060 ext. 1502. www.grouppublishing.com

International Bible Society Bible Catalog. For giving Bibles to new Christians and visitors. Catalogue available: Box 35700 Colorado Springs, CO 80935-3570. Or Call 1-800-524-1588.

Lifeway Church Resources "Providing Biblical Solutions that spiritually transform individuals and cultures." Customer Service Ctr, MSN 113, 127 Ninth Ave. North, Nashville, TN 37234 or call 1-800-376-1140, www.lifeway.com./email: customerservice@lifeway.com.

Good Sense Transformational Stewardship for Today's Church, Willow Creek Publishing. 800-570-9812, www.willowcreek.com.

Zondervan Church Source. Popular books, Bibles and CD-Roms available to churches for gifts to new converts & visitors. Contact www.zondervanChurchSource.com or call (1-800-727-3480).

CURRICULUM SPECIFICALLY FOR NEW BELIEVERS:
New Believer Concepts, Pastor Pancho Flores, Oak Park Assembly, 2073 Oak Park Blvd., Pleasant Hill, CA 94523 (925) 934-3056 (a 3 lesson preliminary new believer Bible study & other excellent materials

James River materials, Sr. Pastor John Lindell, 6100 North 18th Street, Springfield, Mo. 65721-0410 (417)581-5433

DEVOTIONALS:
Magazines: Evangelical Press Ascn.(804) 973-5941 (Trade Assoc. for Christian Periodicals) www.epassoc.org

MAGAZINES:

There are now countless Christian magazines that specialize in (& target) scores of various different areas and interests. A great gift idea for new converts is a pre-paid subscription that targets and profiles either their gender, life-stage interest area, sport or hobby, or life-controlling problem area.

National Ministries Monthly Mailings. Beyond this there are National Ministries Monthly Mailings, specializing in almost every life-gender, life-stage, interest & life-controlling problem area. For example: "Focus on the Family" sends a monthly full-color magazine full of interesting, helpful, family, marriage & children's life-area articles. Most larger ministries publish great monthly or quarterly magazines at no charge. Call their 800 toll-free lines & start the ministry's magazine coming to y-o-u-r new convert.`

Focus On the Family monthly magazine, plus over a dozen specialized magazines for: teens guys, teen girls, children, singles, grandparents, businessmen, doctors, etc.1-800-FAMILY/www.Family.org

"New Man" magazine (81/2 x11" 32 pages) Glossy full color m0agazine. Strang Publications. $3.95. available at www.newmanmagazine.com

"Honor Bound" (for Men) ("8 1/2" by 11" glossy magazine) published by Assemblies of God. 31 pages. Articles by Josh McDowell, Bob Pagett, etc. Available at web site honorbound.ag.org, or 1445 N. Boonville Avenue, Springfie1ld, MO 65802-1894. Or call (417)862-2781 ext. 4170

Pentecostal Evangel. 8 1/2 by 11 glossy magazine published by Assemblies of God. Subscribe at 1-800-641-4310. 1445 N. Boonville Avenue, Springfield, MO 65802

MISCELLANEOUS:

Artwork: Christian Artwork Center, web site. Catalog: Christian Book Distributors. From encyclopedias to various trade paperbacks for popular Christian titles. Available at Box 7000 Peabody, MA 01961-7000 or at www.christianbook.com

Alpha Course: Conferences: Fuller Theological Seminary Ten Week Alpha course introduces the Christian faith for non-churchgoers and those who have recently become Christians. Conferences in many major cities, from Chicago to Las Vegas. Call for details. 1-800-999-9578 or write at Lowell W. Berry Institute for Continuing Education in Ministry, Fuller Theological Seminary, 135 N. Oakland Ave, Pasadena, CA 91182

Christian Radio Programming & Brochure from y-o-u-r nearest local Christian station. 11x3 folded. KCBC 710 AM. Advertises quality Christian Radio for Central & Northern California. Includes schedule of programming, ministry and contact information. 19048 Cleveland Avenue. Oakdale, CA 95361 (209) 847-7700 Every Christian radio station has a available play-list of its programs. Excellent for any new convert's day-of- salvation gift-pack to help them plug in daily to worship, praise, & teaching ministries heard on Christian radio.

Greeting Cards: "Our Church Family Welcomes You." (poem inside and statement: we're blessed to have you!) Published by Dayspring Cards. $2.25 www.dayspring.com

Greeting Cards: "Welcome to the Family of God"!... to a living hope, to a daily peace & to a life of never-ending joys. Rejoicing in your new Life in Christ. Published by Dayspring Cards. $1.75. www.dayspring.com

Jewelry Jesus' Name and Christian theme (dove, cross, etc) rings, crosses, pendants, pins, etc. Commonly available at local Christian bookstores or nationally from Christianbook.com 1-800-Christian

Keychain: "What Would Jesus Do" initials Key Ring": (WWJD), red with silver clasps. 5" long, Available at local Christian bookstores.

Local Area New Christian Resource List: send a self-address stamped envelope to JGM ministries

"New Birth Cerfificate" 8X11, Call your local Christian Bookstore, and locate one, or create one on computer.

Stationery with Poem: "Footprints in the Sand", by Margaret Fishback Powers. Begins: "One night a man had a dream. He dreamed he was walking along the beach with the Lord. Available at local Christian Bookstores.

T-Shirts: many sizes and scores of styles from Christian T-shirts, also see www.christianbook.com or contact/visit your local Christian Book Store. Also contact national ministries (age & interest topic-targeted) for their T's & ideas.

Jesus Poster/Painting: "Jesus Laughing" (comes in 16x20 & other sizes, groups of 20 wallet sized cards of Jesus Laughing. T shirts S-XL. Ralph Kozak. 1-888-294-0674 (231)941-4880:10485 S. Mt. Josh Dr., Traverse City, MI.

"Jesus and The Lamb" Painting & Poster, awesome, sensitive line art drawing, by Kathryn Brown www.Jesusandthelamb.org

"100 Grand" Milk Chocolate French Candy Bar. Can be given in Hospitality baskets to visitors & gift packs to Converts.

MUSIC (PRAISE AND WORSHIP CD'S, TAPES, DVD'S, ETC.):

Intégrity Hosanna Music, Vineyard Worship, and CBD offers closeout and bulk purchase contemporary CD's frequently for $1 or $2 apiece. These make great gifts for new convert snack packs and for visitors. Contact them direct for prices, minimum quantity, details etc.

NEW BELIEVER GIFT-PACKS & SNACK-PACK SAMPLES:

"New Believers Gift Pack", from Pastor Greg Laurie, Harvest Crusades, in Southern California price $10 (-pack of several new believer items given out to thousands of new converts)

New Believers Materials" From Louis Palau Ministries.

New Believer Materials, from Billy Graham Crusades. 1-800-2-Graham

New Believer Snack Packs: Full samples of 6 weekly "snack packs", available for a love gift of $20 Pastor Kathy Dehring, c/o 1st Assembly, 1004 East 16th, Yankton, SD 57078 (605) 664-7567.

TRACTS:

American Tract Society, New York, New York .Write for samples and list of 100's of various, targeted tracts & mini-Gospel messages

"Minutes With God. How to Plan A Daily Quiet Time" 5x7 tract by Robert Foster. About how to begin daily devotions/quiet time with God. Published by NavPress. P.O. BOX 35001 Colorado Springs, CO. 80935.

"Are You Going to Heaven: Two Question Test Reveals Answer". (Tract, 3"6") by Francis Anfuso. Published by Glad Tidings, Christian Equippers International Box 16100, South Lake Tahoe, CA 95706 or call (916)542-1509. Write for catalog.

"Decisiones!" (in Spanish) (Tract, 4"x6") by American Bible Society. Published 1994.

"Despue's Lo Hare' in Spanish (tract, 4"x6") with comics. P.O. Box 164 Lebanon, OH 45036.

"The Funnel" (Tract 3x4") Story of a saved wild-teen alcoholic, now International street minister Denny Nissley. Christ in Action Ministries, Box 4200, Manassas, Virginia 20108. (703) 368-6286.

"High Times" (Tract, 3"x45") tract by Mike Long. Specifically for Street ministry about a drug addict who found Jesus & a better way to live with the Most High. Available through Gainsbrugh Ministries. Send a stamped S.A.S.E.

"Love Takes a Change of Heart" (2"x3" tract). Big red heart on cover, 3 page salvation tract with sinners prayer at end. Printed by Marshall Arts Press (510) 531-5702 3930 Maybelle Ave, Oakland, CA. 94619.

"My Commitment". 5x4 tract organized like a business survey to determine how to be sure you have eternal life. Billy Graham Evangelistic Association. Minneapolis, MN. ISBN 0-89066-295-9 1-800-2GRAHAM

"Now That I'm A Christian I Should Read the Bible". (Tract. 3x5"). 4 pg. Scripture and teaching related to a practice of reading God's Word. Gospel Publishing House:1445 Boonville Avenue, Springfield, MO 65802-1894.

"Now That I'm a Christian I should be a Witness." (Tract 3x5") . Information and teaching related to witnessing and evangelism for New Christians. Ordering info same as above.

VIDEOS:

"The Jesus Video", (84 minute full Life of Christ, professionally done, from Campus Crusade 1-800-29-Jesus, available in over 100 languages. "Jesus Video for Children" separate, designed for children, with children praying the salvation prayer at the end ($14.95)

"Shout to the Lord II": Darlene Zschech, world-renowned singer, author of worship masterpiece "Shout to the Lord", worship leader of Hillsong Music & Hillsong Christian Center, Australia. Also Alvin Slaughter & Ron Kenoly One hour of high energy praise & worship. Hosanna Music, 100 Cody Road, Mobile, AL 36695

Veggie-Tales Videos: Growing children's series of 12 (now more)! Kids love'em with a spiritual, moral Biblical message . Why not have an entire set or two for loan-out, specifically only for your new children's converts, Especially immediately following summer-time, annual Vacation Bible School programs and harvest of souls.

The Visual Bible "Gospel of Matthew": (& Book of Acts) Each a 4 VHS tape series. Entire Gospel of Matthew enacted out beautifully, from Matthew 1:1 to Mathew 28:20. Same with Acts. Reasonably priced., under $100 per series. Great lending out, visual faith-building scriptural/visual input www.visualbible.com

Misc. Gospel Concert videos: Your local Christian Bookstore has scores of recording artist's videos available, from super-alternative as Newsboys to Carman, to new & traditional Black Concert artists i.e. Alvin Slaughter or Kirk Franklin, to the older set's Gaither Homecoming videos. Great as gifts to Converts, but also as a lending library, specifically for your church's new believers to borrow & be blessed by.

Gospel films. Com has 100's of Christian videos available for age groups, topics, etc.

Idea of a video lending library just for New converts at your church. (Or possibly for churches in a given area.)

Chapter 39
"TRACKING: WE DON'T KNOW WHERE THEY ARE...
BUT... WE DO KNOW WHERE THEY ARE NOT!"

It amazes and shocks me, as I travel, to see the number of churches (of all sizes) that fail to "track" their people from Sunday to Sunday! Usually this lack of tracking... and the glaring need for it... is only identified as a "weakness", when growth has stopped! As Sunday AM attendance plateaus... (and decline develops), churches finally, slowly "a-w-a-k-e"... to their damaging "Backdoor" dynamics and preventable losses!

Jesus ever-amazing 1% "tracking" example in Luke 15

Jesus' own example of the diligent shepherd in Luke chapter 15 (& Matthew 18) shows our Lord is "a rewarder of those who diligently seek Him (Hebrews 11:6)".

He is also a rewarder of those who diligently t-r-a-c-k His precious sheep... & precious baby lambs!

*Scripture doesn't tell us he counted...
nor does it tell us: "he didn't!"*

There's no realistic way the diligent Luke 15 shepherd (with 100 sheep) could know only one sheep was missing, without counting! With a flock ever in motion... and scores to keep track of... he may even have needed some sub-shepherds, to count their sub-flocks. This in itself is one of the "open-secrets" of better, more precise tracking! Smaller groups are easier to track... and to lovingly keep track of.

An easy & effective way of tracking lambs is to keep a concurrent list of converts:

In only one church I've spoken at (out of over 500), have I seen a prayer list (in the church lobby) listing the church's very newest converts. Above it was an attractive sign/poster encouraging the church family to pray for ..and connect with... these newest members of God's Kingdom, recently birthed there.

Increase the attention (by intention) ...and you will increase the retention: This, once again, is a matter that the church's new (& developing) Convert Care Task Force and Convert-Care Team would have oversight of. The age-old adage goes: "Everybody's business is often nobody's business! Your Convert-Care Task Force will see to it that the lambs are loved... & fed f-i-r-s-t!

Everybody thought that... "somebody..."

Most of us have not only heard some version of the following, but sad to say, we have seen it acted out in too many church's Convert-Care.

"Everybody thought somebody would do what they all knew anybody could do! Sadly, nobody saw it get done. Everybody thought somebody else was doing it. Nobody wanted to interfere with somebody else's job. Eventually everybody found nobody did what anybody could. Everybody blamed somebody else, but nobody took responsibility for what needed to be done...
by someone ....else!"

Thank God Isaiah didn't say: "Here am I Lord, Send him!"
Rather, Isaiah properly said: "Here am I, Lord, ...send me!" Isaiah 6:8

Make a continually updated
"Convert List" a matter of prayer at monthly
Church Board meetings:

He is also a rewarder of those who diligently t-r-a-c-k His precious sheep... & precious baby lambs!

A great idea is listing a-l-l new converts (& the weekly updating that "lamb-list" for prayer and ongoing nurture)! Make the care of Jesus' lambs... at y-o-u-r church... an ongoing agenda item on the monthly Church Board agenda list!... and part of the monthly Board meeting itself.

This will require creating (& continually updating) week-by-week, month-by-month, year-round, a continually renewed list of the converts that God's blessed your church with!

Bringing the church's "lamb-care" up to a Church Board level responsibility (& matter of monthly oversight), is spreading "like a plague of health"... across the USA. More and more churches are wanting to take the "lamb-care" challenge as seriously as their Lord does! As the attention is increased, the retention dramatically and w-o-n-d-e-r-f-u-l-l-y increases.

One church using this strategy now has a list of each of its converts for the past 9 months. At the beginning of the year, they'd had 50 converts last year. None of the staff even knew these 50 converts' names, much less how they were doing, where they were, who was caring for them & if they were still in the church....in the Kingdom...or worst of all, had perished!

Good "tracking" questions
that need to be asked... and answered!

1) What is our church's retention & the loss factor of converts for this year? For last year?

2) What do we need to change, to be able to detect(& correct) a 10% or 20% loss factor ? (Luke 16:10)

3) Who will be responsible for creating a current list of New (& former converts) at our church?

4) Who will be responsible to our Sr. Pastor (& Church Board) for updating the list of converts ongoing?

5) What church that we know of has the best Convert-Care?

Why can't the answer be... our church...
...when we ask and answer this appropriate question?

6) What would the Lord Jesus Himself change about our church's entire Convert Care Systems, ...if He were really 1,000% in charge and could change anything (and everything) about it... that He desired to?

Chapter 40
"FOLLOW THROUGH & ONGOING EVALUATION"

The poet Carl Sandburg wrote a famous poem that stated: "The fog creeps in on little cat's feet, and then quietly slips back out to sea." It is that way with the Back Door dynamics in churches. Not just with Visitors, New, (Regular and Long-Term) Members... but especially with New Converts!

Newborn baby lambs most easily slip quietly, silently, and usually without a whimper, right through our fingers!

We must ask ourselves the hard questions like: what questions are we n-o-t asking?

Although People don't want to be "tracked"...
they do want to be "missed!"

"Well, Honey, four out of five is not bad!"

We've already told the story of the husband who returns from an afternoon outing with his five kids! His wife says: "Darling, We have five children. I only see four!" To this he replies: "Well, babe... Four out of five's not bad!"

"Four out of five..." is B-A-D!

Like explaining a joke for the fourth time, this above is the "punch line" that the American Church just does not seem to get! For most churches, keeping 80% (4 of 5) of their converts would be millennial, quantum improvement!

Most pastors are caught like deer in high-beam headlights, when asked the simple questions: "How are the new converts and new believers ...Jesus' lambs... doing at your church? How many converts did the church report last year? Who are they? Where are they? How are they doing? Who knows?"

The lights are on, but who's at home? You wouldn't believe the vague answers these questions get.

The "Fish Ladder" Analogy:

Using a word-picture of a "fish ladder" is beneficial here! When a dam is built into a river for flood control (or hydro-electric purposes), the river's fish habitat is totally disrupted! In rivers where the salmon annually "run" back upstream to spawn, construction of a sizeable dam obviously creates an impassable blockage!

Here the Department of Wildlife (or Fish and Games) often steps in and builds a "fish ladder." The "fish ladder" is constructed for o-n-e specific purpose. Its success is evaluated, not on its looks, nor its supposed intent, but o-n-l-y on its ability to accomplish that one solitary purpose!

The Fish Ladder must successfully help the "fish" get past the impasse... of the dam.

The ultimate criteria of the success of the "fish ladder"... is...?

The ultimate criteria of success for a "fish ladder" might be thought to be the "best thinking" that the wildlife engineers (with graduate level degrees) ...can come up with!

Adjustments must continually be made in planning, as to the number of and height, breadth, & length of the sequential steps in the fish ladder. The volume flow & speed of the cascading water, the materials used, height of the steps, resting pools, ...all must factor in... to help... the f-i-s-h climb!

The Fish themselves are the ultimate criteria & judge of the "fish ladder":

In all of these matters, the "fish" themselves are the ultimate criterion & judges of the "fish ladder". Does it work? Does it get the job done... or does it N-O-T get the job done!

One Superintendent in the Pacific Northwest, while I was on a district tour there, told me that healthy salmon in the wilds have been documented to jump (or "climb") up a 10, 12, even 15 feet gap up a waterfall!

An interesting point! The sicker the fish are, the smaller the gaps have to be, for the weaker the fish are, the lower a height distance they would be able to climb!

Each of our church's Convert-Care systems is a like a "fish ladder"!

In the matter of His lambs & their survival Our Lord Himself is a "sanctified pragmatist!"

We must ask (& continually re-ask): "Where are the gap... and linkages"?

In a parallel way, the lambs are the ultimate & o-n-l-y "success" judge of our Convert-Care strategies, methods (& evangelism methods)... as well.

The criteria to evaluate success or "failure" in our Convert-Care methodologies, assumptions, strategies and ministries, is not our theology... n-o-t the stated "intention" of our strategies... n-o-r even our written-on-paper, "lamb-care" mission statements.

It is not even the fact that a given strategy that may have had an impressive, past track-record of past success!

It makes no difference, who has whatever memories of how good these methods "used to" produce lasting fruit... long ago!

The ultimate criteria we must judge the above by,
is quite simply... and o-n-l-y... by Jesus' desire: that we bear
much fruit...fruit that remains!"

How much... of all we do... Is producing: "lasting fruit?" (John 15:16)
Which methods are producing mere statistics, and "vapor fruit!"
What questions aren't we asking that we should be asking...
and what questions are we asking, that now are irrelevant?

The "cold information" is what feeds the "improvement curve:"

Much as we hate it, every massive, past improvement... f-i-r-s-t required massive change.

Much as we hate it, every massive, past improvement... f-i-r-s-t required massive change. As we learned earlier, we cannot improve any more... than we are willing... to change.

Most improvement is outside of our current comfort zones. But God Himself continually expands our learning curve, through our prayer & Relationship-time with Him, through His Holy Spirit changing our thoughts (and our will)... to God's always better... ever-perfect plan and Divine design!

"Let us go back to every city we've been in..."
and see how they are doing." Acts 15:36

Paul wrote in the Book of Acts: "Let us now go back and visit our brethren... (& convert "lambs")... in every city where we have preached the Word of the Lord, and see how they are doing." (Acts 15: 36).

The Apostle Paul was not going to wait around for some other "fruit inspector" to come see his much vaunted, invisible, "vapor fruit." If the methods he was using were n-o-t producing "fruit that remains", Paul was enough of an anointed "sanctified pragmatist", to want to know n-o-w: ...not 5 or 10 years or never!

As a lamb,
Paul received the gentle, relational,
uplifting nurture of Barnabas;
...later in his own Apostolic life...
Paul gladly applied it to Philemon...
and Onesimus.

"As the twig is bent (or nurtured) ...so grows the tree"

Paul nurtured "baby Onesimus", even as Barnabas, so lovingly nurtured "Baby Paul".

Sociologists say abused children often grow up and become child abusers themselves. They also say those gently, relationally nurtured & cared for as children, often grow up to be kind-hearted, gentle, nurturing people as well. So it was, in the case of the Apostle Paul. Barnabas took Paul under his wing and nurtured him gently as a newborn believer. Paul's entire life was molded by Barnabas' world-class lambcare.

> **Paul nurtured "Baby Onesimus", even as Barnabas, so lovingly nurtured "Baby Paul".**

Later in Paul's life, Paul writes Philemon. In Philemon (verse 19), Paul states that he (Philemon) himself was Paul's convert, a "fruit" & result of Paul's own ministry: "that he "owed" his salvation" to Paul's lifework. Setting that aside, Paul gently asks (rather than commands) Philemon (as a slave owner), that he be gentle (& restorative) with Onesimus (Philemon's former, runaway slave who's now returned home!)

Paul asks Philemon to rejoice that Onesimus is now t-h-e-i-r mutual, newborn brother in the Lord!

You see, verse 10 shows us Onesimus is also now a new convert through Paul. Paul calls him: "my son, my own child" (Weymouth). Paul writes: "if he owes you anything, I myself will repay you."

Jesus' criterion & goal was... and is... "lasting fruit": ...not "vapor fruit"!

Our Lord so eloquently and clearly phrased it in His: "I am the Vine and you are the branches" discourse in John 15. Jesus stated clearly that He not only wanted much fruit.

Jesus clearly told us: "In this is My Father glorified,
that you bear much fruit (John 15:8) ...but also...
Jesus said: ..."and that your fruit... remain." (John 15:16B)

Chapter 41
"WE A-L-L WERE LAMBS!"

"RAMBO LAMBO"... and other lamb-care myths

There are many popular, false beliefs making the rounds regarding the rural analogy of the Shepherd, the sheep, and His lambs. We must throw out these false and damaging myths! Perhaps the most deadly, false myth about lambs is: the responsibility-eliminating, sleep-inducing myth of "Rambo-lambo!"

The "Rambo-Lambo" lamb-care myth goes something like this. Through prayer, "anointing", and the "good wishes" of a lazy, 'Laodicean' church, ...this frail, vulnerable, newborn lamb somehow transforms itself overnight... into a "hyper-grace', newborn "full-grown warrior."

Suddenly "lambo" becomes "rambo"...and turns into "Super-lamb"!

Somehow, magically, "lambo" becomes a wolf-chaser and a lion-devourer! In line with this culturally popular fantasy & delusion, there's even a contemporary popular Christian song, in which the chorus repeats: "We need to be lambs that roar, we need to be eagles that soar." It rhymes, but beyond that it flies like an elephant!

"Lambs that roar?"

The very statement: "lambs that roar" is ludicrous, an oxymoron, and a "dead give away"! No one reading this book (or any other book) has ever heard a lamb r-o-a-r. No—one ever will! Lambs do n-o-t- roar... nor do sheep!

Any application to Jesus being both the Lion and the conquering Lamb is true to Scripture... but O-N-L-Y as uniquely applied to Jesus alone as the Eternal Son of God! It is n-o-t even close to being scriptural, to apply that analogy of a "roaring, conquering Lamb"... to a-n-y new believer! There is no such thing as a "rambo-lambo," especially, a new-born believer (& lamb) in God's Kingdom, family and flock!

What are the characteristics of a lamb... once again?

I've previously mentioned the pastor who embarrassed himself in a room full of ministerial peers, at a "Feed My lambs" seminar saying: "What's the big deal? What's the difference between a lamb and a sheep?"

WE ALL WERE LAMBS

Everyone in the room said together with me in a unison response:
"The difference between a lamb & a sheep... is that A LAMB...
I-S... A... B-A-B-Y SHEEP!"

Let's review below, as we draw to a close, some of these specific, life-and-death differences!

Characteristics differences of lambs & sheep

As to:	Lambs are:	Sheep are:
Age:	Lambs are newborn	Sheep once were newborn
	Lambs are days & weeks old	Sheep are years older (1-20 years old)
Strength:	Lambs are weak	Sheep are much, much stronger
Dependence:	100% care (& "Mom-dependent")	Parent independent
Food:	Milk-drinkers	Grass, alfalfa, corn & grain eaters
Food source:	"Baby food only" from Mom	Adult sheep food from the field & from Shepherd
"Care-priority"	Put 1st before the sheep	2ndary care/feeding priority" by Jesus
Time between meals:	"shorter"	Longer time between meals! Self-feeding
Weight	8 pounds	150-300 pounds
Meal size:	Tiny but frequent "milk"	Larger grass & grain meals... less frequently
Gait & motion:	Frolic, skip, leap	Sedate, slower gait: appear almost motionless
Flock position:	The "Future flock"	The "Now" & "strength" of the flock
Defenses:	No defense	Horns, sheepdogs & a Shepherd to defend them!
Knowledge of Predators:	"Wolf & coyote dumb"	"wolf & coyote-smart"
Straying factor:	Prone to stray	Accustomed to stay close to their Shepherd
Dependencies	"Mother-dependent"	Shepherd-dependent
Experience	100% in-experienced	100% Experienced & keen to danger of predators
Teachers:	Must learn everything from elders	Well taught, & now the teachers of the young
Heart	Tender-hearted	Wise and experienced often callous-ed hearts
Reproducibility	Future reproducers of the flock	Current reproducers of the newborns
Benefit to flock	The "future of the flock"	Current $ producers & producers of lambs & wool
Productivity	Must be cared for "24-7"	Givers of Care to newborns & the youngest.
Care Neediness	Receivers of care day & night	Givers of Care to the newborns & the youngest!

Survival Quotient	Protection-less	Protectors
Predator-Desirability	Favorite fast-food of predators	Formerly the "Predator's choice" (long ago)
Durability	Easiest "carry-out" & "to-go" meal	Harder to order "to go" (weight, size & Shepherd)

There was a time, when... we were all... lambs!

There was a time when we...

There was a time... when we didn't know God... or even know that we could... or would even want to... know Him!

There was a time... when we didn't know what the red letters in the New Testament represented

There was a time... when we weren't grown-up sheep! Not one of us!

There was a time... when we never thought we'd live long enough to become a big sheep!

There was a time... when we all once were lambs and knew nothing of the love and security of the Shepherd, the sheepfold, nor of the flock!

There was a time... when we didn't know the whole alphabet, much less the beginning & advanced language of the Kingdom of God and God's Word!

There was a time....when we didn't know.... what we didn't know!

There was a time....when "baby food" was all we could eat...and all we hungered for!

There was a time....when God's people were "relationship-ing' us, and sometimes we didn't even know what they were up to...merely l-o-v-i-n-g us!

There was a time....when satan's howls & predatorial threats "scared us to death!"

There was a time....when as baby lambs....our feelings told us that God had left us for good.... and we believed it!...for a time!

There was a time....when we were baby lambs.... we made foolish "baby-lamb" mistakes!

There was a time....when we, like newborns, needed diapers, baby carriers & baby-care!

There was a time....when we were "milk drinkers" only...& dreamed of the day we'd eat tall, green grass with the other grown-up sheep & rest of the flock!

Now We know... but back then...

Now we know Jesus, our Good Shepherd, will never leave or forsake us... ...but back then, our security was shaken & renewed only day-by-day!

Now we know that when "there's only 1 set of footprints", it was then that Jesus carried us! ...but back then... our feelings ruled us & told us we were all a-l-o-n-e!

Now we can feed baby Christians for weeks on Scriptures we've memorized and love, ...but back then, one memory verse at a time was a huge challenge in itself!

Now we know from years following Jesus, that it is His love keeping us...not our love for Him, ...but back then, it all seemed based on our performance...and our love for Him!

Now we can pray whenever...wherever... and as long as we want.... ...but back then, prayer was a new challenge & five minutes seemed like hours!

Now we know, if we do sin, Jesus' blood cleanses us from all sin when we ask Him to... ...but back then, we ran from... instead of running to... our loving shepherd!

Now we have strong, unshakeable confidence ...but back then, our enemy scared us!

We All Were Lambs

Now, in Jesus' Name, we tell the enemy "where to go & how to get there!"
...but back then, we were scared & discouraged more often than we
care to admit, remember, or share with others... especially new believers!

There was a time... we all were lambs.

Mistakes Lambs Make

Newborn lambs... over-estimate themselves

Newborn lambs... mistakenly also under-estimate the enemy!

Newborn lambs... mistakenly take their Shepherd for granted!

Newborn lambs... mistakenly over-react!

Newborn lambs... also characteristically under-react!

Newborn lambs... take risks that wiser, older sheep would never take!

Newborn lambs... are gullible and naïve!

Newborn lambs... do not know their own limitations!

Newborn lambs... are flighty and impulsive!

Were Y-o-u ever a "baby Christian lamb"? What mistakes did you make?

What "diapers" ever needed 'changed' in your life as a newborn believer?

What "stupid" things did you do, and/or "believe" as a newborn Christian?

What dumb things did you think, say, or act out...when you were a baby Christian?

Were you even ever a real baby Christian?

What embarrassing things did you ever do, think or say, as a new believer?

What were we really like as newborns and lambs?:

(*Question: "If sheep are dumb, then that makes lambs _____?)

"Benevolent amnesia" intercepts embarrassing memories of our own newborn frailty, dependencies, what we didn't know, the details of what we could & couldn't do, when we were newborns

What can a baby do? A baby can't do... a lot more things than it can!

How well can a baby read, write, drive, bank, delegate, plan, phone, talk, write, buy or sell ?

Lord, remind us that we were all lambs... & how dependent we all were!

Somebody carried us... things that break Your heart! Lord, tenderize our hearts... for your precious, tender, baby lambs and their care! Help us recalibrate our care-giving, Lord. Help us remember what it was like in our newborn helplessness, when we all were 100% care-dependent baby lambs, not only dependent on Your perfect care, Lord, ...but also dependent on the care... of the rest of the flock!

Remind us, Lord, of the many, many kind things people did for us, when we all were baby lambs!

Chapter 42
"CLOSING CHALLENGE & JOHN 21:15 PRAYER"

Our Lord Jesus Himself very clearly told Peter: "If you love Me, feed My lambs." We must constantly remind ourselves (& others) that these are not OUR lambs, but His!

Jesus very clearly... and tenderly... called them: "My lambs"
(John 21:15).

In Luke 16:10, Jesus Himself promised:
"He that is faithful in the few, is faithful also in the many"
...and "Because thou has been faithful in that which is least,
I will put you in charge of the many!" (Mt.25:21)

We forget we all once were baby Christians...
WE ALL ONCE WERE LAMBS!

We forget... that someone carried us in their arms... someone loved us without requiring that we love them back. Someone older and established in the "Faith" carried us and loved us onward and upward! Someone "relationship-ed" us! Through that relationship they brought us along in our belief that God truly, deeply cared for us, that He alone had the ultimate, most loving, wonderful plan for our lives.

We must pass on this marvelous care-powered, affirming nurture by which God saw to it we ourselves were "graced"... when we were newborn.! We were all unknowledgeable, frail, naïve, baby lambs ourselves. We must pass on this tender grace to the new lambs in God's flock: ...those He births around us... in our churches, fellowships... and day-by-day, everyday world!

We need to build into our church budgets (as well as into our time, relational and emotional budgets), consistent, dedicated, gentle, relational nurture of His baby lambs: the kind of care Jesus Himself wants... e-a-c-h... of His newborn lambs to receive!

Jesus has specifically commanded us:

If you say you love Me... then f-e-e-d M y l-a-m-b-s!
No excuse will take its place.
No activity will substitute for this loving & intentional
feeding of H-i-s lambs!

Jesus said:
"If you know these things, blessed are you if you do them!
John 13:17

All that's left is to continually ask, pray for & receive our marvelous Lord's continual help, encouragement and guidance. Jesus will help us target & achieve world-class Lamb-Care in days ahead!

Not for just s-o-m-e of His lambs... but for A-L-L: ...e-v-e-r-y-o-n-e... of the lambs He gives our churches! Not just to feed them marginally... not to just get by... but to feed them lushly... as He fed (& daily feeds)... each one of us!

We must never forget... how Jesus so wonderfully and faithfully saw to it we were fed... nurtured & carried... when we ourselves were the newborns... in His flock!

We dare do no less. We must strive to do more for the newborn lambs being birthed around us.

Together, let's go forward now... and w-i-t-h Jesus' great, triumphant and Eternal Joy...

...let us commit afresh to fulfill His command...
to feed HIS precious lambs... FIRST!

Chapter 43
"RECOMMENDATIONS & RESULTS"

"Jonathan. The Good News here is to report that in one year, since we started implementing your material from the "Feed My Lambs" seminar (& FML network materials), ...our retention of 1st time converts improved from 50%... ...to now over 90%! Hallelujah!"

"This material is a real eye opener and has helped me better understand the nature of "lambs. Everyone needs to hear this!"

"Wonderful topic! It spoke to my heart. All members of our congregation need to hear this!"

"Great teaching, good presentation. Do it! A must for all pastors!"

"I appreciate your emphasis on the lambs and look forward to your ministry again in South Dakota". – District Supt. Steve Schaible

"Keep on feeding the shepherds... so we will be more fit to care for the lambs!"

"A revolutionary, Bible-based convert-care seminar that every pastor can benefit from." District Superintendent Steve Brown, S. Carolina Assemblies of God

"The whole Body of Christ needs to hear this seminar! I would recommend this to A-L-L pastors, churches & districts!"

"The best convert–care teaching I've ever had. This is breakthrough teaching for any church & pastor!

"Jonathan's passion for new babes in Christ, along with his sense of humor, was sobering, yet challenging to all that were there. There are many grateful pastors who are already implementing the practical advice shared & beginning to turn their church around in the area of & retention of new converts." Clayton B. Glickert, As't. District Supt., NY Assemblies

"It's exciting to finally hear someone else speak intelligently on the subject of relationship"

"This was time well spent. Host a session and empower your People!" "I appreciate your focus on relationships. The most important thing pastors can do to love their people."

"This event will challenge you! Don't miss an opportunity to let God change your thinking, change your life, & change your church."

"Tremendous! You will not go away the same!"

"This seminar is convicting & eye opening!"

"This material is a real eye opener and has helped me better understand the nature of lambs". Everyone needs to hear this!"

'Every door should open for this. The best teaching I have ever heard!"

"Awesome! You have nothing to lose except converts, and everything & everyone to gain!"

"Yes! Refreshing, much-needed teaching. I nearly perished as a lamb. My spirit's nearly shouting for the need of this!"

"It was one of the most ministry-changing seminars & information of my ministry life"

"This is the most urgent and important word for the Body of Christ today!"

"This reinforced my need to be "w-i-t-h" my leadership and my lambs. Also, to spend time eating, living, not just in church-related activity."

"You shared things in the last two-days that I've never heard before. Extremely helpful!"

"Grasp this relationship concept, it is God's plan. Discipleship goes hand in hand with fellowship and N. Carolina Pastors' recommendations: District Convert-Care "Pilot" Project 2/5/2001

"When Brother Kelly first contacted me about being part of the North Carolina District Convert Care retention program taught by Jonathan Gainsbrugh, to be very honest I was maybe a little resentful about this, about having another job & another list of things I had to do. However, the more I read about this & the more I studied, the more I realized how important this ministry really is. The importance of retaining our new converts and assimilating them into the body of Christ. There is so much scripture that goes along with this in backing this up. Our church has caught this and caught the fire of this and we have a wonderful Convert Care team working toward this. I can see where this would change the way we do business in our churches. There's no reason why we cannot hold on to our converts, the people God sends us and we must do this if we are to survive as a church & as a movement."
Pastor Dave Waterfield, Lighthouse Assembly, Buxton, North Carolina

Hello, my name is Pastor Jim Bedsaul, Pastor of Calvary AG in Mt. Airy, NC. "I want to share with you how I feel about the program Brother Gainsbrugh has brought to us. In John 4:35 the Word of God says: "say ye not four months & then comes the harvest. Behold, I say unto you: "Lift up your eyes & look on the fields, for they are white already unto harvest." We have a great harvest to reap & we're doing a fair job in many areas of reaping this harvest. But what are we doing to maintain& preserve that harvest? It is not acceptable that we lose 90% of the harvest every year. This has got to stop and in order for that to take place, we are going to have to stop doing business the way that we have grown accustomed to doing business. We're going to have to learn to love people. We're going to have to learn to build relationships & I believe that Brother Gainsbrugh has been anointed of God. I believe he has put together a program that is the best that I have ever seen. Whoever may view this tape, I encourage you to support Brother Gainsbrugh. I would like to encourage Supt. Kelly to invite him back to District Council so that all 220 churches in NC can take advantage of this. It's one of the greatest programs I've ever seen. It's done great things in my church & will do the same for yours."

"When I was contacted concerning this program of new converts and creating a New Convert Task Force, to me it was a logical thing to do. I remember the scripture Matthew 28:19 & 20 says to: "go make disciples of all nations, baptizing in the name of the Father, Son and the Holy Ghost, teaching them to obey all things. It presumes the confession and faith in Christ Jesus. The important thing & the emphasis 1st is to make disciples. I must admit that I fell into the category of many preachers & people who just accept the losses. Lots of people get saved; lots of people confess Jesus Christ is their Lord. Few seem to make it work and we are guilty of blaming them for the lack of their survival, which to me is like blaming an infant for not surviving because no one fed it , as if it should have gotten up to feed itself. When new converts get saved, they're compared to babies in Christ. We must feed them, we must disciple them. It's our responsibility to keep them, not theirs to keep coming back, and not theirs to feed themselves. There's lots to do to feed new converts. There's much for them to understand. They don't know what we know. We presume that they know what they should do. We presume that they should automatically just begin to attend and develop the habits, and that all they need for survival but they don't know these things. We much stop presuming that they do. We must get behind a program like this. There needs to be a conscious effort to win people for Christ, not just get them to say the prayer, but go all the way into the Kingdom of God for eternity. This program is necessary. I'm glad for it!"
Pastor Tim Brohier, 1st AG, Andrews N.C.

"For years it had been in my heart that, as I saw people come in and come to an altar and get saved, and then that was the last time I would see them, I knew there was something we could do to better equip these new converts who would come into our churches, say a prayer of faith, put a true trust in Christ, yet seemingly disappear the next week. Too many times I was told that this was just something you have to get used to; something that is just a part of ministry. It's something, that statistically this is what was to be expected. Well, in my heart of hearts, I knew that that was to be expected, but I knew that there was more. And for years I had looked and for years I had diligently searched, studied the word and studied the scriptures. I began to see some things that the Lord was beginning to show and reveal concerning new convert care. But when the opportunity came along and I received contact from the district about a New Convert plan, it was just something I'd been looking for, for years; God just had come in and heard the cry of one of His servants & said: "listen, I've already prepared some things for you; If you'll be open and receive them, these will help your church tremendously to begin to retain more of the converts you have & help effectively build more relationships in the body of Christ. I was thrilled, I was excited, and whenever the call came I jumped at the opportunity. It's been something that has been just tremendously, tremendously re-ignited the passionate side of my heart, not to maintain status quo, but to go on for 100% convert retention knowing that God is not satisfied with just having 50%, He's not satisfied with 30%... He's not satisfied with 10%! He wants a-l-l the sheep to come into harvest so that they may come

and glorify Him and in turn bring more of the harvest in. I commend anyone with a heart & passion, to not only see souls saved, but people discipled after the same manner Christ discipled people...to give credence to what Brother Jonathan is sharing with us. Such fabulous, revolutionary ideas but very simplistic concepts that even the most youngest of converts can grab on to and begin to implement them into their life. "
Pastor Duane Campbell from Faith AG, Hertford, NC.

"I feel very privileged to be part of the Jonathan Gainsbrugh program, as we are learning how to better assimilate new converts into the church family. I believe one of the 1st things that has to be done is: you have to realize that there is a problem. On examining records & seeing what we have done in the past, it becomes clear that we are losing much too large of a percentage of people who are coming into the kingdom. They are falling by the wayside & not being properly cared for as they should. It's somewhat disturbing to see this, but I'm encouraged to know there are ways we can do better at this. We have been examining the ways our Lord ministered & discipled those who followed Him. We can get great insights into how we can better do that. So we are looking into and implementing different things into our church that's enabling us to identify the needs of the new converts as well as the existing members of the church and help them better become more of what God wants them to be. I think this program has been very beneficial to me & opened my eyes to see the real need that exists, and also to look to ways to change the direction we're going, to retain all those new babies the Lord has entrusted to us to nurture for Him & in His Name. I recommend highly this program that Jonathan Gainsbrugh has been introducing to us. I think it will completely turn around any church, any people that have a heart to really disciple God's people & reach the world for Christ. I highly endorse & recommend him."
Pastor Ralph Acevedo, Praise AG, Madison, N.C.

"When I received a letter from the District Office about coming & joining the Jonathan Gainsbrugh ministry here, at first I had a little resentment. I said: "this is for other churches, this is not for me". We we're already retaining about 65% of our people & I was satisfied with that! One day talking on the phone with Jonathan, we were talking about abortion. I said: "God, I refuse to be in the abortion business. "I'm not satisfied with retaining 65%, I want 100%! I do not even want to lose one, because that is the heartbeat of God. I would ask & encourage you to come be on a winning team & partner with us, join with us as we study to understand the knowledge and heartbeat of God, of listening and attending to His sheep. Let me just say, we encourage you to come. We ask Brother Kelly to perhaps have Jonathan back in one of our District Councils to teach & show us concepts & give us knowledge of how to retain the sheep that perhaps we have lost. May God bless you."
Pastor Billy Carlisle 1st Assembly, Wilson. N.C.

Chapter 44
"RESPONSE: ADDING JG & JGM TO YOUR CHURCH'S MINISTRY TEAM"

What if... we all were to network... and to cooperatively work together? What if... we put all this lamb-care information (and much more) at the fingertips of pastors everywhere, working together to fulfil Jesus' tender priority-command to: "Feed His lambs F-i-r-s-t"!

I am a missionary and as such...

I admit that I am a different type of missionary. I want to build the Kingdom of God and help thousands of churches. However, at the same time, I also want to help you at your church.

Like any missionary, I can only go... if somebody will send me. Every missionary has to ask for help, because it helps them realize how dependent they are. It also helps the Body of Christ realize its own total interdependence in going & sending! No missionary goes... unless Godly pastors & churches send!

Missionary to India, C.T. Studd, put it so well when he said: "I'll keep going down into the pit... if you will hold the rope."

It's not easy to ask for help. Everyday I visit the mailbox, and thank God for individuals, pastors, & missions-minded "John 21:15-hearted" churches, who pledge and give monthly, generously & regularly in missions, to help keep JGM ministries and the National Lamb-Care Network on the front-lines... and out on the web on our expanding, Feedmylambsnetwork.org website.

Feedback Page: The Importance of your response

On the following end-page is a tear out (or copyable) response page.

1) Buying copies of this book will help your church (& other pastors) as well as moving us forward here!

2) Positive Comments: Any positive one or two lines (or more) you would write us, will help open doors to other pastors, churches, superintendents and denominations (or area-wide ministerial associations), and would be really appreciated, written or e-mailed.

3) Interested in a seminar in your church (& or area)? If you are, please signify so on the response page with an approximate time of year preference as well. Thanks!

4) Please take the time to share with us your current e-mail address at our feedmylambsnetwork.org web page, e-mail us (or snail mail us).

Whether or not you join the Lamb-Care Network, we can still correspond from time to time at no cost at either end, by e-mail! We will not pass on your e-mail to any other organization or anyone else. I'd like to help your church become a "world class lamb-ery!"

Together, we can do just that!
Together: Your church can become a "World-Class lamb-ery"
And we'd like to be there to help!

When your church joins the JGM "Feed My Lambs Network" & becomes a monthly JGM Ministry missions-partner church, you will automatically receive:

- Audio tapes of the 4-hour *"Feed My Lambs"* seminar (and rights to copy)
- CD 's of the entire 4-hour *"Feed My Lambs"* seminar (and rights to copy)
- 34 page seminar syllabus without answers
  (with permission to copy for your church)
- 34 page seminar syllabus w-i-t-h the answers
  (& permission to copy for your church)
- Reproduceable booklet:
  "How to Start your Convert-Care Task Force"
- Plus 3 unique, reproduceable Church-Health booklets:
  - *"Help Your Church Extend a Warm & Caring Greeting"* (51 pages)
    (one of the best materials on visitor Care and Greeters/
    out-of-print elsewhere, we give you reprinting rights)
  - *"Paradigm Blindness and How To Prevent It"*
  - *"7-Step Hospitality System"*
    (reproduceable for all your Greeters & Hospitality Team members)

Plus continuing, ongoing "Feed My Lambs Network" Partners-Only Benefits:

- All partner gifts in digital, down-loadable format
- on-line quarterly **partners-only** e-letter
- on-line library of lamb-care articles, book reviews,
- feature church-of the-quarter article about other
  "world-class lamb-ery" churches
- **partners-only** access to the Power Point slides of the *"Feed MY Lambs"* seminar

PLEASE ZEROX OR CLIP THIS FEEDBACK PAGE AND RETURN TO:

JGM Ministries, 3450 Palmer Dr., Suite 4 - #302, Cameron Park, CA. 95682
Phone: (530) 344-0299 **Email:** jg@d-web.com or jg@gainsbrugh.org
Web: www.gainsbrugh.org and www.feedmylambsnetwork.org

Bibliography

Barna, George:
    "The Frog and the Kettle"
    "Visitor Friendly Churches"

Cho, Pastor David Yongii:
    "Successful Cell Groups"
    "The 4th Dimension"

Carl George
    "Prepare Your Church for the Future"
    "The Coming Church Revolution"
    "9 tips for Small Group Success"

Haggard, Pastor Ted
    "Flying Fishing, Dog Training and Sharing Christ in the 3rd Millennium"

Huckaby, Henry
    "Experiencing God"

George Hunter's Books:
    "The Celtic Way of Evangelism"
    "Reaching Secular People"

Hurston, Karen,
    "Growing the World's Largest Church", Gospel Publishing House
    "Breakthrough Cell Groups"

Hybels, Bill and Lynn
    "Reinventing the Church"
    "Fit To Be Tied"

Matheson, John Ed
    "Every Member In Ministry"

Swartz, Christian.
    "Natural Church Development"
    Church Smart Resources, 350 Randy Rd., Ste 5, Carol Stream, Il. 60188

Sweet,Leonard:
    "AquaChurch"
    "Carpe Manana"
    "Soul Tsunami"
    "Soul Salsa"

Warren, Rick:
    "The Purpose Driven Church"
    "The Purpose Driven Life"

Feedback & Response Page

❏ Yes! We would like more information on adding JGM Ministries to our church's ongoing ministry team.

❏ Please send us more information on joining the national Feed My Lambs Network.

❏ Please send us your current JGM Ministry Resources Catalogue with information on other JGM Ministry books, audio tape & CD Series, Videos, consulting, etc.

❏ We are interested in you presenting a seminar
      ❏ in our church   ❏ in our area

  ❏   Feed My Lambs Seminar

  ❏   Closing Your Church's 7 Backdoors

  ❏   Other: ❏ Small Groups ❏ Mobilizing Members in Ministry
                ❏ Relationships: the key to Health and Growth
                ❏ A Church–Health Audit and Clinic
                ❏ Evangelism In the 3rd Millennium
                ❏ Paradigm Blindness and How to prevent and cure it

❏ We would like to receive your occasional e-mail updates on new lamb-care ideas, contacts, strategies and innovation.

❏ We would like pricing info to order _____ copies of "The Lamb's Book"

❏ Please call us with details of bulk-order discount pricing

❏ The quantity we are interested in ordering is:
      ❏ 5   ❏ 10   ❏ 15-20   ❏ 50+   ❏ 100+   ❏ other

———————————————— **PLEASE PRINT** ————————————————

Sr. Pastor's name: _____

Church name: _____

Denomination: _____ Sun Am size: _____

Person if other than Pastor: _____

Ministry at church: _____

Mailing address: _____

City _____State _____Zip _____

PH#:(Ch.) _____ (Hm) _____

Time frame you'd like a seminar:
      ❏ Soon   ❏ Spring   ❏ Summer   ❏ Fall   ❏ Winter Year:_____

PLEASE ZEROX OR CLIP THIS FEEDBACK PAGE AND RETURN TO:
JGM Ministries, 3450 Palmer Dr., Suite 4 - #302, Cameron Park, CA. 95682
Phone: (530) 344-0299 **Email:** jg@d-web.com or jg@gainsbrugh.org
Web: www.gainsbrugh.org and www.feedmylambsnetwork.org